For the Common Good

FOR THE COMMON GOOD

Popular Politics in Barcelona, 1580–1640

LUIS R. CORTEGUERA

Cornell University Press

ITHACA AND LONDON

This book is published with the aid of grants from the Program for Cultural Cooperation between Spain's Ministry of Culture and Education and United States Universities, and from the Scholarly Publications Revolving Fund of the University of Kansas.

First published 2002 by Cornell University Press

Printed in the United States of America

Library of Congress Cataloging-in-Publication Data

Corteguera, Luis R.
  For the common good : popular politics in Barcelona, 1580–1640 / Luis R. Corteguera.
     p. cm.
Includes bibliographical references and index.
  ISBN 0-8014-3780-6 (cloth : alk. paper)
  1. Barcelona (Spain)—Politics and government. 2. Spain—Politics and government—1556–1598. 3. Spain—Politics and government—1598–1621. 4. Spain—Politics and government—1621–1665. 5. Central—local government relations—Spain. 6. Catalonia (Spain)—History—Revolution, 1640—Causes. I. Title.
  DP402.B29 C67 2001
  946'.7204—dc21   2001007148

Cloth printing   10 9 8 7 6 5 4 3 2 1

Contents

Illustrations

Figures

Maps

Preface

In 1640 popular violence in Barcelona transformed the history of Spain and consequently that of the rest of Europe. In June, crowds of agricultural laborers and city artisans murdered a royal judge and the viceroy of the northeastern Spanish principality of Catalonia. In the days and weeks that followed, continued rioting paralyzed the principality's royal government and forced the Spanish monarchy to send royal troops to put down the revolt. By Christmas, as the king's troops approached the city, five royal judges of Barcelona's highest court had been stabbed, shot, or defenestrated, and the rest had fled for fear of a similar fate. Less than a month later, Catalans severed their allegiance to the Spanish monarchy and elected France's Louis XIII as their new king.

The start of the Catalan Revolt of 1640 is the concluding episode of my sixty-year history of popular politics in Barcelona. As the principality of Catalonia's political center and its most populated city, Barcelona had a long history of active popular politics. More than half of its 30,000 to 40,000 inhabitants were artisan men and women who lived and worked within walking distance of the viceregal, Catalan, and city administrations. Master artisans sat in the city council—the Consell de Cent—and formed the core of the city's guard, the principality's largest militia. The "people," as artisans were often called, also had a tradition of participating in protests and riots that would pose a threat to the ties between Catalonia and the Spanish monarchy beginning in the second half of the reign of Philip II (1556–98).

Beginning around 1580, rising prices and food scarcity raised fears about the possibility of popular disorders in Barcelona. The Consell de Cent tried to improve conditions in the city by adopting a variety of measures that royal authorities opposed, claiming they would encroach on the king's sovereignty. For their part, the royal government sought to redress its precarious financial situation in Catalonia in ways that Catalans insisted would undermine their laws and liberties. By the early 1590s, conditions for most inhabitants in Barcelona were on the brink of a crisis just as the relations between Catalan and royal authorities reached new lows. The two sides averted an open confrontation, largely to avoid the fate suffered by the neighboring Kingdom of Aragon, which royal troops invaded in 1592 to quell a rebellion against the monarchy. But as Spain's economy declined during the reign of Philip III (1598–1621), and as the monarchy's involvement in foreign wars increased under Philip IV (1621–65), the need to fix royal finances in Catalonia regained urgency. Aimed at increasing the principality's share of the war effort, the royal policies of Philip IV's principal minister, the count-duke of Olivares, rekindled Catalans' concerns about the loss of their liberties. Violent protests in Barcelona worsened the already strained relations with Madrid until the situation reached a turning point in 1640. The revolt of 1640, and the twelve-year war that followed, became the Spanish monarchy's worst internal crisis in the seventeenth century.

In telling the history of popular politics in Barcelona between 1580 and 1640, I have sought to address two central problems. The first problem is one faced by all historians of popular culture: how to decipher the meaning of the political actions, ideas, and language of people who lived hundreds of years ago and often left few records explaining their motivations and intentions. Fortunately, James Amelang pointed out to me the variety of sources by and about Barcelona's artisans (which I discuss below). In addition, the methods of cultural historians such as Natalie Zemon Davis and E. P. Thompson, as well as more recent works on popular resistance by William Beik, Suzanne Desan, and James C. Scott, offer important guidance in the study of popular ideas and actions. In the chapters that follow, I present a wide range of ideas expressed by artisans regarding their duties as subjects, the nature of justice and privileges, and the obligation of rulers to govern well—ideas that inspired and influenced artisans' political actions. These findings do not support the view that common people inhabited a different political world from that of their rulers and social superiors. Historians have often contrasted the formal and institutionalized aspects of high politics to spontaneous and violent popular politics. Yet common people were no more inclined to violence than aristocrats, whose interest in warfare, hunting, and dueling did not make them more peace-loving. Popular and elite forms of politics in fact shared fundamental assumptions about what constituted good government, justice, and the duties of rulers and subjects. Thus I would argue, following Roger Chartier's definition of popular culture, that we should see popular politics not as "opposed to that of the notables, but as a repertory of themes and acts ready for use by people of a variety of social levels (not necessarily in like fashion)."[1] What qualified certain political actions, ideas, or language to be "popular" was not that they were associated with artisans or peasants, but rather that contemporaries described the social standing of certain political actors with such imprecise terms as "common," "ordinary," or "plebeian."[2]

The second problem involves how to incorporate popular politics within the political history of early modern Europe. Above all, I focus on two areas in which popular politics, to use John H. Elliott's words, "made a difference" in early modern politics.[3] One area concerns the relations between central governments and outlying territories in what historians refer to as "composite monarchies": amalgams of territories, often with distinctive laws, institutions, and culture, linked by their allegiance to the same monarch.[4] Peasant revolts or urban protests could have a decisive impact on the future of a composite monarchy either by encouraging a rift between a monarch and the ruling elite of an outlying territory or by fostering an unexpected alliance between the two to suppress popular disorders.[5] A second area where popular politics could have a significant impact on politics involved the proper functioning of government. From the quiet disregard of official orders to the public refusal to pay taxes, the actions of ordinary people could have serious repercussions if they thwarted gov-

---

1. Roger Chartier, *The Cultural Origins of the French Revolution*, trans. Lydia G. Cochrane (Durham, N.C., 1991), 142–43.

2. Wayne te Brake, *Shaping History: Ordinary People in European Politics, 1500–1700* (Berkeley, 1998), 6–7. On the imprecision of these and other terms, see E. P. Thompson, "The Patricians and the Plebs," in *Customs in Common: Studies in Traditional Popular Culture* (New York, 1993), 16–96.

3. Referring to early modern peasant revolts, Elliott writes: "But we should not, I believe, be afraid to ask the apparently brutal question: did they make any difference? Or, indeed, *could* they make any difference, in a world in which technological backwardness had at least as much to do with the condition of the populace as exploitation by an oppressive ruling class?"; John H. Elliott, "Revolution and Continuity in Early Modern Europe," in *Spain and Its World, 1500–1700* (New Haven, 1989), 102.

4. J. H. Elliott, "A Europe of Composite Monarchies," *Past and Present* 137 (November 1992), 48–71; Xavier Gil, "Noves visions sobre velles realitats de les relacions entre la capital i els territoris a les monarquies europees dels segles XVI i XVII," in *El Barroc Català: Actes de les jornades celebrades a Girona, desembre 1987* (Barcelona, 1989), 23–45; Xavier Gil, "Visió europea de la monarquia espanyola com a monarquia composta, segles XVI i XVII," *Recerques: Història, Economia, Cultura* 32 (1995), 19–43; H. G. Koenigsberger, "The Crisis of the Seventeenth Century: A Farewell?" in *Politicians and Virtuosi: Essays in Early Modern History* (London, 1986), 149–68.

5. Te Brake, *Shaping History*, 15–16.

ernment policy. Even though the mundane details of everyday government might seem worlds apart from the loftier concerns of high politics—be they war and diplomacy, the state of finances, or church and state relations—the two political spheres were inseparable. This was especially evident in capitals such as London and Paris, where the proximity of crowded streets to the great halls of power made it difficult for one to ignore the other. These same circumstances existed in territorial capitals such as Barcelona, Bordeaux, and Naples, although in these cities political life was further complicated by the dynamic of the relations between monarchy and territories.

This study of artisans and politics has required comparing and contrasting very different kinds of documentation. The disparate papers of master artisans' craft confraternities—found in Barcelona's municipal archive, the Arxiu Històric de la Ciutat—include books recording confraternity meetings, official correspondence with local and royal authorities, and papers from court trials, all of which reveal a great deal about artisans' political ideas and language. However, more often than not, this documentation says little or nothing about major political events, not even during times of crisis. In contrast, the voluminous papers of Barcelona's Consell de Cent—also in the municipal archive—offer crucial information about political events in the city but often ignore the impact of popular politics in order to highlight the consensus in the city and the effectiveness of its officials. This is especially true of differences between artisan representatives and those from Barcelona's elite in the city council, where, to maintain secrecy, individual votes were not recorded. One must therefore turn to a variety of additional sources to clarify important details. Contemporary diaries and chronicles, a significant number of which remain unpublished in libraries in Barcelona, Madrid, and Paris, provide eyewitness accounts of riots. Catalan municipal and regional archives occasionally had correspondence dispatched from Barcelona that revealed interesting information about conditions in the city. The state papers found in the castle archive of Simancas, west of Madrid, helped clarify the extent of popular opposition to military levies in the 1630s, during the war between the French and Spanish monarchies. But some of the best information about popular politics in Barcelona comes from the enormous collection of papers of the Council of Aragon, the agency in Madrid that oversaw royal policy in Catalonia. The council received detailed reports about rumors circulating in Barcelona, incidents of street violence, and differences between the interests of city authorities and popular demands. These documents, located in Barcelona's Arxiu de la Corona d'Aragó, are especially valuable because they observe popular politics in light of the relations between Catalans and their kings. The fact that this documentation is abundant between 1580 and 1640 determined to a large extent this book's chronological boundaries.

After Chapter 1's description of the place of Barcelona's artisans in politics and their relations to key political players, each subsequent chapter examines an episode between 1580 and 1640 when Barcelona's popular politics had an impact on the relations between Catalonia and the monarchy. While describing those events, I also analyze specific actions, ideas, and language that characterized artisans' politics. Thus, Chapter 2 analyzes the concept of the "common good" in a petition campaign to Philip II organized by master craft confraternities in the 1580s to combat high prices in Barcelona. Chapter 3 discusses artisans' notions of political representation expressed during and after the Corts of 1585. Chapter 4 focuses on popular notions of patriotism revealed in demonstrations and riots between 1588 and 1591. Other chapters examine artisans' understanding of privilege (Chapter 5), justice (Chapter 6), resistance (Chapter 7), and revolt (Chapter 8). Chapters are arranged chronologically, covering the years 1580–92 (Chapters 2–4), and 1599–1640 (Chapters 5–8). The book concludes with the start of the Catalan Revolt of 1640, not because I believe the events prior to it made the rebellion inevitable but because it is the clearest expression of how popular politics could make a major difference in the political history of early modern Europe.

Finally, I have written the book as a narrative to link the often complex evolution of events in Barcelona to the analysis of the motivations and character of popular politics. I hope, nonetheless, that excitement and drama do not make the reader lose sight of the fact that what happened involved human beings, whose minds and true intentions no historian can ever fully claim to know.

Many individuals, programs, and institutions have helped me to complete this book. The following provided the generous financial support that allowed me to travel to Spain to conduct research: the Fulbright-Hays Program in Spain, the Program for Cultural Cooperation between Spain's Ministry of Culture and Education and United States Universities, the Council on Regional Studies at Princeton University, the Generalitat de Catalunya, Cleveland State University, the National Endowment for the Humanities, the Joyce and Elizabeth Hall Center for the Humanities at the University of Kansas, and the University of Kansas. It is not possible here to acknowledge the assistance of all the staff at archives and libraries in Spain, the United States, and France, but I am especially grateful to Maria Angels Solà and the late Dolors Florensa of the Arxiu Històric de la Ciutat de Barcelona, Laureà Pagarolas of the Arxiu Històric de Protocols de

Barcelona, and Isabel Aguirre of the Archivo General de Simancas. Barbara Shortridge and Darin Grauberger of the University of Kansas Cartographic Services produced the maps. At Cornell University Press I would like to thank the careful editing and suggestions of John Ackerman, Teresa Jesionowski, and Susan Tarcov.

Teachers, colleagues, and friends have offered valuable comments on all or parts of this book. They include James Amelang, Lisa Bitel, Barbara Corbett, Natalie Zemon Davis, John H. Elliott, Antonio Feros, Jesús Gascón Pérez, Xavier Gil, Anthony Grafton, Bernat Hernández, Karen Hellekson, William Jordan, Richard Kagan, Sabine MacCormack, Peter Mancall, Roger Manning, Jason Mayerfeld, Carolynn Nelson, Miquel Pérez Latre, Theodore K. Rabb, Teófilo Ruiz, Eva Serra, Helen Szathmary, Jane Szathmary, Joyce Thomas, Susan Whyman, and Bartolomé Yun. Individual chapters benefited from discussions at Princeton University, Cleveland State University, the Society for Spanish and Portuguese Historical Studies, and the Early Modern Seminar, Medieval Society, and Social and Economic History Seminar of the University of Kansas. My deepest gratitude goes to Marta Vicente Valentín for her many comments, constant help, and encouragement. I dedicate the book to her.

I wish to thank the Kenneth Spencer Research Library at the University of Kansas for permission to reproduce illustrations from rare books belonging to its extraordinary Special Collections. Parts of this book have been previously published. Parts of Chapters 1 and 8 appeared in "Violence and Identity in Sixteenth- and Seventeenth-Century Barcelona," *Mediterranean Studies* 7 (1998): 179–90. An earlier version of Chapter 2 appeared as "Popular Politics in Composite Monarchies: Barcelona Artisans and the Campaign for a Papal Bull against Hoarding (1580–1585)," *Social History* 26, no. 1 (January 2001): 22–39 <http://www.tand f.co.uk>. Parts of Chapter 6 were published in "The Painter Who Lost His Hat: Artisans and Justice in Early Modern Barcelona," *Sixteenth Century Journal* 29 (1998): 1021–40.

LUIS R. CORTEGUERA

Barcelona, September 2001

Abbreviations

I. Archives and libraries

AADD	Archives diplomatiques (Ministère des Affaires Étrangères, Paris)
ACA	Arxiu de la Corona d'Aragó (Barcelona)
AGS	Archivo General de Simancas
AH	Arxiu de l'Hospital de la Santa Creu (Barcelona)
AHCB	Arxiu Històric de la Ciutat de Barcelona
AHCC	Arxiu Històric Comarcal de Cervera
AHCG	Arxiu Històric de la Ciutat de Girona
AHPB	Arxiu Històric de Protocols de Barcelona
AMV	Arxiu Municipal de Vic
APL	Arxiu de la Paeria de Lleida
BC	Biblioteca de Catalunya (Barcelona)
BNM	Biblioteca Nacional (Madrid)
BNP	Bibliothèque Nationale (Paris)
BUB	Biblioteca Universitària de Barcelona

II. Other abbreviations

AR	Audiència Reial
C	Consellers
CA	Consell d'Aragó
CC	Consell de Cent
CP	Correspondence Politique
DACB	*Dietari del Antich Consell Barceloní*
Delibs.	Deliberacions
E	Estado
F Bon.	Col.lecció de Fullets Bonsoms
G	Generalitat
GM	Guerra y Marina
Gremis	Documentació Gremial Corporativa
LC	Lletres Closes

LCO	Lletres Comunes Originals
leg.	*legajo*
llig.	*lligall*
MHE	*Memorial Histórico Español*
RB	*Rúbriques de Bruniquer*

For the Common Good

CHAPTER ONE

Artisans in Politics

Pride and Freedom

"In Barcelona the wives of simple cobblers were pointed out to me, with whom the ladies of the nobility could scarcely compete. They suck pride with their milk."[1] The twenty-five-year-old Swiss medical student Thomas Platter, the son of John Calvin's famous printer and the brother of the distinguished physician Felix Platter, reached this conclusion during a trip to Catalonia in 1599. The young Platter was both outraged and fascinated by Barcelona's artisans.[2] He described taverns full of rowdy men drinking and playing cards. In the streets, large crowds watched acrobatic performances on their way to theaters or whorehouses. Yet in this city of many vices and temptations, Platter also found industrious inhabitants who made pottery, jewelry, shoes, and boots. He watched with pleasure the busy shops of apothecaries, tailors, and barbers. Nevertheless, he disdained the way even ordinary women dressed luxuriously, and he labeled Spain as "the vainest nation I have ever seen."[3]

---

1. *Journal of a Younger Brother: The Life of Thomas Platter as a Medical Student in Montpellier at the Close of the Sixteenth Century*, trans. Seán Jennett (London, 1963), 227.

2. On the Platter family, see Emmanuel Le Roy Ladurie, *The Beggar and the Professor: A Sixteenth-Century Family Saga*, trans. Arthur Goldhammer (Chicago, 1997).

3. Platter, *Journal*, 227.

Platter may have exaggerated, but Barcelona's artisans, especially masters, cared as much as any noble about their titles, demeanor, and ranking. Master resellers *(revenedors)*, for example, called their officers "honorable,"[4] and in 1626 the shoemakers' officers saw fit to welcome King Philip IV with a retinue worthy of a prince: a master in a purple coat bearing a silver boot, the confraternity officers carrying staffs and wearing golden caps, a treasurer, forty-two masters, and a standard-bearer with a flagpole on top of which sat a golden lion holding a silver boot on its raised paw.[5] Master artisans were also intensely protective of their place in the city's guard. Master shoemakers regarded their "grandiose" company's position as "a most ancient possession"; hatters attacked the mercers for allegedly taking up their place; and gardeners warned city authorities that if the auctioneers *(corredors de coll)* failed to take their assigned position in the company, "many men will be in danger of dying."[6]

To Platter and other foreigners, such behavior would have been consistent with what they described as Catalans' arrogance, disobedience, and violent temper. In 1466, a Bohemian traveler named Schaseck went so far as to declare Catalans "a perfidious and scoundrelly race of men; they profess Christianity but are worse than any heathen."[7] Early in the sixteenth century, the Florentine humanist Francesco Guicciardini averred that Catalans had "a reputation of being fierce and bellicose"[8] because they had privileges that allegedly sheltered bandits and inhibited efforts by the king to punish them. Because Barcelonese had more privileges than anyone else in Catalonia, their arrogance allegedly bordered on disloyalty. In 1525, the Venetian humanist Andrea Navagero insisted that most of Barcelona's privileges "were hardly fair" because they allowed the city's rulers to abuse "even the emperor himself."[9] Likewise, one diplomat from Artois wrote in 1582 that those privileges "undermine[d] significantly the greatness and majesty of kings" and fostered among Barcelona's citizens a "propensity to take

---

4. AHCB Gremis 45-19 ("Llibre d'examens" 1613–28), fol. 1.

5. AHCB Gremis 1-93 ("Llibre de consells" 1625-36), fols. 27–28.

6. AHCB Gremis 1-93 ("Llibre de consells" 1625–36), fols. 18–19; AHCB C III-4 (Guerra i política), no. 81: "Informe. . . sobre un motín" (1596); AHCB Gremis 2-6 (council minutes of the confraternity of the gardeners of the Portal de Sant Antoni, 1552–87), 87r.

7. *The Travels of Leo of Rozmital,* trans. Malcolm Letts (Cambridge, 1957), 139. On Catalans' alleged violent character, see Luis R. Corteguera, "Violence and Identity in Sixteenth- and Seventeenth-Century Barcelona," *Mediterranean Studies* 7 (1998): 179–90.

8. Francesco Guicciardini, *Viaje a España* (1511), trans. José María Alonso Gamo (Valencia, 1952), 43.

9. Andrea Navagero, *Il viaggio fatto in Spagna et in Francia* (Venice, 1563), 3r.

arms," even against their own monarchs.[10] Platter was aware of the supposed link between Barcelona's privileges and its citizens' character. As an example, he told how during the entrance ceremony for King Philip III in 1599, the city would not allow their ruler to enter as king but only as count of Barcelona. Barcelona's citizens "are so intractable about this privilege," Platter added, "that they would go over to the king of France rather than renounce their right."[11]

Not surprisingly, Catalans strongly denied all accusations of disloyalty. Such insults came primarily from French and Italian authors, "enemies of the Spaniards and in particular of the Catalans," insisted Andreu Bosc, a lawyer from Perpinyà, who in 1628 published a nearly six-hundred-page compendium of Catalans' honors, titles, and privileges. With remarkable erudition, he presented one quotation after another by non-Catalans about Catalans' many virtues, including the following praise by Miguel de Cervantes: "[T]he courteous Catalans [are] angry people, terrible and peaceful, gentle; who easily give up their lives for honor, and to defend both exceed themselves, which is to exceed all the nations of the world."[12] This was how Catalans liked to see themselves: courageous fighters at home and abroad, loyal subjects willing to sacrifice their lives for their monarchs, and above all, a free people. In fact, the seemingly incongruous mix of anger and gentility described by Cervantes was a mark of the sense of entitlement to the honor, respect, and dignity—even the nobility—belonging to those who were free.[13] Yet being free did not mean Catalans could not obey their rulers; on the contrary, their obedience was all the more laudable because it was voluntary rather than forced.[14] Proof of their obedience and loyalty was their many privileges, which, contrary to the opinion that they fostered unruliness and disobedience, were "testimony" and

10. Philippe de Caverel, *Ambassade en Espagne et en Portugal en 1582* (Arras, 1860), 197.

11. Platter, *Journal,* 228.

12. Andreu Bosc, *Sumari, index o epítome dels admirables y nobilíssimis títols de honor de Catalunya, Rosselló, i Cerdanya* (Perpinyà, 1628; facsimile edition, Barcelona-Sueca, 1974), 37, 39. Bosc quoted from Cervantes's novel *Los trabajos de Persiles y Sigismunda,* bk. 3, chap. 12.

13. Bosc claimed all Catalans were noble, like the Basques; *Sumari,* 73. Jesús Villanueva López offers an interesting discussion of Catalan claims to "universal nobility" (*hidalguía universal*) in his licentiate thesis, "Los orígenes carolingios de Cataluña en la historiografía y el pensamiento político del siglo XVII" (Universitat Autònoma de Barcelona, 1994), 45.

14. Bosc, *Sumari,* 58, 73. For a similar notion of liberty expressed by Aragonese writers, see Xavier Gil, "Aragonese Constitutionalism and Habsburg Rule: The Varying Meanings of Liberty," in *Spain, Europe, and the Atlantic World: Essays in Honour of John H. Elliott,* ed. Richard Kagan and Geoffrey Parker (Cambridge, 1995), 160–87.

"external signs" of centuries of countless services to their kings.[15] Not long after Bosc, the Augustinian priest and writer Gaspar Sala explained to the French the Catalans' understanding of privileges:

> In Catalonia what are called privileges mean something very different. Privileges are the graces, prerogatives, and liberties granted by kings broadly or individually, that is to say, to Catalonia as a whole, or on the contrary, to a city, town, or place, a church, a community, or individual persons. These privileges have the force of law, and are made by means of a contract that the king may not revoke.[16]

Privileges, history, and the ties to their kings were therefore closely linked to each other, and Catalans saw all three as essential to how they lived and who they were.

Barcelona's artisans shared Catalans' pride in their identity and way of life. Pau Pedrola, a master mercer from Barcelona, wrote about the "great fame" *(tant bona fama)* of the "Catalan nation" contained in the chronicles and conquests of Catalonia.[17] Artisans could also claim Barcelona's greatness and glory as their own because it was their city and homeland, "my *pàtria*," in the words of Esteve Gilabert Bruniquer.[18] This seventeenth-century chronicler was by profession a notary, which in Barcelona made him an *artista*, an artisan belonging to a select group of "arts" that included druggists, barber-surgeons, and makers of wax candles. In 1630, after more than thirty years of service to the city council, this notary finished a history of Barcelona that remains one of the most ardent expressions of love for the city. In all his years of work, Bruniquer declared in the book's preface, his sole aim had been to "serve my pàtria and sacrifice myself for it, as a holocaust, with all my dedication." That sacrifice included searching for every piece of evidence that would demonstrate beyond doubt that Barcelona had the best government, that its officials were the most dedicated, that its noble families were the most valiant warriors, and that its people were the most Christian—in short, that it was a city without parallel.[19]

---

15. Bosc, *Sumari*, 8. He also defines privilege as "retribution and payment" for services (58) and "reward [*premi*] for the work and favor in the public and common interest" (510).

16. BNP Français 705: "Estat de la Catalogne: Mémoire de Mr. l'Abbé de St. Cugat sur les affaires de la Principauté" [1644?], fol. 17.

17. BC F. Bon. 6558: *Molt Illustres Senyors Diputats del General de Catalunya* (Barcelona, 1626), fol. Av.

18. Esteve Gilabert Bruniquer, *Relació sumaria de la antiga fundació de la Ciutat de Barcelona* (Barcelona, 1885), 9. Bruniquer wrote this work in 1630, but it remained unpublished until the nineteenth century.

19. In return, Barcelona named a street in the neighborhood of Gràcia after him.

Barcelona's greatness also owed much to its artisans. This busy industrial and commercial port of 30,000 to 40,000 inhabitants had become rich and powerful in large part because of artisans' hard work.[20] There were more than one hundred different trades and crafts in virtually every imaginable economic sector—textile, leather, metal, construction, transportation, and many more (see Appendix 1). Known as "mechanical arts" because they required the use of the hands, these trades included professions common to other European cities, such as carpenters, smiths, shoemakers, and weavers, but also others that might not seem consistent with our image of an artisan—for example, market gardeners *(hortolans)* and sailors.[21] Officially, they were all *menestrals,* or "mechanics," that is, men who worked with their hands, although colloquially they were simply called *oficials:* men of the trades. Altogether, masters, journeymen, and women artisans headed nearly half (48.53 percent) of the families in the city,[22] and their spouses, children, relatives, or servants most likely shared their work and were therefore artisans as well. They lived and worked for the most part in three- and four-story buildings along narrow streets *(carrers)* bearing the names of their trades: Carrer dels Escudellers (potters), Carrer de la Freneria (harness making), Carrer de la Tapineria (clog making), and so on. Some trades had long concentrated in certain neighborhoods, such as the shoemakers and cobblers, two of the oldest crafts in the city, who had for centuries lived near the cathedral. To the north, by the conventual church of Sant Agustí Vell, the numerous wool clothiers, weavers, tanners, and skinners had their workshops. Not far away, the doors of the beautiful Church of Santa Maria del Mar opened to the Carrer de l'Argenteria, named after the silversmith shops on this street that looked down to the sea. On the waterfront were the poorer and densely populated neighborhoods of La Marina and La Ribera, where large numbers of sailors, fishers, and skippers worked in the city's busy port and fish market. They too called their neighborhoods their pàtria, expressing their

20. For Barcelona's population between 1580 and 1640, see Antoni Simon and Jordi Andreu, "Evolució demogràfica (segles XVI i XVII)," in *Història de Barcelona,* ed. Jaume Sobrequés i Callicó, 8 vols. (Barcelona, 1991–97), 4:111–12.

21. For two overviews of Barcelona's trades and craft confraternities, see Pedro Molas Ribalta, *Los gremios barceloneses del siglo XVIII* (Madrid, 1970) and Pierre Bonnassie, *La organización del trabajo en Barcelona a fines del siglo XV* (Barcelona, 1975).

22. Figures are based on the analysis of the 1516–17 census in Jorge Nadal and Emilio Giralt, "Barcelona en 1717–18: Un modelo de sociedad pre-industrial," in *Homenaje a Don Ramón Carande,* 2 vols. (Madrid, 1963), 2:289. Albert García Espuche has recently pointed out problems with the findings of Nadal and Giralt; see *Un siglo decisivo: Barcelona y Cataluña, 1550–1640* (Madrid, 1998), 79–80.

sentiments not with notary Bruniquer's literary enthusiasm but rather with loud shouts cried in their streets.[23]

Artisans' sense of pride came not only from being Catalan and being from Barcelona. Artisans enjoyed privileges as both signs of their service to God, king, and pàtria and a guarantee of the freedom necessary to continue that service forever. That service was not limited to working at their trades. Artisans' nearly eighty confraternities had contributed much to the city's religious life by taking part in public processions, the worship of saints, and acts of charity. Craft confraternities gave artisans the opportunity to worship God and perform acts of charity.[24] Master artisans also served in the city council and in the city's guard, where they defended Barcelona from attack and went to war to fight for their king. Privileges enabled artisans in craft confraternities to elect officers freely, establish rules, and meet without the presence of any religious or lay authority; they also allowed artisans to regulate their trades, determine who could exercise a trade, and punish any infractions (see Appendix 3 for a list of confraternity officers).[25] The idea that artisans' privileges guaranteed freedom might at first seem difficult to understand because historians have long described such privileges as monopolies. Yet that was not how artisans saw it. Explaining the reason for their privileges, master wool clothiers claimed that privileges guaranteed their freedom to practice their trades: "It is a most just and reasonable thing that all who. . . live by the same art or trade have a certain form and order. . . so that all. . . may live comfortably and without prejudice of some over others."[26]

History and Privileges

Privileges also reminded artisans that their distinct place in Barcelona was intimately bound to the history of their city and of Catalonia. Each craft

23. On La Ribera, see Albert Garcia i Espuche and Manuel Guàrdia i Bassols, *Espai i societat a la Barcelona pre-industrial* (Barcelona, 1986), 27–29, 37. According to the tanner Miquel Parets, rioters in La Ribera cried "*Visca la pàtria*" during a riot in 1629; *De los muchos sucesos dignos de memoria que han ocurrido en Barcelona y otros lugares de Cataluña*, in *MHE*, vols. 20–25 (Madrid, 1888–93), 20:41. On the concept of *pàtria*, see James S. Amelang, "People of the Ribera: Popular Politics and Neighborhood Identity in Early Modern Barcelona," in *Culture and Identity in Early Modern Europe (1500–1800): Essays in Honor of Natalie Zemon Davis*, ed. Barbara Diefendorf and Carla Hesse (Ann Arbor, 1993), 119–37.

24. For a discussion of the place of artisans' confraternities in Barcelona's religious life, see Henry Kamen, *The Phoenix and the Flame: Catalonia and the Counter Reformation* (New Haven, 1993), 165–67.

25. In most cases, masters' confraternity officers (*prohoms* or *cònsols*) were chosen from the bags held in city hall containing the names of masters' candidates to the Consell de Cent. The names were chosen at random, following the system of *insaculació* (lottery) used in the election of city officials.

26. ACA Reial Audiència Plets Civils 5968: confraternity of wool weavers versus confraternity of wool clothiers (1594–1606).

confraternity maintained its own archive of documents, which included minutes of council meetings, lists of members, copies of trade ordinances, and privileges. The tanners and skinners had privileges granted to them in 1401 by King Martin copied in red and black ink on parchment, and together with other ordinances the privileges were bound in a book with a heavy leather cover, studs, a lion design, and a big clasp.[27] Other confraternities had similarly fancy volumes, some of which are on display at Barcelona's Museum of History.

The city's long and distinguished history was palpable in the heavy Roman ruins, the fine Gothic churches, and the respectable houses of Barcelona's patrician families in the Carrer de Montcada.[28] To the notary Bruniquer, the city had been fated for greatness from its distant origins. Four hundred years before the foundation of Rome, Barcelona began its existence at the hand of the Egyptian Hercules—not to be confused with the younger Greek hero claimed by the Spanish Habsburg monarchy as its founder.[29] However, it was centuries after the Roman Empire had disappeared that the relatively modest Roman town of Barcino began its glorious ascent.[30] The Arabs had overrun the Visigoth kingdom of the Iberian Peninsula in the eighth century, when Christian fighters came down from the Pyrenees and began the slow process of reclaiming territories to the south. Among those Christian warriors, the counts of Barcelona became the dominant force in northeastern Iberia during the ninth and tenth centuries, turning their still modest town into the undisputed capital of Catalonia. By the twelfth century, the counts of Barcelona had also become kings of Aragon, making the Catalan capital a royal court in an aggressive and expanding monarchy.

Catalans, and especially the people of Barcelona, were the driving force behind this expansion. Catalan warriors and Barcelona's merchants proved able servants to the kings of Aragon in the conquest of the Balearic Islands

27. It appears that most documents in this volume date from the late fifteenth or early sixteenth century, and that later ones were copied on blank sheets possibly left for that purpose; AHCB Gremis 35-90 ("Ordinacions. . . dels blanquers," 1422–1710).

28. James S. Amelang, "El Carrer de Montcada: Canvi social i cultura popular a la Barcelona moderna," *L'Avenç* 18 (1979): 56–60.

29. Bruniquer, *Relació sumaria*, 13–14. Bruniquer does not give the source for his claim about the Egyptian Hercules, whom Herodotus discusses in his *History of the Persian Wars*, bk. 2, chaps. 43–44. Bruniquer cites Pere Tomich (or Pedro Tomic), whose *Historias e conquestas dels. . . reys d'Aragó e comtes de Barcelona* (first published in 1495) describes the foundation of Barcelona by the more familiar Hercules. (I am grateful to Lynn H. Nelson for these references.) On the Habsburg dynasty's identification with Hercules, see Jonathan Brown and J. H. Elliott, *A Palace for a King: The Buen Retiro and the Court of Philip IV* (New Haven, 1980), 160.

30. For an overview in English of Barcelona in the Middle Ages, see T. N. Bisson, *The Medieval Crown of Aragon: A Short History* (Oxford, 1986).

and Valencia, two territories where Catalan became the dominant language. Whereas the kings of Castile continued the Reconquista against the Arabs until 1492, during the thirteenth and fourteenth centuries the kings of Aragon embarked on an easterly expansion across the Mediterranean to Sardinia, Sicily, Naples, and the Greek duchies of Athens and Neopatria. All of these lands, together with the old territories of Catalonia and the kingdom of Aragon, became known as the Crown of Aragon.

In return for helping their rulers enlarge their power and reputation, the count-kings granted important privileges to the citizens of Barcelona. As early as 1118, Ramon Berenguer III, the count of Barcelona (1093?–1131), awarded the first commercial privilege to the "men of Barcelona" for their assistance in suppressing a revolt in his Provençal territories.[31] In 1249, following the conquests of Majorca and Valencia led by Catalan forces, King James I the Conqueror (r. 1213–76) granted the city a privilege recognizing a council with a considerable measure of self-rule. The municipal regime evolved quickly, and before the end of James's reign, Barcelona had in place two institutions that would govern the city for the next five centuries: the *consellers* (counselors) and the Consell de Cent (Council of the Hundred). By 1257, artisans from at least nineteen trades had eighty-five (out of two hundred) representatives in the city council,[32] and later artisans would also serve as consellers.

In addition to allowing artisans to participate in their city's government, Barcelona's rulers recognized artisans' growing importance by granting privileges to various trades. As early as the twelfth century, the city's artisans made armors, arrows, catapults, lances, swords, shields, bridles, and harnesses.[33] However, the earliest royal privileges went to artisans in trades increasingly involved in commerce. In 1200, King Peter II (r. 1196–1213) recognized the confraternities of tailors, weavers, and skinners, in 1203 that of the shoemakers, and in 1211 that of the masons.[34] With conquest came new economic opportunities for Barcelona. By the middle of the thir-

---

31. Stephen P. Bensch, *Barcelona and Its Rulers, 1096–1291* (Cambridge, 1995), 224.

32. Antonio de Capmany y de Monpalau, *Memorias históricas sobre la marina, comercio y artes de la antigua ciudad de Barcelona,* ed. E. Giralt and C. Batlle, 3 vols. (Barcelona, 1961–63), 1:451. According to Carme Batlle Gallart, there were more than twenty trades represented; *L'expansió baixmedieval (segles XIII–XV),* vol. 3 of *Història de Catalunya,* ed. Pierre Vilar (Barcelona, 1988), 125–26.

33. Bensch, *Barcelona and Its Rulers,* 184–87.

34. Bonnassie, *Organización del trabajo,* 13; on the shoemakers, see Joan-F. Cabestany i Fort, "Els mestres sabaters i la Confraria de Sant Marc (segle XIV)," in *Homenaje a Jaime Vicens Vives,* 2 vols. (Barcelona, 1965–67) 2:75–84; and Philip Banks, "The Origins of the 'Gremi de Sabaters' of Barcelona," *Quaderns d'arqueologia i història de la ciutat* 18 (1980): 109–18.

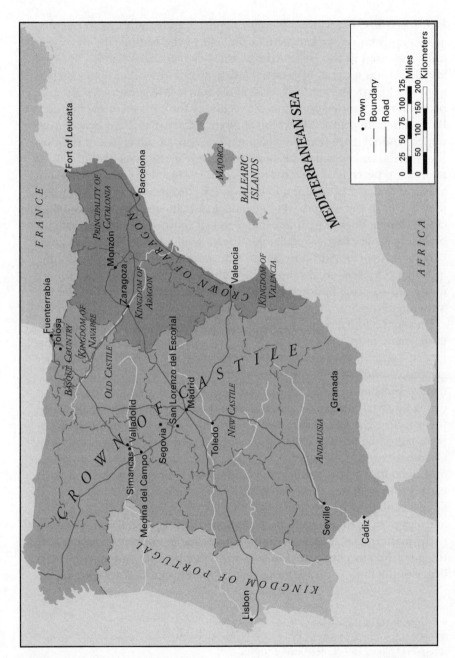

MAP 1. Iberian Peninsula

teenth century, Barcelona's skinners exported hides and furs to regional and long-distance markets, and at the end of the century the first cloth mills appeared in the city.[35] Around the year 1300, Barcelona exported abroad several varieties of cotton textiles (mixed with other fibers, such as wool and linen). During the course of the fourteenth century, wool textile production expanded dramatically, becoming the city's principal industry. By the fifteenth century, Barcelona had thousands of artisans in dozens of trades producing woolens, cotton and linen canvas, silk veils and ribbons, shoes, glass, and countless products made of iron, tin, and silver. In all, as many as 80 percent of the city's population made a living from working in artisanal trades.[36] In addition to its industry, the city rose as a major maritime power in the western Mediterranean, challenged only by the Italian city of Genoa. Beginning in the late eleventh century, Barcelona's artisans built ships that crisscrossed the Mediterranean hauling wares and combatants to Cyprus, Alexandria, and Constantinople. The city's shipping industry centered on the impressive shipyard *(drassanes)*, whose large fourteenth-century building with its monumental arches today houses the Museum of the Sea.[37]

During the fourteenth and fifteenth centuries, kings granted master artisans many more privileges, allowing them to establish new confraternities. In 1395, there were forty-five such organizations, and their number grew to seventy-three in the following century.[38] In principle, their objective was for their members to perform acts of charity and pray together for divine intervention for the protection of their persons, their families, and their trades. The successive waves of bubonic plague that hammered Europe beginning in 1347 had inspired such organizations throughout Latin Christendom. But Barcelona's confraternities also allowed artisans a second objective: to organize better and make greater demands on their earthly rulers. Master artisans were thus able to pull resources together and appeal to their rulers for greater input in the city's government. In 1451 and 1453, they sent delegations to Alphonse V (r. 1416–58), who listened to the masters' claims and saw in those demands an opportunity to counter the powerful city patriciate. Consequently, in 1454, he granted royal privileges to the craft confraternities that increased significantly their repre-

---

35. Bensch, *Barcelona and Its Rulers*, 191, 299.

36. Antoni Riera i Melis and Gaspar Feliu i Monfort, "Activitats econòmiques," in Sobrequés i Callicó, *Història de Barcelona*, 3:150.

37. On the first shipbuilding activities in Barcelona sponsored by count Ramon Berenguer I (1035–76), see Bensch, *Barcelona and Its Rulers*, 116.

38. Riera i Melis and Feliu i Monfort, "Activitats econòmiques," 3:150.

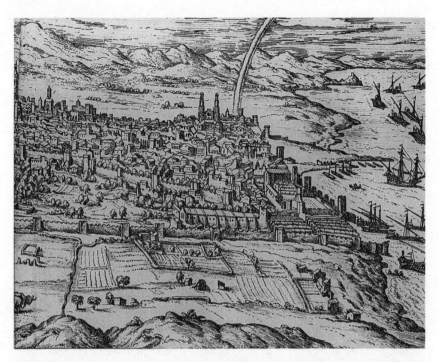

FIGURE 1 Detail of a view of Barcelona from the nearby mountain of Montjuïc drawn in 1567. To the right, on the port, is the complex of buildings that formed the drassanes (shipyard). The two high towers further back belong to the church of Santa Maria del Mar, in the Ribera neighborhood, which had a large concentration of artisans. From Georg Braun and Frans Hogenberg, *Civitates orbis terrarum*, 6 vols. (Cologne, 1572–1617), vol. 1, plate 5. Courtesy of the Kenneth Spencer Research Library, University of Kansas.

sentation in the Consell de Cent (32 artistes and 32 menestrals out of the council's 144 members) and among the consellers (one artista and one menestral out of five consellers; see Appendix 2).[39] Artisans had become a powerful force in the city, thanks to royal support.

Unfortunately for artisans, this period of significant legal and political gain was accompanied by the scourges of plague, economic instability, and political turmoil. Between 1348 and the end of the fifteenth century, Barcelona suffered more than a dozen outbreaks of the plague. The city's

39. These events are discussed further in Chapter 2.

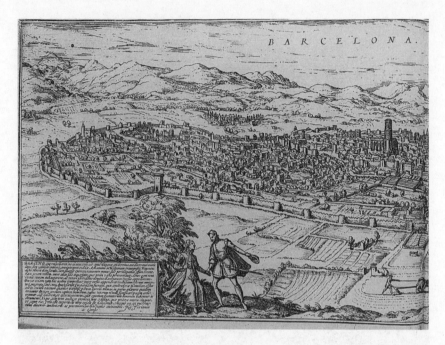

FIGURE 2 Detail of a view of Barcelona in 1567. The high tower on the right is the cathedral's. Within the city walls in the foreground, the Raval neighborhood still had numerous open fields. From Georg Braun and Frans Hogenberg, *Civitates orbis terrarum*, 6 vols. (Cologne, 1572–1617), vol. 1, plate 5. Courtesy of the Kenneth Spencer Research Library, University of Kansas.

thriving industry and trade managed to overcome such adversity and do relatively well through the middle of the fifteenth century. Catalan ships continued to export cloth and other artisan-produced items all over the Mediterranean. Nevertheless, merchants and artisans worried about the city's economic well-being, especially in view of mounting foreign competition that was supplanting Catalan goods in Flanders and Andalusia and that threatened their standing elsewhere. In the 1450s, Catalans felt confident that if the Consell de Cent adopted protectionist measures, Barcelona would overcome its commercial enemies. That confidence, however, was shattered by the start of civil war in 1462. Barcelona became the epicenter of a ten-year civil war involving King John II (r. 1458–79), Catalonia's elite, and serfs *(remences)*. At the height of that conflict, Catalans severed their allegiance to their king and successively elected three foreign princes as counts of Barcelona, none of whom could defeat John.[40] The conflict dragged on, and the city had to withstand a siege and the plague. When the fighting came to an end in 1472, the city welcomed back King John as its rightful ruler, and in return the king did not repeal Catalonia's laws or the city's privileges. The plague and years of fighting had long-lasting effects. Barcelona's population declined from 50,000 in 1340 to 20,000 in 1477.[41]

Two decades had passed since the end of the civil war when Ferdinand and Isabella welcomed Christopher Columbus back from his first voyage to the Indies at the old royal palace of the kings of Aragon in Barcelona. The city, however, had little to rejoice in from this meeting. The Genoese admiral's conquests and profits would belong exclusively to Castile. Moreover, Barcelona was in no position to turn wholeheartedly to this new imperial venture. Twenty years of peace had given the city an opportunity to rebuild its economy and reestablish good ties to the monarchy. Ferdinand the Catholic (r. 1479–1516) had promoted a reorganization of the city's institutions—including the reduction of artisans' power in the city's political institutions—to maintain a certain degree of stability and forever prevent the conflicts that had marred his father's reign. In 1498, he granted a privilege that fixed artisans' representation in the Consell de Cent for the next century and a half (see Appendix 2). Nevertheless, even those reforms could not restore Barcelona to its former glory and preeminence in the Crown of Aragon. Valencia had surpassed it as the principal Iberian port on the Mediterranean. In addition, new, more pressing concerns in the much larger and more populated Crown of Castile were drawing the monarch's attention away from Catalonia. King Ferdinand made long visits with Isabella to Castile to manage the affairs of that kingdom, and after she died in 1504, he settled there as regent to his daughter Joanna ("the Mad") until his death in 1516.[42]

Ferdinand's successor and grandson, the nineteen-year-old Charles of Habsburg (1500–1559), arrived in Catalonia's capital in 1519 as the new king of Castile and Aragon. He had come for the traditional swearing-in ceremony as count of Barcelona to promise to observe all of the principality's laws and respect its privileges. The city celebrated the presence of

40. Catalans elected as counts of Barcelona King Henry IV of Castile (1462), Peter, constable of Portugal (1463), and René of Anjou, duke of Provence (1466).

41. Bisson, *Medieval Crown*, 165.

42. On Catalonia's changing fortunes during the reign of Ferdinand the Catholic, see Núria Sales, *Els segles de la decadència (segles XVI–XVIII)*, vol. 4 of *Història de Catalunya*, ed. Pierre Vilar (Barcelona, 1989), chap. 1.

their new ruler and prayed for his long and prosperous reign. Yet during his stay, news arrived of the young monarch's election as Charles V, Holy Roman Emperor, the newest and greatest of his long line of titles. His territories already extended from Sicily to the Netherlands, from the Austrian Habsburg lands to the Caribbean Antilles. That same year, Hernán Cortés would initiate the conquest of Mexico, and Ferdinand Magellan set out on an expedition that in time would extend Spanish authority as far as the Philippines.[43]

In this vast empire, Barcelona and Catalonia remained strategically significant. As a frontier territory bordering France, the Habsburg dynasty's chief rival, the principality remained vitally important to the defense of Spain. Around 1570, Barcelona also became a departing point for troops and American silver en route to central and northern Europe; it was also a relay point for courier service from the Netherlands and communications between Spain and Italy.[44] The successors of Charles V acknowledged Catalonia's importance during successive royal visits, but these visits became rare after the middle of the sixteenth century. The fortunes of Barcelona's artisans accompanied those of their city. They could no longer sustain the industrial and commercial growth that had made Barcelona a powerhouse in the late Middle Ages. The city could no longer claim to be one of the dominant ports in the western Mediterranean, even at a time when the Mediterranean was losing its commercial preeminence to the Atlantic. But Barcelona's artisans remained important, though in a more modest way. Thousands of men and women continued to work in their trades and pay taxes. Exports of leather goods and textiles still arrived in Sicily, Naples, and increasingly Seville, where they were shipped to the American colonies.[45] Slowly, and perhaps unwillingly, Barcelona's artisans introduced changes in their ways of doing business in order to survive, at

43. For an overview of Spanish expansion abroad during Charles V's reign, see John Lynch, *Spain, 1516–1598: From Nation State to World Empire*, 2d ed. rev. (Oxford, 1991), chap. 5.

44. On the passage of silver (and troops) from Barcelona to Genoa, see Fernand Braudel, *The Mediterranean and the Mediterranean World in the Age of Philip II*, trans. Siân Reynolds (New York, 1972), 1:487–93; and Pierre Vilar, *La Catalogne dans l'Espagne Moderne*, 3 vols. (Paris, 1962), vol. 1, chap. 2. On the movement of Spanish troops to northern Europe, see Geoffrey Parker, *The Army of Flanders and the Spanish Road, 1567–1659: The Logistics of Spanish Victory and Defeat in the Low Countries' War* (Cambridge, 1972), 51 (figure 6), 59. On Barcelona's link in the courier service from the Netherlands to the Spanish court, see Geoffrey Parker, *The Grand Strategy of Philip II* (New Haven, 1998), 48.

45. On Barcelona's trade with Seville and America, see García Espuche, *Un siglo decisivo*, 347–60.

least until better times came along. Meanwhile, they found in their history and privileges not dusty relics of a lost past, but inspiration for their future actions—and more important, the means to undertake them.

Politics

By 1580, the challenge to Barcelona's artisans, and Catalans in general, was how to maintain the freedom, the laws, and the privileges gained in the course of many centuries. In this sense, old strategies gave way to new ones. The monarch's continued absence meant that Catalans could not rely as readily on the Corts—the principality's representative assembly— and that any direct appeals to the king would take longer.[46] Major problems in the principality therefore remained unresolved, causing serious long-term difficulties. The prolonged separation from the king also reduced opportunities to ask for and receive honors and privileges—a situation that frustrated Catalans as well as many other subjects of the Spanish monarch. However, in his absence, Catalan authorities, empowered by their laws and privileges, might enjoy greater freedom of action. This was the other side of royal absenteeism: the possibility of acting first and offering explanations later. Artisans took stock of this situation and adapted their strategies accordingly. They appealed to city and Catalan authorities for quick action but never surrendered their desire to seek royal privileges or justice.

Artisans, however, were not passive observers of political events; on the contrary, in defending their interests or voicing their concerns, they could in turn impact politics in Barcelona. This was true not only in the case of master artisans who took part in their city's government. Masters and journeymen, poorer and better-off artisans, men and women of the trades—they were all part of what contemporaries described as the *poble menut*, the "little people," whose actions were of great concern to those responsible for maintaining order in the city.

The wider political significance of the little people in general and artisans in particular depended on the complex relations among the major political institutions in Barcelona. Simply put, politics in Barcelona were dominated by the sometimes uneasy dynamic among city, Catalan, and

46. Joan Lluís Palos discusses the impact of the growing infrequency of the meeting of the Corts on the Catalan political system in "El fracàs de les Corts," chap. 7 of *Catalunya a l'imperi dels Àustries: La pràctica de govern (segles XVI i XVII)* (Lleida, 1994).

royal authorities. During the sixteenth and seventeenth centuries, three major players dominated the city's political life: first, Barcelona's Consell de Cent headed by its five consellers; second, the Diputació presided over by its *diputats,* sometimes in close cooperation with Catalonia's nobility and clergy represented in its estates, or *braços;* and third, the viceregal administration, headed by the viceroy with the assistance of the judges of the royal Audiència.

On the one hand, the Consell de Cent had great authority over most affairs in Barcelona.[47] Occasionally it wanted to extend that authority beyond the city's walls to the rest of Catalonia, particularly in economic and commercial matters such as grain supplies, the export of raw materials, and the import of foreign manufactured goods. The two most effective channels to resolve those concerns were the king and the Catalan Corts, neither of which had any special predisposition to act quickly or favorably toward the city. If pressured for action and impatient for results, Barcelona's consellers might simply act on their own, disregarding the indignation such actions might produce in viceregal authorities and the rest of Catalonia.

On the other hand, the Diputació ideally acted in the interests of all Catalans.[48] Strictly speaking, the Diputació was a committee of the Corts. Well before the sixteenth century, it had become a permanent institution of great authority housed in a large palace behind the cathedral. Its primary duties were the collection and administration of taxes voted by the Corts, but it also oversaw the defense of Catalan laws and liberties. Three diputats presided over the Diputació, one for each *braç* (estate) in the Corts: ecclesiastic *(braç eclesiàstic),* noble *(braç militar),* and representatives from towns and cities *(braç reial).*[49] Although in theory the Diputació represented all Catalans, in practice it was not rare to find clear differences between Barcelona's policies—or more precisely, the Consell de Cent's—and those of the nobility, the clergy, and especially other Catalan towns, who did not like how the capital tried to lord over them. Yet more often than not, the Diputació's prime concern was to ensure that royal officers did not violate Catalan laws and privileges. Consequently, diputats and the viceregal ad-

---

47. For an early modern perspective on the workings of the Consell de Cent, see Bruniquer, *Relació sumaria.* For an overview in English, see James S. Amelang, *Honored Citizens of Barcelona: Patrician Culture and Class Relations, 1490–1714* (Princeton, 1986), 22–33.

48. On the Diputació, or Generalitat, see Víctor Ferro, *El dret públic català: Les institucions a Catalunya fins al Decret de Nova Planta* (Vic, 1987), chap. 6; Palos, *Catalunya a l'imperi,* chap. 8.

49. On the *braços,* see Ferro, *Dret públic,* chap. 5.1, and Palos, *Catalunya a l'imperi,* chap. 6.

ministration were often at odds, and on several occasions between 1580 and 1640, their disputes became major political crises.

Compared with the two powerful city and Catalan institutions, the viceregal administration felt its resources were inadequate for the magnitude of its duties: to protect the king's patrimony, to dispense justice, and to make certain that the principality's defenses were ready.[50] To carry out these tasks, a viceroy counted on a relatively small number of officials consisting of judges, fiscal agents, and a few guards. Although viceroys stood for the monarch—his alter ego—they faced considerable limitations. They could not grant privileges or generally make major decisions without consulting the king and his ministers in the Council of Aragon in Madrid, often a slow process that tested many viceroys' patience. Viceroys were especially at a disadvantage when, as was often the case, they were aristocrats from outside the principality.[51] Catalans' pride in their freedom and privileges appeared to them to be petulant stubbornness, even disloyalty. Many viceroys bitterly complained about the difficulty of carrying out their duties properly, interrupted at almost every step, it seemed to them, by Catalan punctiliousness regarding their laws and privileges. The viceroy's greatest aid lay in the judges of the Audiència, the royal court of appeals for Catalonia. This tribunal consisted of about a dozen magistrates whose duties included judging civil and criminal cases; but as members of the viceroy's Royal Council, they also advised him and when necessary executed royal orders.[52] By far the greatest limitation on the power of all royal officers in Catalonia was the dismal situation of the royal finances in the principality.[53] To increase revenues, the Corts had to be convened, but more often than not officials resorted to measures that Catalans considered illegal.

The relationship of Barcelona's artisans to these three players varied greatly, and it was this relationship that shaped artisans' strategies for political action. They felt the closest affinity by far to the Consell de Cent, where they had considerable representation, access to city offices (see Appendix 2), and close ties to the consellers through the city guard and other

50. On the viceregal administration, see Ferro, *Dret públic*, chap. 2; Jesús Lalinde Abadía, *La institución virreinal en Cataluña (1471–1716)* (Barcelona, 1964).

51. Between 1520 and 1700, only six of fifty viceroys were Catalan; Palos, *Catalunya a l'imperi*, 39.

52. On the Audiència and the Royal Council, see Ferro, *Dret públic*, 108–19, and Joan Lluís Palos, *Els juristes i la defensa de les Constitucions: Joan Pere Fontanella (1575–1649)* (Vic, 1997), 21–29.

53. Bernat Hernández, "Un assaig de reforma del sistema fisco-financer de la monarquia a Catalunya: L'impost del quint sobre les imposicions locals, 1580–1640," *Manuscrits* 14 (1996): 297–319.

areas of city government. After 1454, thirty-two menestrals and an equal number of artistes sat in the Consell de Cent, and after 1498 the two artisan estates alternated in the office of fifth conseller.[54] This meant that artisans could participate in major decisions taken by one of Catalonia's most powerful institutions. Nevertheless, artisans were not always in agreement with the policies of the Consell de Cent. What James Amelang has called the city's oligarchy—noble "honored citizens" and knights, doctors of law and medicine, and merchants—were expected to have, and usually did have, the dominant voice in the council; they sometimes supported policies that artisan confraternities opposed. Such differences were inevitable, partly because the eighty or so craft confraternities in Barcelona had competing interests, but also because the oligarchy and artisans had different sets of priorities that were not always possible to reconcile.

Artisans' organizations—the craft confraternities and colleges—therefore remained crucial vehicles for expressing artisans' needs and defending their privileges. Those privileges guaranteed artisans' organizations considerable autonomy of action, and their officers constantly expressed their views to city authorities on all matters concerning their members, including fiscal and commercial policies, aid to the city's poor, and participation in public ceremonies. In addition, confraternities and colleges had resources to sue the city or lobby royal authorities for privileges. Perhaps even more important, artisans could put together the resources to appeal to the Audiència to defend their privileges from challenges by competitors or the Consell de Cent's policies. Thus, the royal tribunal became an important ally of artisans to balance the city's seemingly undisputed authority over trade matters.

Occasionally, master artisans might find in the Diputació another ally against commercial or economic policies instituted by the Consell de Cent. For instance, because one of the principal revenues collected by the Diputació came from taxes on textiles, the diputats and master wool clothiers (who finished and traded in woolens) paid special attention to any ordinances voted by the city council that might affect cloth manufacture. Master artisans also found in the Diputació minor posts, but the important offices in this institution—the diputats, the *oïdors* (who supervised accounts), and lawyers—were Catalan ecclesiastics, nobles, and members of the ruling oligarchies from Barcelona and other towns. The Diputació's position tended to reflect the concerns of this Catalan elite, which often differed greatly from those of the poble menut of Barcelona. Diputats and

---

54. Josep M. Torras i Ribé, *Els municipis catalans de l'Antic Règim, 1453–1808* (Barcelona, 1983), 63–64.

delegates from the braços might consider it natural to defend the privileges and laws of the principality, but on the whole, artisans had a far better chance of having their concerns heard in the Consell de Cent than in the Diputació. In return, it was the consellers rather than diputats who expected to command the support of artisans if necessary.

For all its privileges and independence of action, the Consell de Cent cherished the power it derived from commanding the wills of Barcelona's poble menut. The poble menut—or more specifically, the masters of the craft confraternities—formed the core of the city's guard, which was the largest defensive organization in the principality.[55] Service in the guard's companies offered artisans an important source of pride, and the companies followed orders from the conseller *en cap*. In an emergency, he could call as many as ten thousand men to defend the city. Although the viceroy was the "captain general" of Catalonia, he had nowhere as many soldiers at his disposal as did the consellers. In the 1550s and 1560s, viceroys had attempted and failed to put the city guard under their military control. Viceroys had to content themselves with a small number of royal guards in the drassanes.[56] Only in 1652 did viceroys have a permanent garrison of soldiers in a fort on the mountain of Montjuïc that overlooked the city. In an emergency, it was the Consell de Cent's bells to which the companies responded. Likewise, in case of disputes between the viceroy and the Diputació, the artisans of Barcelona followed the lead of the city council.

The Consell de Cent's command over the guard did not mean it controlled the people of the city because, according to royal officers, "among the people there is a variety of types, and the menestrals are the more in line with reason because their aim is to maintain their state quietly, which does not happen with the other part of the little people."[57] Masters, journeymen, and women and men workers did not all share the same sense of loyalty to city authorities. As would happen time and again, artisans might be on both sides of street disorders, taking part in the violence and attempting to quell it. Even the consellers could not claim that their command over masters' companies was perfect. After all, the guard was made up of civil-

---

55. On Barcelona's guard, see BC F. Bon. 10848: "Ordre militar [d]els puestos als quals las compañias. . . han de acudir. . . " (Barcelona, 1623); Jordi Vidal Pla, "Les formes tradicionals de l'organització armada a la Catalunya dels s. XVI i XVII: Suggerències per a una investigació," *Manuscrits* 3 (1986): 105–16.

56. According to I. A. A. Thompson, in 1583 there were only 150 men on the Catalan frontier; *War and Government in Habsburg Spain, 1560–1620* (London, 1976), 75.

57. "Porque en el Pueblo hay distinción de gentes y los que son menestrales ques la parte más puesta en razón porque llevan la mira a continuar su estado con quietud, lo que no sucede en la otra parte de Pueblo suelto"; ACA CA llig. 287 no. 133: *consulta* of the Junta de Estado y Ejecución, 18 June 1640.

ians, not soldiers, and either jealousy among men of different trades or dis-
agreement with orders might result in acts of insubordination. Such incidents were rare, but nonetheless serious violence and disorders could have
a severe impact on Barcelona's politics, especially at moments of great tension among the city, Catalan authorities, and royal officials. At those times,
the Consell de Cent's ability to maintain order could be its greatest evidence of power, but its failure could be a sign of its weaknesses. Rarely did
the Diputació and the viceroy try to undermine the Consell de Cent's authority over the people of the city; not only was that difficult, but it was playing with fire. Yet at moments of crisis, royal authorities might feel desperate enough to try to undermine the Consell de Cent's broad base of support
by offering artisans privileges or threatening to take the Audiència away
from Barcelona.

Artisans' impact on the city's complex political life therefore hinged on
aligning themselves with a higher authority or threatening to act violently.
Barcelona's craft confraternities could not usually exert much influence
over its own artisans and the rest of the poble menut, or over the city's powerful lay and religious institutions. But as much as those institutions dis-
liked it, the poble menut sometimes appeared to have a mind of its own
that, like a beast or a monster, would not listen to reason, only to threats
and force. This image of the poble menut as monster, however, betrayed
the respect and the fear it could inspire among the powerful, which alerts
us to an important conclusion: to understand major events in the city's history requires paying close attention to what artisans and the rest of the
people were doing.

Myth and Action

Above the political conflicts in Barcelona, the ultimate arbiter was the
monarch himself. The viceroy residing in Barcelona represented the king
in Catalonia, but the viceroy never replaced the king. For all Catalans, and
especially for the citizens of Barcelona, whose city government and day-
to-day lives were in large part dependent on royal privileges, the king
often had the last word. The Consell de Cent acted on the basis of its privileges without seeking royal approval; yet it also depended on the king to
carry out significant reforms in government, which might require a new
privilege to replace an old one. In a dispute with the viceroy, the king's
decision could either help the Consell de Cent proceed with its policies
or create additional roadblocks. Similarly, although the Diputació considered its interpretation of Catalan laws and privileges authoritative, it
could not supplant the monarch, who despite his physical absence re-

mained at the heart of the principality's political and legal foundation. Catalans could govern themselves, but they also needed and wanted their monarch.

For Barcelona's artisans too, the king remained central despite his physical absence. Artisans wanted royal justice because it could help them defend their interests and achieve what they believed was fairness. Only the king could grant privileges. All subjects desired a monarch who fit the image of the protector of his people, the dispenser of justice, the source of gifts and rewards. Such myths, which for so long were considered a sign of subservience and naïveté, could also serve as inspiration for action. The "just king" offered a standard against which to measure the living king and his government and ministers.[58] As the political scientist James C. Scott has pointed out, myths and dreams can be empowering if only because they can allow people, especially those who live under repressive circumstances, the opportunity to imagine an alternative reality and therefore aspire to something more, something better.[59]

The monarchy fostered its own myths, which were intended to heighten the image of the ruler, giving him an almost superhuman quality.[60] It was not that monarchs everywhere thought they could somehow brainwash their subjects into believing fairy tales that would keep them subjugated, but rather that rulers everywhere considered myths, political ceremonies, and the cult of their images essential to fostering the loyalty and love that bound ruler and subject more tightly than anything else could.

For all the Spanish monarchy's insistence on detachment from its subjects and strict etiquette, kings always remained willing to support the myths and dreams of their subjects by allowing them to present petitions, seek royal justice, and participate in the magnificent spectacles of royal entrances and processions. The very same conditions that made the king divine and therefore distant from other human beings made the monarchy more, not less, accessible in spirit. What greater difference than that between lowly, sinful human beings and the Lord God Our Father—and yet it was to that divine monarch that all Christians could direct their pleas, if not directly, then through the intercession of the Virgin Mary and the

---

58. On the myth of the just king, see Peter Burke, *Popular Culture in Early Modern Europe* (London, 1978), 151–52; E. J. Hobsbawm, *Primitive Rebels: Studies in Archaic Forms of Social Movement in the Nineteenth and Twentieth Centuries* (1959; reprint, New York, 1965), 119–20.

59. James C. Scott, *Weapons of the Weak: Everyday Forms of Peasant Resistance* (New Haven, 1985), 333.

60. Antonio Feros, " 'Vicedioses, pero humanos': El drama del Rey," *Cuadernos de Historia Moderna* 14 (1993): 103–31.

countless patron saints. The king, like God, remained the last recourse, but it was one monarchs liked their subjects to count on.

Between 1580 and 1640, the Spanish monarchy had important reasons to demonstrate that it cared about Barcelona's artisans. Unlike Castilian cities, where the monarchy might hope to buy influence by appointing allies to city councils or by coopting local officials to the king's service, Barcelona remained out of the king's control.[61] The consellers and the Consell de Cent were elected by lottery, and the names went into the candidates' bags according to a series of procedures intended to prevent interference. Without this avenue of influence, the Spanish monarchs appear to have had few options available except the typical threats of retribution and promises of rewards, especially privileges.

But ever since the days of the count-kings, the rulers of Barcelona had seen in artisans potential allies against the powerful city elite. This is not to say that the monarchy ever acknowledged such a strategy. Rulers in general feared that to encourage the people to stand up to their social superiors might prove that the cure was sometimes worse than the disease. Yet in regard to certain important policies, it is clear that the Spanish monarchy wanted to encourage the impression that artisans sometimes might have more to gain from the king than from the Consell de Cent. Although all monarchs from Ferdinand the Catholic through Philip IV issued declarations agreeing that the Consell de Cent had exclusive authority over all matters involving the craft confraternities, they never once stopped the Audiència from admitting appeals by artisans' organizations. Kings realized how much artisans and the rest of Barcelona's citizens valued their access to the tribunal, and more than once kings tried to coerce them into compliance with royal wishes by threatening to transfer the appeals court to another city. In addition, monarchs never once gave up the promise of privileges, whether to the craft confraternities or to artistes and menestrals in the form of an additional artisan conseller. The notion of the king as a source of gifts and justice was consistent with the image of the monarchy the Habsburgs wanted to project, but this notion also became an effective way to try to garner popular loyalty in Barcelona; the kings used it to pressure the city and Catalan authorities.

Ultimately, however, it is essential to consider artisans as important political players in their own right, even if their role was sometimes small. This

61. I. A. A. Thompson, "Patronato real e integración política en las ciudades castellanas bajo los Austrias," in *Imágenes de la diversidad: El mundo urbano en la Corona de Castilla (s. XVI–XVIII)*, ed. José Ignacio Fortea Pérez ([Santander], 1997), 475–96.

is not to say that what artisans thought and did determined the larger outcome of Barcelona's politics and the relations between Catalonia and the
Spanish monarchy. That would be an exaggeration. But to say that popular politics did not always count in the big game of high politics does not
mean they did not count some of the time, and as it turned out, they mattered at crucial moments between 1580 and 1640.

CHAPTER TWO

For the Common Good of Barcelona

A round 1580, the inhabitants of Barcelona saw with concern the un-stoppable rise of prices of flour, bread, and other basic goods, which many blamed on the shameless greed of unidentified hoarders. If prices continued to climb, it would not be long before crowds of hungry and desperate people began to riot throughout the city. Existing laws prohibiting hoarding and price speculation in Catalonia had apparently failed. The situation seemed grave enough that traditional solutions did not seem to work anymore. Frustrated, city authorities and master artisans began to consider seriously the proposal to request a papal bull excommunicating anyone involved in hoarding and speculation. Perhaps the terrible threat of spiritual condemnation might prove more effective than laws and ordinances. At the same time, the bull would have force beyond Barcelona's territory, where city officers had no authority and most of the grain imports came from. But in order to obtain the papal condemnation, King Philip II had to request it for Barcelona, and so convincing him to do so became the final goal of the campaign for the papal bull against hoarding.

The campaign for the bull against hoarding offers a first look at the complex dynamics of city politics in the late sixteenth century and artisans' place in it. The Consell de Cent, the Diputació, and Catalonia's clergy and nobility debated the merits of the bull and sent delegates to meet with King Philip II in order to discuss the proposal. Master artisans relied on their craft confraternities to lobby city and royal officers in favor of the bull; they also raised funds and used them to send delegates to influence the monarch's decision. Supporters and opponents of the bull tried to convince the king that the bull would benefit or harm the "common good," and although master artisans' confraternities did not use those words, there was no doubt they understood the significance of them.[1] To do their part for the common good had been the reason for the foundation of their confraternities, and it was their duty as loyal subjects to act for the common good by praying and working honestly at their trades. When necessary, artisans felt that duty was reason enough to meet with people of authority to voice their views on important matters. Moreover, the arguments and the language used by proponents and detractors of the bull give us a sense of how artisans saw themselves as political actors, as well as their relationship to city authorities and to their king.

The Evils of Hoarding

The duties of the consellers of Barcelona—the five men who presided over the city's government—"consist above all of three things": first, to keep the city "supplied and stocked with wheat and other food" and to ensure that these goods are not sold at "immoderate prices"; second, to defend "the privileges and prerogatives of the city"; and third, to maintain "peace and kindness among [Barcelona's] citizens and subdue them in case of discord."[2] The notary and chronicler Esteve Gilabert Bruniquer arrived at this statement in 1630, after over thirty years of service to Barcelona and meticulous research on its history and government. He did not explain why he believed that the consellers' principal duty was to keep the city stocked with food. Perhaps the reasons were obvious. Without food a city could not survive, no matter how many privileges it had; and hungry citizens would not live peacefully for long. Yet this ranking of priorities also underscores another, more important idea—namely, that the principal duty of all rulers was to work for the good of their subjects.

However, by 1580, rising prices made it increasingly difficult for Barcelona's consellers to carry out their first and most basic duty. Between

1. For the medieval origins of the notion of the common good or the common utility, see Ernst H. Kantorowicz, *The King's Two Bodies: A Study in Mediaeval Political Theology* (Princeton, 1957); Gaines Post, *Studies in Medieval Legal Thought: Public Law and the State, 1100–1322* (Princeton, 1964). For two different early modern perspectives, see Peter Blickle, *The Revolution of 1525: The German Peasants' War from a New Perspective,* trans. Thomas A. Brady Jr. and H. C. Erik Midelfort (Baltimore, 1985); and Lyndal Roper, " 'The Common Man,' 'the Common Good,' 'Common Women': Gender and Language in the German Reformation Commune," *Social History* 12 (1987): 1–22.

2. Esteve Gilabert Bruniquer, *Relació sumaria de la antiga fundació y cristianisme de la Ciutat de Barcelona* (Barcelona, 1885), 36.

1561 and 1580, the price of wheat in the city nearly doubled, while other food prices rose between 10 and 50 percent. In addition, during the same period, wages failed to keep up with the rise in prices. By 1580, the wages of masons and carpenters could pay for only half of the bread and wheat they could buy twenty years before.[3] The consellers confessed that although the city lost fifty thousand lliures annually to keep bread prices low, the poor suffered "extreme misery and hunger."[4]

The reasons given for this rise in prices have changed over time. Later historians have pointed to such variables as the flood of American precious metals into Spain, rapid population growth, and monetary disparities between Catalan and foreign currencies.[5] Late-sixteenth-century Catalans often cited bad weather and natural disasters.[6] Another repeated explanation centered on human greed. "Those who have wheat for sale always wish for a bad year": so went an anonymous Catalan song published around 1566.[7] But even in a good year, unscrupulous, avaricious people were believed capable of causing wheat scarcity and high prices by hoarding grain. According to one "true story" recounted by a preacher, a merchant "hoarded as much wheat as he could and would not sell it to those who needed wheat." In punishment, one night the devil unleashed a cloud of flies that devoured the merchant's face and took his soul. The preacher warned: "This is the justice of that sovereign judge against this bad Christian hoarder."[8]

Some believed even clergymen were not immune from the temptation to hoard. In 1579, the consellers blamed high bread prices in Barcelona

3. Prices for the five-year periods of 1561–65 and 1576–80 are from Gaspar Feliu Montfort, *Precios y salarios en la Cataluña moderna,* 2 vols. ([Madrid], 1991), 1:37, *cuadro* III.1 (price of wheat), chaps. 3, 5, 6 (prices of cereals, wine, and oil), and vol. 2, chap. 4 (salaries of masons and carpenters).

4. AHCB CC VI-61 (LC 1578–80), fol. 115: Consellers to Tomàs Pujades, 9 October 1579.

5. Earl J. Hamilton, *American Treasure and the Price Revolution in Spain, 1501–1560* (Cambridge, Mass., 1934). For a critique of Hamilton's thesis in relation to Catalonia, see Pierre Vilar, *La Catalogne dans l'Espagne Moderne,* 3 vols. (Paris, 1962), 1:548, 554–57.

6. Núria Sales, *Els segles de la decadència (segles XVI–XVIII),* vol. 4 of *Història de Catalunya,* ed. Pierre Vilar (Barcelona, 1989), 254. Barcelona also complained that stocking galleys and excessive export licenses issued by viceroys often depleted the principality of basic goods and caused prices to rise; Vilar, *Catalogne,* 1:556–57.

7. *Cobles nouament fetes sobre los forments y usures ab un villancet* (Barcelona, n.d.), facsimile edition, in *Pliegos Poéticos del s. XVI de la Biblioteca de Cataluña,* ed. José Manuel Blecua (Madrid, 1976).

8. BC F. Bon. 10771: Juan Salazar, *Siguese un caso notable, y verdadero de cono* [sic] *los dsablos* [sic] *se han llevado a un mercader agavellador de trigo, porque no se quiso confesar* (Barcelona, 1603).

on the greed of monks and cathedral canons in the city. A long memorandum by the consellers to Pope Sixtus V complained that these clerics would "hoard all the wheat they could" to force prices up and sell their excess wheat and bread for profit. The consellers wanted the pope to prohibit such practices, which caused great suffering to the poor.[9] Yet the pope was reluctant to limit the clergy's privilege to buy grains and make bread.[10]

In August 1580, Tomàs Pujades, Barcelona's ambassador to the pope, informed the consellers that he had found a way to combat clerical hoarding that would win the pontiff's blessing. Pujades explained that in 1578, Pope Gregory XIII issued a *motu proprio,* or declaration, against hoarding to the city of Zaragoza, the capital of the kingdom of Aragon. The declaration threatened anyone who hoarded grains and other basic goods with excommunication.[11] Ambassador Pujades argued that Barcelona should request a similar motu proprio, "not just for the good of the city but of the entire province of Catalonia." The declaration would "tacitly" make "unlawful the business clerics have of selling bread made with the wheat they store." So convinced was Pujades of the merits of his idea that he had discussed it with the pope, who agreed to entertain the request as long as it came, in writing, from the Spanish king or the viceroy of Catalonia. The moment their letter arrived in Rome, Pujades assured the consellers, the pope would grant Barcelona its motu proprio.[12]

In Barcelona, Pujades's good news could not have arrived at a better time. That year's bad harvest would tempt many to hoard wheat. The scarcity of grain forced Barcelona to import six thousand *cafissos* (over one hundred thousand liters) of wheat from Aragon alone.[13] But convincing Francesc de Montcada i Folc de Cardona, count Aitona and viceroy of Catalonia, to request the papal motu proprio proved more difficult than expected.[14]

9. AHCB CC VI-61 (LC 1578–80), fol. 115: Consellers to Tomàs Pujades, 9 October 1579.

10. AHCB CC X-48 (LCO 1580–84), fol. 114: Pujades to Consellers, 29 May 1581.

11. I have not been able to locate Felipe de Urríes y Urríes's *Declaración de motu propio que concedio la Santidad de Gregorio XIII en Roma a 14 de mayo de 1578 en materia de panes y frutos* (Lleida, 1579).

12. AHCB CC X-48 (LCO 1580–84), fol. 63: Pujades to Consellers, 23 August 1580. Pujades enclosed a copy of the motu proprio he was requesting, but I have not found this or any other copies of the document.

13. AHCB CC VI-62 (LC 1580–82), fols. 37v–38r: Consellers to King, 21 November 1580. 1 *cafís* = 17.5 liters.

14. The count of Aitona became the first marquis of Aitona in 1585; Pere Molas i Ribalta, *Catalunya i la Casa d'Àustria* (Barcelona, 1996), 152.

After several failed attempts to secure the letter for the pope, on 28 January 1581 the consellers led a large delegation to the viceregal palace to discuss the matter with Aitona. The consellers once more insisted that the motu proprio would be "a good thing for all the inhabitants of Catalonia, especially for the 'little people' [*lo poble menut*]." Aitona agreed that nothing would please him more than "to punish and eradicate hoarders." Still, he could not say when he would write the letter for the pope.[15] Aitona's delay was not entirely his fault. The viceroy had felt compelled to consult on the matter with King Philip II, who was busy with the conquest of the kingdom of Portugal.[16]

After six months of waiting for the letter, ambassador Pujades in Rome began to worry about the fate of the motu proprio. On 20 March, he wrote to the consellers:

> May God forgive Your Magnificencies and your predecessors, but if you had expediently sent me the letter from the king or the viceroy—which has delayed me and which I am still waiting for—the matter would have been settled and Your Magnificencies would have the motu proprio in hand.[17]

He implored the consellers to forward the letter immediately. Pujades also urged them to maintain strict secrecy on the matter, warning that "if the monasteries and clergy hear about the effect of the motu proprio, all hell will break loose; and whereas now we have one enemy, we will have one hundred."[18]

But it was too late to keep the motu proprio a secret. In December 1580, the Barcelona Cathedral chapter had already discussed news of a "grace and provision to prevent the lease of wheat and other crops in the present principality."[19] Catalan nobles did the same a month later. These nobles and clerics were suspicious of the consellers although not certain of what they were up to. But if, as Pujades feared, the clergy and the nobility decided to oppose the papal declaration, they had the necessary institutional backing to do so. The braç eclesiàstic and the braç militar represented the ecclesi-

---

15. *DACB*, 5:258.

16. AHCB CC VI-62 (LC 1580–82), fols. 58v–59r: Consellers to Pujades, 16 March 1581. Spanish troops invaded Portugal in August 1580. In April 1581, the Portuguese Cortes recognized Philip II as their king.

17. AHCB CC X-48 (LCO 1580–84), fol. 100: Pujades to Consellers, 20 March 1581.

18. AHCB CC X-48 (LCO 1580–84), fol. 111: Pujades to Consellers, n.d. [1 May 1581].

19. *Dietaris de la Generalitat de Catalunya*, vol. 3 (1578–1611), ed. Josep Maria Sans i Travé (Barcelona, 1996), 83 (20 December 1580).

Philippus König hochgeborn
Von Gott dem Herrn ist erkorn/
Daß er regier mit Helden Mut/
Vil Königkreich vnd Jnseln gut.

FIGURE 3 Philip II, age 61, in armor. From *Historien der Königkreich Hispannien, Portugal, und Aphrica* (Munich, 1589), German translation of *Dell'unione del regno di Portogallo alla corona di Castiglia,* a work about the union of Portugal to Castile by Girolamo Franchi di Conestaggio (pseudonym for Juan de Silva, count of Portalegre?) (Genoa, 1585). Courtesy of the Kenneth Spencer Research Library, University of Kansas.

astic and the noble estates, respectively. Clerics and nobles could call meetings of their own braç to discuss the motu proprio and appoint delegates to denounce it before religious or secular authorities. Moreover, two representatives from each braç—known as diputats, or deputies, and oïdors, or keepers of accounts—ran the powerful Diputació, the body created to administer taxes and defend Catalan laws and liberties. Presiding over the Diputació was a clergyman, the *diputat eclesiàstic,* who could also send ambassadors to the king and the pope to lobby against the motu proprio.

In March 1581, Barcelona noble Joan Ferrer de Claravalls, the Diputació's ambassador to the papal court, paid a visit to ambassador Pujades. Ferrer wanted to know if the motu proprio could in any way harm the laws of Catalonia or the Diputació. If so, he had instructions to oppose it. Pujades refused to reveal the contents of the document, alleging that he was not authorized to do so.[20] Nevertheless, by June even Barcelona's shoemakers knew that the motu proprio sought by Pujades and the consellers was similar to the one issued to the city of Zaragoza a few years before.[21]

Although Catalan nobles, clerics, and members of the Diputació lacked specific details about Barcelona's motu proprio, they feared the worst. They did not object to the condemnation of hoarding wheat and other goods; rather, they worried that the declaration sought by the consellers might also affect agricultural production and rents from the land. These complaints are similar to those made by critics of the Zaragoza motu proprio in the kingdom of Aragon. Aragonese opposition to their papal declaration affirmed that peasants, merchants, and all landowners suffered important losses after the implementation of the papal declaration.[22] Moreover, Zaragoza's motu proprio had a clause restricting the lease of lands used for growing those goods. The aim was to prevent speculation and hoarding. But critics of the Zaragoza motu proprio insisted that it seriously affected the lease of lands. It appears that Catalan clerics and nobles worried Barcelona's motu proprio might have similar restrictions and affect their land rents. Because most nobles and ecclesiastic landowners did not work the lands themselves but leased them, the papal declaration might seriously reduce their income. The Barcelona Cathedral chapter warned the Diputació that the motu proprio would be "a very great prejudice to the land. . . , to ecclesiastics' rents, and to religion."[23] Ambassador Pujades informed the consellers that those restrictions in the leasing of lands or rents were true of the Zaragoza motu proprio but not of the one he sought for Barcelona.[24] However, the fact that neither Barcelona's ambassador in Rome nor the consellers made the text of the papal declaration public made it difficult to counter those claims.

20. AHCB CC X-48 (LCO 1580–84), fol. 100: Pujades to Consellers, 20 March 1581.

21. AHCB Gremis 1-91 ("Llibre de consells" 1578–82), fol. 19: shoemakers' confraternity council, June 1581.

22. Gregorio Colas Latorre and José Antonio Salas Ausens, *Aragón en el siglo XVI: Alteraciones sociales y conflictos políticos* (Zaragoza, 1982), 559–67. I am grateful to Jesús Gascón Pérez for this reference.

23. *Dietaris de la Generalitat*, 3:92 (9 August 1581).

24. AHCB CC X-48 (LCO 1580–84), fol. 115: Pujades to Consellers, 29 May 1581.

In August 1581, there were rumors that the new viceroy of Catalonia had finally given the consellers the letter for the pope. The Sicilian Carlo de Aragona e Taglavia, prince of Castelnuovo and duke of Terranova, had recently arrived in Barcelona as viceroy of Catalonia to succeed the count of Aitona, who had taken the post of viceroy of Valencia. Although the duke of Terranova had not given the consellers the letter for the pope, the Diputació seemed to believe the rumor that he had and ordered its ambassador in Lisbon—where Philip II had installed his court as the new king of Portugal—to be ready to campaign against the motu proprio.[25] Meanwhile, Pujades waited in Rome, wondering if he would ever see the letter for the pope.

Master Artisans and the Motu Proprio

By the end of the summer of 1582, the motu proprio against hoarding seemed to have no future. It had been nearly a year and a half since the consellers had asked the viceroy for the letter in favor of the papal declaration. The viceroy's inaction, together with the mounting opposition from the clergy, the nobility, and the Diputació, seemed to discourage the consellers from pursuing the matter any further.

The consellers had failed to win the motu proprio and were also failing in their duty to keep the city stocked with wheat at moderate prices. By the end of 1581, torrential rains had ruined much of the harvest, and the visit of Empress María, the widow of Emperor Maximilian II and Philip II's sister, had diverted the already scarce resources to feed the large entourage accompanying her.[26] The following spring of 1582, the price of a *quartera* of wheat, which ordinarily went for 28 to 30 sous, rose to 40 sous and continued to rise daily.[27] Drought conditions during the summer of 1582 contributed to yet another poor harvest. In September, the consellers described Barcelona's desperate situation as follows:

> Within days wheat and other goods have risen to such high prices that the poor are almost dying of hunger; and what is worse, wheat cannot be procured for money; and in the markets of the present city it has been a long time since any [wheat] has been unloaded; . . . the people of the present city remain very afflicted and oppressed.[28]

25. *Dietaris de la Generalitat*, 3:92 (14 August 1581).
26. AHCB CC VI-62 (LC 1580–82), fol. 122: Consellers to King, 28 November 1581.
27. *DACB*, 5:303.
28. *DACB*, 5:336.

The olive harvest had also failed; and whereas "the poor in times of want of bread can alleviate their need with herbs and oil," now they would have to do without.[29]

In the midst of these terrible conditions during the second half of 1582, Barcelona master artisans took up the initiative to win the motu proprio against hoarding. In September, they discussed the problem of hoarding with city officials.[30] That same month, officers from several master artisans' craft confraternities came together.[31] Although few details exist about what happened at those meetings, they almost certainly addressed the subject of the papal declaration. In fact, as early as June 1581—fifteen months before the first known public meeting of confraternity officers—the master shoemakers had approved a meeting between their officers and those of other confraternities specifically to discuss the motu proprio.[32] But it was sometime in November or December of 1582 that master artisans at one of these gatherings proposed the extraordinary measure of sending their own delegates to Lisbon to request the king's support for the motu proprio.[33]

These large gatherings of master artisans, which may have had as many as seventy participants, raised concerns among Barcelonese, Catalan, and royal authorities.[34] Allegedly, those who took part in those meetings posted inflammatory libelous flyers on street corners, sang provocative songs, and even started fistfights after discussing the motu proprio. Officers of the Diputació wanted the viceroy to restore the peace; they also decided to send an envoy to Lisbon to dissuade the king from supporting the papal declaration, "given that the confraternities and the people [*gent popular*] of this city are so united and in agreement to request this grace."[35] Joan Pau Ciurana, a knight and the Diputació's regent of accounts, would undertake that mission. Likewise, the nobility's braç militar sent Don Galceran d'Alentorn to Lisbon "to argue the dangers of the motu proprio."[36]

29. *DACB*, 5:338.

30. AHCB Gremis 1-91 ("Llibre de consells" 1578–82), fols. 30–31: shoemakers' confraternity council, 22 September 1582.

31. *RB*, 2:154.

32. AHCB Gremis 1-91 ("Llibre de consells" 1578–82), fol. 19: shoemakers' confraternity council, June 1581.

33. ACA CA llig. 261 no. 32: *memorial*, February 1583.

34. For the number of participants at master artisans' meetings, see ACA CA llig. 343: instructions to Joan Pau Ciurana, 7 December 1582.

35. *Dietaris de la Generalitat*, 3:133 (2 December 1582).

36. Ibid., 3:133–34. D'Alentorn's name is given in AHCB CC X-48 (LCO 1580–84), fols. 227–28: Lentisclà to Consellers, 30 December 1583 (i.e., 1582; the calendar year began on Christmas Day).

Barcelona canon Dr. Miquel Bonet would do the same in the name of the braç eclesiàstic.[37]

Master artisans' meetings may have also contributed to the consellers' renewed interest in seeking the papal declaration against hoarding. After more than eighteen months without any significant action on the matter, on 22 November 1582 the consellers drafted a letter to Philip II urging him to request the motu proprio from the pope because it would result in "great abundance of . . . wheat and other goods" in Catalonia.[38] Barcelona notary Nicolau Lentisclà would deliver the consellers' letter to the king.[39] Lentisclà would also take additional letters asking for the support of two influential men in the royal court: the count of Chinchón, one of the king's most trusted men, and Dr. Miquel Terçà, regent of the Council of Aragon—the royal council that reviewed policy in Catalonia and the other territories of the Crown of Aragon.[40]

If the consellers hoped that sending an envoy to Lisbon would discourage artisans from doing the same, masters responded by choosing three delegates to meet with the king: a shoemaker named Villaseca, veil maker Terrats, and notary Jaume d'Encontra.[41] Unfortunately, aside from their names and professions, little more is known about these men, except for d'Encontra, who would become fifth conseller in 1587–88.[42]

Unfortunately, no records of these meetings have survived to reveal the exact reasons for master artisans' support of the papal declaration. High food prices must have hurt many artisans and their families, whose incomes often could not keep up with the rising prices.[43] High prices and the problem of hoarding affected master artisans not just as consumers but also as producers. The scarcity of olive oil, for instance, affected the important wool textile industry, since it was "necessary in Catalonia for the manufacture of woolens, which cannot be made without this oil."[44] The hoarding

37. ACA CA llig. 342: Concili Provincial de Tarragona to King, 9 December 1582. The letter mistakenly describes Bonet as canon of Tarragona Cathedral.

38. AHCB CC VI-63 (LC 1582–84), fols. 16–17: Consellers to King, 22 November 1582.

39. AHCB CC VI-63 (LC 1582–84), fols. 19–20: instructions to Nicolau Lentisclà, n.d. [25 November 1582].

40. AHCB CC VI-63 (LC 1582–84), fols. 17–18: Consellers to Chinchón, 25 November 1582; and Consellers to Terçà, 25 November 1582.

41. ACA CA llig. 261, no. 34: *consulta*, n.d. [between June and 6 September 1586].

42. Jaume d'Encontra worked as a notary for the confraternities of master carders and master tanners (*blanquers*); see AHPB Jaume d'Encontra, "Libro de negocios de la Cofradía de Carderos" (1576–1608), and BC AH: Jaume d'Encontra, "Causa Pia dels Blanquers instituïda per Jaume Figuerola" (1552–89).

43. See note 3 above.

44. *DACB*, 5:338. Spinners and weavers used oil to lubricate wool fibers to prevent threads from breaking.

of raw materials was a recurring concern among the city's trades.[45] Because the motu proprio condemned the hoarding of wheat and other *vitualles*— a term roughly equivalent in English to "victuals" or "goods"—the papal declaration could conceivably also condemn the hoarding of raw materials necessary to master artisans.[46]

No doubt master artisans' decision to send their own delegates to the king also resulted from frustration with the consellers' unsuccessful efforts to win the motu proprio. But frustration, hunger, and fear cannot fully explain the artisans' choice of actions. These meetings, which took place over the course of several months, had precedents in the aims and activities of Barcelona's craft confraternities.

Craft Confraternities and the Common Good

Most of Barcelona's inhabitants had some connection to the city's craft confraternities. Some offered services, including tavern keepers, sailors, and stevedores. This diversity of professions led to a diversity of confraternities. Some confraternities were large and old, such as those of the shoemakers and the wool clothiers *(paraires),* both of which dated from the fourteenth century and had up to two hundred active members.[47] Most had well under one hundred confreres; a few were so small that they disappeared for lack of members.

Craft confraternities had three principal duties: to worship God, to perform acts of charity, and to regulate their trades. Those duties, moreover, derived from the ideal notion that artisans should do their part for the common good of Barcelona. As confraternities pointed out, trades existed for the "good and utility of the public" *(bé y utilitat de la cosa pública).*[48] Con-

45. Vilar discusses Barcelona artisans' concerns about the hoarding of raw materials in *Catalogne,* 1:560.

46. For the use of *vitualles* in relation to the motu proprio, see AHCB Gremis 1-91 ("Llibre de consells" 1578–82), fol. 19: shoemakers' confraternity council, June 1581; and AHCB CC VI-63 (LC 1582–84), fols. 19–20: instructions to Nicolau Lentisclà, n.d. [25 November 1582], fol. 19.

47. For the number of wool clothiers, see AHPB Francesc Jovells, "L[l]ibre dels. . . parayres" (1517–45). For the shoemakers in the early seventeenth century, see AHCB Gremis 1-3 ("Llibre de promenia" 1615) and 1-92 ("Llibre de consells" 1613–24).

48. Foundational privilege of booksellers (*llibreters*), transcribed in *Gremios y cofradías de la antigua Corona de Aragón,* vol. 41 of *Colección de documentos inéditos del Archivo de la Corona de Aragón,* ed. Francisco de Bofarull y Sans (Barcelona, 1910), 2:361. See also Ferdinand the Catholic's 1506 privilege in Jaume Vicens i Vives, *Ferran II i la ciutat de Barcelona, 1479–1516,* 3 vols. (Barcelona, 1936–37), appendix in vol. 3. For a European perspective on craft confraternity privileges, see Antony Black, *Guilds and Civil Society in European Political Thought from the Twelfth Century to the Present* (Ithaca, 1984).

fraternities served the public good by regulating production. Their religious and charitable activities also served the spiritual and moral good of the city.

In all major city churches, craft confraternities had chapels dedicated to their trades' patron saints and decorated with religious paintings and sculptures. Given the significance of the cult of saints in Catholic tradition, the feasts of these patron saints were an important part of the city's spiritual and festive calendar. Those ceremonies brought together members of a trade, their relatives, devotees of the saint, and other Christians who cared to participate in worship. The large confraternity of shoemakers had masses in honor of each of their five patron saints. For the feast of St. Mark (25 April), their principal patron saint, shoemakers decorated their chapel in the cathedral with flowers and oranges and invited religious and secular authorities to their services.[49] Confraternities also played a central role in religious processions, especially that of Corpus Christi (in late May or early June), the city's most important. In that procession, masters paraded imaginative floats, danced, or simply marched with their flags and wearing their best clothing in honor of God and for the spiritual well-being of their city.

Craft confraternities practiced various forms of charity, depending on their resources. Many paid for the burial expenses of poor masters and offered dowries to masters' daughters.[50] Shoemakers paid for medicine for sick masters and distributed bread among the city's poor for the feast of All Souls (2 November).[51] During the famine of 1522, wool clothiers, shoemakers, and possibly others imported wheat from Italy to feed the hungry—something they had to do twice, as pirates intercepted their first shipment of grain.[52]

---

49. See Aurelio Capmany and Agustín Duran y Sanpere, *El gremio de los maestros zapateros* (Barcelona, 1944). The other patron saints were Anianus, Crispin, and Crispinian. The patron saint of the shoemaker apprentices was the former Barcelona shoemaker apprentice Salvador d'Horta, whose cult dated from the late sixteenth century and was canonized in 1938.

50. For dowries, see AHCB Gremis 1-183 ("Bossa de les donzelles" 1548): shoemakers' list of "maidens"; and AHPB Francesc Jovells, "Libre dels. . . parayres" (1517–45): wool clothiers' council, 22 January 1541. For masses for the dead, see AHCB Gremis 1-2 ("Llibre de promenia" 1612): shoemakers' book of accounts.

51. On payments of medicines, see AHCB Gremis 1-93 ("Llibre de consells" 1625–36), fol. 72r: shoemakers' council, 1627.

52. AHCB Gremis 1-90 ("Llibre de consells" 1522–25), fols. 1r–2r: shoemakers' council, 1522; and AHPB Francesc Jovells, "Libre dels. . . parayres" (1517–45): wool clothiers' councils, 11 May and 24 June 1522.

Craft confraternities had a third purpose: to protect masters and the public from abusive trade practices. For example, confraternities guarded against the hoarding of raw materials, which endangered artisans' freedom to practice their trades.[53] They also ensured the quality of goods and services "for the good of the public" *(lo bé de la cosa pública)*.[54] Thus craft confraternities awarded titles of master and policed professional activities to guarantee the public's interest. Similarly, when proposing trade ordinances to city authorities or seeking confraternity privileges from the king, master artisans insisted that they were for the good or well-being of the city.[55]

In order to do their part for the good of the city, confraternities had the privilege to convene members in council, often in a church or guildhall. At these meetings, masters discussed trade matters, organized religious activities, administered confraternity funds, and elected officers. These officers had legal powers to represent their fellow masters before city and royal authorities. Confraternities hired notaries and lawyers to give them legal advice. Masters also elected delegates *(síndics)* to take cases to courts of justice and petitions to the king.

Since the fourteenth century, Barcelona's artisans had been sending delegates to their kings in the name of the common good of their city. In 1386, master artisans were part of a delegation *(sindicat)* that sought King Peter IV's support for major reforms to Barcelona's government. The proposals, which the king accepted, were intended "for the good governance and benefit of the. . . city and for the public good."[56] Likewise, in 1451 and 1453, master artisans from Barcelona sent delegates to King Alphonse V in Naples to petition further changes in the government of the city. These delegates represented the "Syndicate of the Three Estates and the People," a group formed primarily by masters from the city's craft confraternities, along with

53. For regulations against hoarding raw materials, see Jaime Carrera Pujal, *Historia política y económica de Cataluña: Siglos XVI al XVIII,* 3 vols. (Barcelona, 1946–47), 2:155, 161, 170.

54. Foundational privilege of the silk veil weavers *(teixidors de vels de seda)* in *Gremios y cofradías,* 2:356. See also Pierre Bonnassie, *La organización del trabajo en Barcelona a fines del siglo XV* (Barcelona, 1975), 34.

55. For references to "public interest" or "common good" in sixteenth-century trade ordinances, see AHPB Pere Jovell, "Primus liber . . . paratorum lane" (1552–62): wool clothiers' council, 6 November 1562; Carrera Pujal, *Historia política,* 2:150 (1521 woolens' ordinance), 153 (1539 leather guilders' *[guadamassilers]* ordinance), 160 (1584 silversmiths' ordinance).

56. Quoted by Carmen Batlle Gallart, "La proyectada reforma del gobierno municipal de Barcelona (año 1386)," in *VII Congreso de Historia de la Corona de Aragón* (Barcelona, 1962), 3:150.

some merchants and a few honored citizens, all of whom were critical of the city council. In the words of one of its spokesmen, the Barcelona merchant Ramon Guerau, the syndicate sought three things: "the praise of God, the service and honor of the crown, and the public good."[57] In response to their demands, Alphonse V issued a privilege in 1455 that gave artisans permanent representation in the city council and two councilorships.

From the late Middle Ages through the seventeenth century, the claim to act for the common good of Barcelona, which was at the heart of confraternities' charitable and professional activities, also became crucial to artisans' participation in politics. It provided the arguments to demand and defend everything from major concessions from the king to more limited actions by city authorities. For instance, saddle makers *(freners)* refused to support two candidates for city office because they did not believe that the two men would act for the "benefit of the public" *(nols havien per bons ne a profit del públich).*[58] Shoemakers urged the consellers to oppose a privilege sought by the tanners and curriers *(blanquers i assaonadors)* to limit leather imports because the liberty to import leather in Barcelona "brought utility and benefit to the public thing and its prohibition . . . great harm to it."[59] Likewise, velvet makers *(velluters)* argued before the consellers that it would be "very beneficial and convenient to the public good" to prohibit the import of foreign textiles.[60]

Master artisans' familiarity with the language of the common good confirms that it was not exclusive to city and royal authorities; it also reveals one of the ways master artisans saw their role in politics. Concern for the good of Barcelona entitled artisans to address their rulers and present petitions or make demands. In his 1581 encomium to Barcelona, the humanist Dionís Jeroni de Jorba claimed that his fellow citizens

> only care about the good, not only public but also private. . . . Nobles and knights take to their duties; merchants conduct their affairs legally, not seeking their interest but the common good [*el bien público*], which they hold above all else. Priests and religious persons live modestly; artisans of all trades

---

57. Carmen Batlle Gallart, "La ideología de la 'Busca.' La crisis municipal de Barcelona del siglo XV," *Estudios de Historia Moderna* 6 (1955): 172.

58. Quotation from 1452 in Carmen Batlle Gallart, "La 'busca.' Aspecto de la reforma municipal de Barcelona," in *Homenaje a Jaime Vicens Vives,* 2 vols. (Barcelona, 1965–67), 1:338.

59. AHCB Gremis Municipal, Sabaters box: "Memorial. . . als. . . consellers," n.d. (sixteenth century).

60. BC F. Bon. 5151: *Advertiments ab los quals se mostra esser molt vtil, y convenient al be publich de tot lo Principat de Cathalunya y Comtats de Rossello, y Cerdanya, lo prohibir vestir, y calsar de tota sort de Robes fabricades fora Regne* (n.p., n.d. [between 1619 and 1630]).

do not disparage their savings one bit; thus vagabonds cannot be found, for everyone lives most happily and contentedly.[61]

Because the aim of both rulers and subjects was to do their part for the common good, all their actions had to be consistent with this principle. Throughout the debate on the motu proprio, supporters and detractors argued how it would or would not be for the common good.

From this perspective, the confraternities' campaign for the motu proprio can be seen as yet another way in which masters were doing their part for the common good of the city. Despite the lack of any direct statements, their decision to call special meetings and elect three delegates to ask Philip II to support the motu proprio is consistent with earlier campaigns by master artisans.

During the second half of December 1582, advocates for and against the motu proprio got ready to embark on the long trip from Barcelona to Lisbon. In the Portuguese capital, they would try to present their arguments to the king in person. Others who could not go to Lisbon would express their opinions in writing. But the fate of the motu proprio now rested in the hands of Philip II.

Lobbying the King

After more than two years, by December 1582 Philip II's stay in Portugal was nearing its end. With his authority now established over the kingdom, he could turn his attention to his many other concerns, including Barcelona's request for a motu proprio against hoarding.

Philip II had not made public his opinion on the matter, but he had given some thought to Barcelona's petition. According to a memorandum written by the Council of Aragon probably between June and December 1582, the king's initial reaction to the motu proprio was positive.[62] Never-

61. Dionysio Hieronymo de Iorba [Dionís Jeroni de Jorba], *Descripción de las excellencias de la muy insigne ciudad de Barcelona*, 2d ed. (Barcelona, 1589), fol. 4.

62. ACA CA llig. 261 no. 32: *consulta*, n.d. A chronological index card in the ACA (known as "Fitxes d'en Miquel") dates the document as 26 December 1582, although I could not find this date anywhere in the *consulta*. The enclosed (undated) letters addressed to the count of Olivares as ambassador to Rome and to the duke of Terranova as viceroy of Catalonia suggest that the *consulta* dates from the second half of 1582, since the count took up his position in June 1582 and the duke left his post at the end of 1582. The fact that the document does not mention that various emissaries from Barcelona went to see the king in December 1582 also leads me to believe that the *consulta* was written prior to their arrival in Lisbon.

theless, he wanted to know the opinions of the present and former viceroys of Catalonia, as well as those of the Catalan nobility and clergy, before making a decision. Viceroy Terranova had written to the king in support of Barcelona's petition and to inform him that the Catalan clergy and nobility proposed to defer a discussion of the motu proprio until Philip II convened the next Catalan Corts, the principality's representative assembly. Enjoying legislative, judicial, and fiscal powers, the Corts could well discuss a matter that would affect all of Catalonia. But because the Corts had representatives from the braç eclesiàstic and the braç militar, opponents of the papal declaration would probably muster enough votes to reject Barcelona's demand. The Council of Aragon immediately recognized the intention behind this proposal by the clergy and nobility: "It seemed only to aim for their own interest [*proprio* (sic) *interés*], because the clergy and military [the nobility] held all the grain; and that it was more just to take into account the common [interest] and the poor than the others."

Considering that the viceroy's letter had provided enough information about the position of Catalan nobles and clergymen, the council decided that it was time to act. It drafted three letters in the name of Philip II. One informed the duke of Terranova of the king's decision in favor of Barcelona's request. However, the viceroy was advised to keep the decision a secret, "given the risk that if the diputats as well as others who want to oppose it learn the news they might take action and prevent it." Another was a letter of instructions addressed to the king's ambassador in Rome, the count of Olivares. And the third was the long-desired letter to the pope, asking him to grant Barcelona—and Valencia!—the same papal declaration against hoarders given to Zaragoza some years before.[63]

This was precisely what the consellers and the craft confraternities wanted from the king. The Council of Aragon had agreed entirely with the argument that the motu proprio was for the common good and therefore that the objections of the Diputació, the nobility, and the clergy should be dismissed as motivated purely by their own interest. The Council of Aragon also seemed under the impression that the king would agree with that conclusion. However, the king did not respond to the council's memorandum, or if he did, his response has been lost. More important, the letters were certainly not sent.

If the king had been too busy to answer the council's memorandum, the arrival of advocates for and against the motu proprio in Lisbon forced the king to address the matter again. On 28 December, Philip II met with

---

63. The three unsigned and undated letters are in ACA CA llig. 261, no. 32.

the consellers' emissary, the notary Nicolau Lentisclà, who had just arrived in Lisbon four days before. Lentisclà had fallen ill during his trip, and he may not have been in the best condition to make a strong argument before the king, who refused to make any promises regarding the motu proprio. The next day, Lentisclà received orders from the king to go to Madrid, where Philip II had forwarded the matter to the Council of Aragon. Lentisclà also found out that the envoys sent to Lisbon by the clergy, the nobility, and the Diputació had already arrived in Madrid, although he did not say if they had met with the king. They were moved only by "particular interests" rather than by the good of God and the king, wrote Lentisclà to the consellers. Their involvement and the fact that he could not find out anything new about the status of his petition clearly concerned him. Commenting on the prospects for his mission, all Lentisclà could do was hope that "Our Lord will guide and direct it to his service and the benefit of the . . . City."[64]

Joan Pau Ciurana, the Diputació's envoy, had instructions to describe the supporters of the motu proprio as people who cared only about their "particular interests" while disregarding the interest of the king and having no concern for "the conservation of constitutions and laws" or "the universal and public utility, benefit, and tranquillity of all the Principality." He could not be more specific about the papal declaration's negative effects because the text was not known.[65]

Other critics of the motu proprio also sent letters to the king. One such letter came from Paulo Pla, a Barcelona canon, who had met Philip II in 1566.[66] Rather than defend the common good, Pla stated, the papal declaration would "cause greater harm to poor people" because its supporters "looked more to their particular interest than to the public one, even when these people might think otherwise." He warned the king that the motu proprio might "damage the royal jurisdiction" and that the papacy had no business meddling in Catalonia's affairs.[67] He recommended two measures instead: first, to fix prices to prevent their rise, and second, to defer a decision on the papal declaration to the next meeting of the Corts.

---

64. AHCB CC X-48 (LCO 1580–84), fols. 227–28: Lentisclà to Consellers, 30 December 1583 [i.e., 1582].

65. ACA CA llig. 343: instructions to Joan Pau Ciurana, 7 December 1582.

66. Pla had been on a mission involving the adoption in Catalonia of the decrees of the Council of Trent, which after nearly two decades had finally approved sweeping reforms in the Catholic Church; see Joan Bada, *Situació religiosa de Barcelona en el s. XVI* (Barcelona, 1970), 209. In 1585, Philip II made Pla regent of the Barcelona Audiència.

67. ACA CA llig. 261 no. 17: Paulo Pla to King, Montblanc, 16 December 1582.

Hernando de Toledo, the duke of Alba's natural son and former viceroy of Catalonia (1571–79), also wrote to the king upon learning that the delegates of Barcelona's craft confraternities were on their way to Lisbon. He warned against the intervention of the papacy, because "what Your Majesty can do with your power should not be done by another hand." Rather, the viceroy should issue a proclamation against hoarding, something he had done in 1579 during his tenure as viceroy.[68]

During the first week of February 1583, Philip II received another memorandum from the Council of Aragon. This second memorandum expressed urgency about the need to resolve Barcelona's rapidly worsening economic and social problems. The Council of Aragon recommended that Philip II not wait any longer for the opinions of the clergy and nobility, who were known to be hostile to the papal declaration. In a clear reference to the meetings of craft confraternity officers, the memorandum painted a grim picture of how desperate the people of Barcelona had become:

> The people suffer great want because of the lack of bread, to the point of organizing meetings, putting up placards, and refusing to say under what authority they do what they do; and all of this, together with the indignation they feel toward the rich and those they believe are the cause of their continuing hunger—as well as the greed of many good-for-nothings—will be enough for some, in case of a riot, to rob the city bank, which is reputed to be rich, and the Diputació, and the rest of the rich people. It is most evident that this city may be lost and that a civil war may take place—with its subsequent disorders and excesses and many travails and losses—if it is not prevented.[69]

The Council of Aragon proposed that, in order "to remedy such a grave danger," the king request the motu proprio immediately, because "it is convenient and necessary that, on this occasion, the people be given satisfaction in order to calm them and keep them within the obedience and love they feel for Your Majesty." Furthermore, the memorandum insisted that it would be fair and most beneficial to the public good if the king were to give "the poorest and saddest part" of the populace the thing they petitioned for.

As was his custom, Philip II scribbled his response to the Council of Aragon's recommendations in the memorandum's margins. First, he ordered that no action be taken before he heard from the Catalan nobility

---

68. ACA CA llig. 261 no. 17: Hernando de Toledo (who signed as Prior of Saint John [Grand Prior of Castile of the Order of Saint John of Jerusalem]) to King, Valparaíso, 20 December 1582. For his proclamation, see *Dietaris de la Generalitat*, 3:729–32.

69. ACA CA llig. 261 no. 32: *memorial*, February 1583.

and clergy. Second, in the meantime, the viceroy should issue more proclamations against hoarding in an attempt to address the most immediate
problems. And third, the king categorically refused to see the men sent by
the craft confraternities: "Let them go to the representatives [*jurados*], who
normally ask for and deal with what is convenient to the city."

On 7 February 1583, Lentisclà reported to the consellers that the delegates of Barcelona's craft confraternities had left Lisbon. Their mission to
see the king had failed, although they still did not know whether the king
would request the motu proprio. According to Lentisclà, the Council of
Aragon awaited "the papers or writings of those who had come to his
majesty in Lisbon to oppose the motu proprio." He believed that the king
might make a final decision within days.[70]

Less than three weeks later, the consellers relayed what must have been
disappointing news to ambassador Pujades: Lentisclà "had not been able
to obtain the letter they had requested from the king for his ambassador
in Rome."[71] As far as the consellers were concerned, the campaign for the
motu proprio had been lost.

King and Artisans

On 14 July 1584, over a year after Barcelona's consellers had concluded
that there would be no motu proprio against hoarding, the Council of
Aragon again urged Philip II to request the papal declaration. Viceregal
proclamations were insufficient to stop the problem of hoarding, stated
the council's memorandum; only the threat of spiritual sanction might end
this recurring problem. Moreover, the measure would be for the good of
the principality "and especially of the poor, who are in such need of being
protected, favored, and assisted."[72] But the king remained steadfast in his
position not to support the council's view. Instead, he offered a terse response that reveals the reason for the council's memorandum: "Order the
return to Barcelona of the delegate. . . of the confraternities" and "tell him
that this business will stay under my care." It appears that one of the three
delegates from Barcelona's craft confraternities who had gone to Lisbon—
whose name is not given—went on to Madrid, where the king settled his

70. AHCB CC X-48 (LCO 1580–84), fols. 202–3: Lentisclà to Consellers, 7 February
1583. Sadly, the letter has virtually disintegrated.
71. AHCB CC VI-63 (LC 1582–84), fol. 46: Consellers to Pujades, 26 February 1583.
Lentisclà returned to Barcelona on 13 March; *DACB*, 5:346.
72. ACA CA llig. 261 no. 91: *consulta*, "Sobre la execución de los motus proprios q[ue]
prohíben los agabellamientos de trigos y otras vituallas," 14 July 1584.

court in April 1583 after spending nearly three years in Lisbon. This means that the confraternities' delegate had been in Madrid for over a year, perhaps hoping to see the king, and that his presence moved the Council of Aragon to once more discuss the matter of the motu proprio. Although the delegate's fate is unknown, perhaps Philip II's response finally convinced him that it was time to put the matter to rest and go back home.

At first sight, Barcelona master artisans' appeal to Philip II conforms with what some historians have termed "naïve monarchism."[73] From Spain to Russia, in the early modern and modern periods, popular myths expressed the belief that if subjects could tell their monarchs about their plight, monarchs would give them justice and protection.[74] Yet the debate over Barcelona's motu proprio calls into question whether such ideas were exclusively popular or entirely naïve. Scholars and statesmen throughout Europe insisted on the duty of rulers to care for their subjects' well-being.[75] According to the Spanish political writer Baltasar Alamos de Barrientos, "The Prince, to govern well, should be tutor, not lord, of his vassals and kingdom."[76] The Spanish diplomat and writer Diego de Saavedra Fajardo would later write, "Subjects were not born for the king but the king for the subjects."[77] Since the late fourteenth century, Barcelona artisans had appealed to their kings' duty to defend the common good when they presented demands and petitions, and if they persisted, it was not because they were naïve but because in the past monarchs had responded favorably.

Did Philip II conclude that the motu proprio was not for the common good? His opinion on the matter remains unclear. In deciding not to take action, the king seemed to side with the Catalan nobility and clergy. However, the king may have simply wanted to take his time. "When the prince

---

73. For a discussion of "naïve monarchism," see David Martin Luebke, *His Majesty's Rebels: Communities, Factions, and Rural Revolt in the Black Forest, 1725–1745* (Ithaca, 1997), 149–50.

74. E. J. Hobsbawm, *Primitive Rebels: Studies in Archaic Forms of Social Movement in the Nineteenth and Twentieth Centuries* (1959; reprint, New York, 1965), 119; and Yves-Marie Bercé, *History of Peasant Revolts: The Social Origins of Rebellion in Early Modern France*, trans. Amanda Whitmore (Ithaca, 1990), 248–49.

75. On the foundations and diffusion of this duty, see Howell A. Lloyd, "Constitutionalism," in *The Cambridge History of Political Thought, 1450–1700*, ed. J. H. Burns with Mark Goldie (Cambridge, 1991), 254–97.

76. Antonio Pérez [Baltasar Alamos de Barrientos], *Aforismos sacados de la historia de Publio Cornelio Tácito*, ed. Modesto Santos (Barcelona, 1991), no. 19, p. 57. This work was probably finished in 1594 but was published in 1614; José Antonio Fernández-Santamaría, *Reason of State and Statecraft in Spanish Political Thought, 1595–1640* (Lanham, Md., 1983), 225 no. 16.

77. Diego de Saavedra Fajardo, *Empresas políticas*, ed. Francisco Javier Díez de Revenga (Barcelona, 1988), 136: *empresa* 20. The first edition dates from 1640.

is asked something of importance," advised Alamos de Barrientos, "he should not respond at the time, but ask for time to think about it; so that it appears a matter of convenience and not only his own will."[78] Perhaps this unwillingness to act immediately is the only explanation why Philip II did nothing to support the motu proprio for Barcelona. Yet he also rejected the insistent demands of Aragonese nobles and towns to repeal Zaragoza's motu proprio against hoarding.[79] At the same time, by not explicitly rejecting the papal bull, he encouraged Barcelona's master artisans to continue to hope that perhaps they might still convince the king to favor it.

Philip II's opposite decisions regarding Zaragoza and Barcelona point to yet another possible consideration. In a letter to the king, Barcelona's canon Paulo Pla stated that since the Aragonese were "more free" (*más libertados*) from royal authority than the Catalans, "and [because] Your Majesty's ministers and officers there [in Aragon] lack the absolute power they have here [in Catalonia], it may be that the papal declaration might be more convenient in Aragon than in Catalonia."[80] Relations between the Spanish monarchy and the Aragonese nobility had worsened over the years, and perhaps the king thought the papal bull would give him greater leverage in curbing their freedom. Relations between the monarch and the Catalan nobility and clergy had not always been cordial, and in 1567 and 1578 there had been serious clashes in Barcelona over the Inquisition and the reform of the Mercedarian Order. But between 1580 and 1584 tensions had waned, so that perhaps Philip II saw little to gain from angering Catalan ecclesiastics and nobles by favoring Barcelona's master artisans. Of course, in the future conditions in the principality might change, and so it was best to leave the matter of the motu proprio unresolved for the moment and raise it again later to drive a wedge between the artisans of Barcelona and the ecclesiastic and noble braços and diputats. As Wayne te Brake has pointed out, early modern rulers were more likely to champion the interests of "ordinary people" when it seemed convenient to undermine the strength of the local elites.[81]

However, although the king's decision—or lack of one—meant the end of the campaign for the motu proprio, the high prices and fear of scarcity that had inspired the proposal in the first place had not disappeared. If anything, conditions were becoming worse, so that by the second half of

---

78. Alamos de Barrientos, *Aforismos*, no. 462.
79. Colas Latorre and Salas Ausens, *Aragón en el siglo XVI*, 559–67.
80. ACA CA llig. 261 no. 17: Paulo Pla to King, Montblanc, 16 December 1582.
81. Wayne te Brake, *Shaping History: Ordinary People in European Politics, 1500–1700* (Berkeley, 1998), 15.

1584, the specter of a crisis in Barcelona returned. In August of 1584, the viceroy reported that "the want [of wheat] is greater than anything this principality and its counties have ever seen; not even the very old remember anything like it."[82] In Flix, a territory on the Ebro River belonging to the city and a major supplier of wheat, the harvest had yielded nothing; fearing the possibility of riots, the consellers imported wheat from France at a high price.[83] Drought and famine in the wheat-producing pre-Pyrenean region of the Urgell, in the northwestern corner of Catalonia, forced its inhabitants to look for food elsewhere.[84] The Jesuit chronicler Pere Gil pitied the stream of famished people that reached Barcelona in search of respite: "They had yellow and green faces. . . from eating only herbs."[85] In November 1584, the count of Miranda still hoped that the king would support the motu proprio.[86] To add to the uncertain economic conditions in the city, starting in 1585 the relations between Philip II and Catalan elites would begin to deteriorate under the weight of a number of complex constitutional debates. Under those circumstances, the king would listen to Barcelona's artisans for the good of the crown.

Obedience and the Common Good

The campaign for the motu proprio brought to an end what had been one of the most effective forms of popular political action in Barcelona in the late Middle Ages. This would turn out to be the last time that master artisans' confraternities acted in concert to make claims before their king. Their next major joint effort would take place more than a century later, in 1699, when delegates of Barcelona's confraternities presented a series of claims to the viceroy of Catalonia.[87] The lack of more efforts of this kind was in part a consequence of the events in the early 1580s. As will be seen in the following chapter, the Corts of 1585 would prohibit such meetings specifically to prevent the repeat of the craft confraternities' activities in

---

82. ACA CA llig. 343: Miranda to King, 11 August 1584.

83. AHCB CC VI-63 (LC 1582–84), fols. 279, 281: Jurats of Flix to Consellers, 27 June and 16 July 1584.

84. *Dietari de Jeroni Pujades*, ed. Josep Maria Casas Homs, 4 vols. (Barcelona, 1975–76), vol. 4, fol. 120. Jeroni Pujades took this information from his father's diary.

85. *Pere Gil, S.I. (1551–1622) i la seva Geografia de Catalunya*, ed. Josep Iglésies (Barcelona, 1949), 299; Sales, *Segles de la decadència*, 254.

86. ACA CA llig. 343: Miranda to King, 14 November 1584.

87. BC F. Bon. 2760: Luis de Valencià Balart, *Excelentissim Señor: Lo Syndic de las confrarias de la present Ciutat de Barcelona. . .* (n.p., 1699).

favor of the papal bull against hoarding. But perhaps the law was unnecessary. Despite the attention they received, the master artisans' campaign had failed. In addition, future experience would teach masters' organizations that it might be easier and more profitable to secure more modest concessions that fulfilled the particular interests of their own trades.

Nevertheless, the events between 1580 and 1584 point to other ways in which artisans managed to voice their concerns and make demands. Artisans usually addressed the powerful consellers first. As officers charged with caring for the well-being of Barcelona's inhabitants and the maintenance of order in the city, the consellers were most likely to listen to artisans' pleas and complaints. If artisans could secure the support of the city's chief officers, they significantly improved their chances of success. But if the consellers and the Consell de Cent took no action, artisans had few other options. Through their craft confraternities, they could appeal to royal authorities or even the king. Clearly, the chances of securing his support were slim. Like most monarchs, Philip II had little desire to encourage the "little people" in the villages, towns, and cities of his territories to challenge their social superiors and immediate figures of authority. But at the same time, his unwillingness to reject Barcelona artisans' demands outright perhaps betrays a desire to keep alive his subjects' hope that their ruler cared about them and that if subjects followed the appropriate channels, he was willing to listen to them.

Throughout the episode of the motu proprio against hoarding, the notion of the common good helped to articulate the arguments for and against the proposal. City, Catalan, and royal officials made constant references to it. Although none of the surviving documents related to this episode indicates that master artisans cited the common good, it is clear that they knew the term, and what is more important, how to use it. In their relations with the king and Barcelona's city authorities, artisans repeatedly appealed to the common good to support an ordinance or to request a privilege. In other words, artisans saw their duty to the common good as a reason for political action.

Peter Blickle found that German peasants of the early sixteenth century used the common good as a "code word" to make demands about economic relief, justice, and good government.[88] Similarly, in her study of resistance to military levies in seventeenth-century Castile, Ruth MacKay underscores the close connection between the common good and the duties of the king and all of his subjects, including commoners: "The com-

---

88. Blickle, *Revolution of 1525*, 156.

mon good, one of the fundamental measures of law in early modern Spain, assumed the coexistence of authority and liberty and required that both king and kingdom be accountable to that criterion."[89] Subjects, from powerful aristocrats to poor villagers, had a duty to denounce injustice, and even to refuse orders if they contradicted the common good. This notion of "active obedience," as the Spanish historian José Antonio Maravall described it, extended to Barcelona's master artisans.[90] They too had a duty to call on city authorities to act against hoarding and high prices; to regulate their own professional activities to avoid abuses; to denounce injustice in courts of law; and if necessary, to appeal to their king to support a good proposal. Their actions, and those of other commoners throughout early modern Europe, confirm that ordinary men and women could see themselves as political actors and behave accordingly.

89. Ruth MacKay, *The Limits of Royal Authority: Resistance and Obedience in Seventeenth-Century Castile* (Cambridge, 1999), 1.

90. José Antonio Maravall, *Teoría del estado en España en el siglo XVII,* 2d ed. (Madrid, 1997), 340. See also MacKay, *Limits of Royal Authority,* 23.

CHAPTER THREE

Who Speaks for the People of Barcelona?

O n 19 January 1585, Philip II left Madrid with a large entourage for Zaragoza, where he would give his daughter Catalina Micaela in marriage to Charles Emmanuel, duke of Savoy. In addition to Catalina Micaela, the king brought along his eldest daughter, the Infanta Isabel, and his nine-year-old son, Prince Philip—the future King Philip III. The wedding would take place at Zaragoza Cathedral on 11 March. After several weeks of festivities, the royal family would then head for the capital of Catalonia, from where Catalina Micaela and the duke of Savoy would sail to Italy. Barcelona expected the king to arrive in the city in early May.

Philip II's visit to the principality would be his first in more than two decades. No king in recent memory had been away as long from Catalonia. Philip told Catalans that revolts in the Netherlands and Granada, war against the Turks at sea, and the conquest of Portugal had prevented him from coming back sooner.[1] Those who remembered the king from his last visit would see a much older man. When he left the principality in 1564, although twice a widower, the king was thirty-seven years old. Now almost fifty-eight, he had survived four wives and several children. His own father, the Emperor Charles V, died when he was fifty-eight. Philip II was older, but also more powerful. During his years away from Catalonia, the treasure

---

1. Philip II's convocation speech before the Corts on 28 June 1585, in *Dietaris de la Generalitat de Catalunya*, vol. 3 (1578–1611), ed. Josep Maria Sans i Travé (Barcelona, 1996), 742–44. On Philip II's plans for a visit in 1578, see A. W. Lovett, *Philip II and Mateo Vázquez de Leca: The Government of Spain (1572–1592)* (Geneva, 1977), 192.

from the New World had doubled, and the conquest of the Philippines meant that the "Prudent King," as he was known, possessed an empire where the sun never set.[2]

Catalans rejoiced at the news that their king would finally come back and that once again they would be able to demonstrate their fidelity, to petition for (and, they hoped, to receive) royal honors, and to carry on important business that required the monarch's presence. The debate in the early 1580s over the merits of the motu proprio against hoarding had underscored the need to convene the Catalan Corts in order to address major economic and constitutional issues. The king's return would make that possible. His presence would also make it easier for Barcelona's officials and master artisans to request privileges they considered necessary for the proper functioning of the city's government and of its trades.

Ironically, the significance of Philip II's visit in 1585 highlights the fact that Catalans had less access to their monarch than ever before. This was a matter of great concern particularly to Catalan nobles, who resented missing out on the honors and benefits enjoyed by Castilians by virtue of their proximity to the ruler—a frustration shared by nobles in Aragon, in Valencia, and in territories beyond the Iberian Peninsula.[3] The problem was not limited to the Habsburg monarchy. As Sharon Kettering notes for seventeenth-century France and Linda Levy Peck for early Stuart England, access to the early modern monarchs was essential for subjects to tap the bounty of patronage available to those present at court.[4] Rulers recognized their subjects' services with gifts and honors to foster in them a sense of loyalty that would be expressed in turn with future services. Those fortunate to have access to the royal fountain of rewards could act as brokers for their own clients to take part in this exchange of gifts and services.

The desire for royal rewards and honors was not unique to the political elite. Even commoners fairly low in the social hierarchy, such as the majority of Barcelona's master artisans, wanted their share of those rewards.

2. Geoffrey Parker, *Philip II*, 3d ed. (Chicago, 1995), 146.

3. John H. Elliott, *The Revolt of the Catalans: A Study in the Decline of Spain, 1598–1640* (Cambridge, 1963), 72–74. For the Kingdom of Aragon, see Xavier Gil Pujol, "Olivares y Aragón," in *La España del Conde Duque de Olivares,* ed. John Elliott and Angel García Sanz (Valladolid, 1990), 584. But as I. A. A. Thompson, points out, "Castilians themselves seem to have felt short-changed by the monarchy"; "Castile, Spain, and the Monarchy: The Political Community from *Patria Natural* to *Patria Nacional*," in *Spain, Europe, and the Atlantic World,* ed. Richard L. Kagan and Geoffrey Parker (Cambridge, 1995), 139.

4. Sharon Kettering, *Patrons, Brokers, and Clients in Seventeenth-Century France* (Cambridge, 1986); Linda Levy Peck, *Court Patronage and Corruption in Early Stuart England* (London, 1993).

FIGURE 4 The royal fountain of favors: "Reward those who are worthy, for the kingdom shall thus flourish and subjects shall be encouraged." From Andrés Mendo, *Príncipe perfecto y ministros ajustados* (Lyon, 1662), emblem 35. Courtesy of the Kenneth Spencer Research Library, University of Kansas.

Although they had more limited access to royal patronage, their expectations too were more modest. Artisans did not ask for the grants of land and appointments to high office usually reserved for nobles and ministers, but they did want privileges that would confer honors, increase political participation, and have potential economic benefits.

Between 1585 and 1587, Barcelona's master artisans sought different ways to drink from the royal fountain of rewards. The entrance ceremonies and religious processions in honor of Philip II's visit would allow artisans to express, through performance, their desire to exchange services for royal gifts. They also conveyed that message by other, and perhaps more direct, means. Master artisans sent their own lobbyists to the Corts of 1585 to secure privileges for their craft confraternities. Artisans in the Consell de Cent relied on brokers with greater access to that patronage, above all the conseller en cap, the city's delegates to the Corts, and Barcelona's ambassadors. These officials, however, might be susceptible to pressures and corruption and as a result might fail to deliver any gifts. In addition, most of these men belonged to the city's elite and might consider artisans' requests inappropriate. But when artisans tried to bypass these brokers in unconventional ways, tensions erupted in the city.

Closely tied to the efforts to secure royal privileges were competing claims to speak for the people of Barcelona. The city's elite—the honored citizens, knights, and doctors of law and medicine—and master artisans, at times joined by the merchants, disputed who had the authority to represent the true interests of the city before the king. These two views of the people would clash in 1586, a dispute that would require the king's intervention.

Barcelona Welcomes Its King

The Consell de Cent planned to welcome Philip II and his family with a lavish entry ceremony followed by three days of festivities in honor of the king.[5] In case he arrived at night, masters from the confraternities would escort him with one hundred torches. Musicians would play in streets and squares lit by bonfires. There would also be dancing and a large procession with the participation of clergymen and master artisans from craft confraternities. The city council built a covered wooden bridge with large windows behind the royal palace for the royal family to watch fireworks in the port. The most humble inhabitants would also do their part. A city ordinance required that shops remain closed and that "each one dress as well as possible" in honor of the king.[6] Even the economic situation contributed to the celebratory mood. After years of rising prices, scarcity of goods, and a growing number of poor, in 1585 and 1586 prices stabilized and the harvests were the best in years.[7]

---

5. On the preparations for the royal entrance, see *DACB*, 5:417, and *Llibre de les solemnitats de Barcelona*, ed. Agustí Duran i Sanpere and Josep Sanabre, vol. 2 (Barcelona, 1947), 38–41.

6. Ordinance quoted in *Llibre de les solemnitats*, 2:43 n. 1.

7. For prices, see Gaspar Feliu Montfort, *Precios y salarios en la Cataluña moderna*, 2 vols. ([Madrid], 1991), vol. 1, chaps. 3–5, and vol. 2, chaps. 3–4. For the harvests, see *Pere Gil, S.I. (1551–1622) i la seva Geografia de Catalunya*, ed. Josep Iglésies (Barcelona, 1949), 299.

The royal visit loomed large because it stood for what the relationship between ruler and subjects was all about: the communion—in the sense of exchange or rapport—between the king and his people.[8] This communion was based on the monarch's promise to uphold his duties in return for his subjects' fidelity. During royal visits, this communion became palpable in a number of ways. One of them involved the exchange of *mercès* for *serveis*—that is, of favors for services.[9] Kings traditionally granted numerous honors and privileges, whereas in the Corts Catalans voted the royal subsidy to finance the viceregal administration. Similarly, ceremonies organized during royal visits revolved around the theme of mutual exchange and obligations between subjects and ruler. Gestures, symbols, and gifts made visible the ties that bound the king to his people. In this sense, to paraphrase Clifford Geertz, royal ceremonies were "not an echo of a politics taking place somewhere else" but rather "an intensification of a politics taking place everywhere else."[10]

As final arrangements for the royal entry into Barcelona were still under way, the consellers received news that Philip II had decided to forgo the entry ceremony. The prince and the Infanta Isabel were ill, and the king feared a long ceremony would worsen their condition. This was a serious blow to the consellers and to the city, which had invested much effort in the royal welcome. But attempts to change the king's mind failed. On 7 May, around seven in the evening, the enormous convoy of royal carriages and guards entered the city and rushed without a ceremony to the residence of the king and his family during their stay in Barcelona.

Word of Philip II's arrival sent the Barcelonese rushing to the streets to see him. According to the notary Francesc Guamis, Barcelona's official chronicler of the royal visit, "the entire people" of Barcelona ran down the Rambla, one of the city's main thoroughfares, to catch a glimpse of the king.[11] The initial excitement did not last long. The quick and subdued royal entry was a disappointment. According to the Flemish chronicler Enrique Cock, who was also an archer in Philip II's guard, "the consellers were angry, for they felt they had been tricked; the citizens were angry because His Majesty had not entered in triumph; everybody was angry that the con-

---

8. Carmelo Lisón Tolosana, *La imagen del rey (monarquía, realeza y poder ritual en la Casa de los Austrias)* (Madrid, 1991), 170. On early modern royal entrances, see Roy Strong, *Art and Power: Renaissance Festivals, 1450–1650* (Berkeley, 1984).

9. Elliott, *Revolt of the Catalans*, 41.

10. Clifford Geertz, *Negara: The Theatre State in Nineteenth-Century Bali* (Princeton, 1980), 120.

11. *Llibre de les solemnitats*, 2:44–45.

fraternities had not greeted him."[12] "That night," Cock recalled, "there was great silence in the city, despite the many miraculous things worth seeing everywhere."[13]

The lack of a joyous reunion between Philip II and Barcelona led to rumors that the king was unhappy with the city. He allegedly resented the consellers' refusal to assign a place of honor in the entry ceremonies to the duke of Savoy and to the grandees in the royal entourage.[14] According to another rumor, Barcelona's bishop Dimas Lloris had warned the king that the consellers intended to disregard his majesty's wishes for the occasion — a charge the bishop denied.[15] The day after Philip II's arrival, city officers had the opportunity to gauge the king's mood for themselves. At four in the afternoon, the consellers led a large delegation of city officers to kiss Philip II's hand. Clad in their new robes of scarlet velvet lined with golden cloth, the consellers would be the first to welcome the king in the name of the city. At the palace where the royal family stayed, the count of Chinchón took the officers to a room where the monarch awaited them. Philip II stood alone, wearing black clothes, a hat of the same color, boots, and his sword. After the customary courtesies and kisses, conseller en cap Jaume Vila told the monarch that "the city was greatly pleased and received a great honor [*mercè*] from his happy and much expected arrival." Vila also informed him that prayers were being said for the health of the royal family. The king, who had "a very happy expression and a very gracious and serene smile," thanked them for their prayers and bid them "Godspeed, friends."[16] They then went to kiss the hands of the prince and the infantas before returning to city hall.

Relieved by the king's apparently good humor, the consellers immediately ordered music to start and bonfires to be lit all over the city. They also made arrangements for a large procession as soon as the health of the royal family improved and the weather allowed it.

On Saturday, 11 May, five days after the king's arrival, the rest of the city took to the streets to welcome Philip II. They did so with a procession modeled after the annual feast of Corpus Christi celebrated in late May or early June. But whereas in the latter the city worshiped the body of the heavenly

12. Quoted by Henry Kamen, *The Phoenix and the Flame: Catalonia and the Counter Reformation* (New Haven, 1993), 80.

13. Henrique Cock, *Relación del viaje hecho por Felipe II, en 1585, á Zaragoza, Barcelona y Valencia*, ed. Alfredo Morel-Fatio and Antonio Rodríguez Villa (Madrid, 1876), 128.

14. *Memòries de Jeroni Saconomina (1572–1602)*, in *Cavallers i ciutadans a la Catalunya del cinc-cents*, ed. Antoni Simon i Tarrés (Barcelona, 1991), 203.

15. *Llibre de les solemnitats*, 2:50–51.

16. Ibid., 48.

king, Barcelona now honored the presence of their king on earth with a
mix of sacred and worldly symbols in a setting both solemn and playful.[17]
At two in the afternoon, the consellers went to the cathedral to see the procession off. Moving slowly along the city's narrow streets, the procession
reached the royal palace near the port, where Philip II, the infantas, and
their guests watched from large windows. A group of loud drummers led
the way, followed by two dragons spitting firecrackers and a troupe of festive demons. Behind them, twenty-two horsemen clad in rich outfits accompanied a flag bearing the city's coat of arms. Next came the "poor" carrying candles and a float with a castle that fired loud rockets. This was only
a prelude to the master artisans' craft confraternities. Weeks before the
procession, the consellers had sent orders to each confraternity to make
the best effort to impress the king. They even offered to pay for musicians
to accompany each confraternity. Yet masters needed little encouragement:
they enjoyed the opportunity to show off before the whole city and to honor
their king.

During the procession, some sixty confraternities carried their official
flag or ensign, at the top of which was tied a bouquet or some other present for the king. As each group passed by the window from which Philip II
watched, its flag bearer approached him with the offering. Wool weavers
presented the king with a golden eagle, hosiers *(calceters)* and gardeners
(hortolans) offered figures of their patron saints, cutlers *(daguers)* gave a
golden knife, and so on. The king had the various gifts collected, sometimes by the infantas, and brought to the boy Prince Philip, who was still
not feeling well and lay in sickbed. When the Infanta Isabel went to take a
beautifully gilded pelican—a symbol of Christ—offered by the mattress
makers, the sudden flight of little birds released from the pelican's pouch
caught her by surprise. The birds let loose slips of paper with a message for
the king: "Whoever refuses this refuge and flees from its subjection, to him
liberty is prison."[18] The message underscored the wish of subjects to be
bound to their king as they were to God.

Philip II seemed pleased by the confraternities' gestures. According to
Enrique Cock, "His majesty [had]. . . a happy expression and put on a good
face to the people passing."[19] This presentation of gifts to Philip II was one
of the rare occasions when master artisans could go in person to their king,

17. The procession in the king's honor did not accompany the consecrated host, in contrast to the Corpus Christi festivities; see *Dietaris de la Generalitat*, 3:154 (6 May 1585). On
the Corpus Christi processions in Catalonia, see Kamen, *Phoenix of the Flame*, esp. 181–86.

18. *Llibre de les solemnitats*, 2:53.

19. Cock, *Relación del viaje*, 130.

not just as members of their confraternities, but also as the people of Barcelona. Most of the time, the consellers reserved that honor for themselves. But during the three hours that it took the confraternities to pass before Philip II, the people approached their king without their official intermediaries.

After the confraternities' intervention came the final and most solemn part of the procession. Members of the city's religious orders and clergy carried candles, crosses, and figures of Christ and the saints. The bishop brought the formal part of the procession to an end. Behind him followed the people of the city.

The long Saturday procession was the first of three days of public festivities in honor of Philip II. On the afternoons of Sunday and Monday, the craft confraternities came before the king with new dances and floats, trying to outdo each other. The sifters *(garbelladors)* sang praises to the monarch and performed a special dance using their large sieves. But instead of sifting grain, masters tossed sweets in the air and then to the onlookers in the streets before bowing to the king. The sailors pulled a ship on wheels with many sails, which shot large rockets when it passed before the royal family. Fishers *(pescadors)* had a large boat, which they decorated with fabric and flags. Inside the boat, six men pretended to catch live fish, which they offered to the public along with candy. Blacksmiths brought the city's *víbria,* a mythological female dragon that spit fire, while butchers tied a young bull with ropes and made him "dance." In return for their performances, the king offered coins to each confraternity.[20]

This exchange between king and artisans in the streets of Barcelona mirrored the exchange of royal favors for subjects' services.[21] Yet it would be wrong to assume that master artisans were content simply with Philip II's small monetary gift, which many did not even accept. They, along with many other Catalans, would seek much greater favors during the meeting of the Corts, which the king had convened for the end of May.

However, the royal family's stay in Barcelona extended longer than anticipated. Public and private celebrations in their honor continued for the rest of May and the early part of June. Finally, on 13 June, Catalina Micaela boarded the galleon that would take her and the duke of Savoy to Italy. The sight of Philip II's tearful farewell to his daughter brought an emotional end to a spectacular five-week royal visit to Barcelona.

20. The gift consisted of ten coins of 8 rals, or about 160 sous, presumably to each confraternity; *Llibre de les solemnitats,* 2:56–57. The daily wage of a Barcelona master mason in 1585 was between four and five sous; Feliu Montfort, *Precios y salarios,* 2:89, *cuadro* IV.1.
21. Elliott, *Revolt of the Catalans,* 41.

The Quest for Royal Favors

As the galleons of the duke and duchess of Savoy set sail eastward, Philip II headed west to Monzón, a small town in Aragon close to the border with Catalonia. For the king, the most important stage of his extended visit to his eastern Spanish territories now began. He convened what were known as the General Cortes of Aragon: the simultaneous meeting of the representative assemblies of Aragon, Catalonia, and Valencia. Despite the name, each assembly conducted business independently.

Catalans and the king had a staggering list of issues that had accumulated since the last Corts in 1563–64. Reforms were needed in the Diputació, and the continuing problem of banditry in the countryside required urgent attention. Some of the most contentious matters concerned the Inquisition and the reform of monastic orders.[22] The dire state of royal finances in Catalonia and the reform of the Audiència, the royal court of appeals in Barcelona, also required immediate action.[23] The Corts provided the occasion for the equally important exchange of favors for services between king and Catalans. The favors included titles of nobility and other honors given to individual people. To Catalan towns in particular, royal privileges were fundamental to the workings of their governments.[24]

Barcelona's government rested on royal privileges granted over several centuries, and major reforms to the city's regime depended on additional privileges. Barcelona's representatives in the Corts considered winning those royal privileges among their most important duties.

Master artisans also sought royal privileges for their craft confraternities. As with Barcelona's city government, most craft confraternities came into existence through royal privilege; and subsequent privileges served to confirm older ones as well as to introduce changes in their trades.

---

22. For example, Catalan delegates to the 1585 Corts demanded that officials exercising civil jurisdiction not be "familiars"—that is to say, lay officials of the Inquisition. The monarchy agreed to this demand; see Henry Kamen, *The Spanish Inquisition: A Historical Revision* (New Haven, 1997), 147. On Barcelona's tribunal of the Inquisition, see also William Monter, *Frontiers of Heresy: The Spanish Inquisition from the Basque Lands to Sicily* (Cambridge, 1990), chap. 5.

23. On royal finances, see Bernat Hernández, "Un assaig de reforma del sistema fisco-financer de la monarquia a Catalunya: L'impost del quint sobre les imposicions locals, 1580–1640," *Manuscrits* 14 (1996): 297–319. On the rise of litigation slowing the Audiència, see James S. Amelang, "Barristers and Judges in Early Modern Barcelona: The Rise of a Legal Elite," *American Historical Review* 89 (December 1984): 1276.

24. Víctor Ferro, *El dret públic català: Les institucions a Catalunya fins al Decret de Nova Planta* (Vic, 1987), 149.

Barcelona's craft confraternities therefore found it expedient to send delegates *(síndics)* to Monzón to seek royal privileges and other favors from Philip II, even though city authorities did not approve such actions. The delegates from the college of apothecaries would win a privilege, and masons *(mestres de cases)* and other confraternities would try to do the same.[25] Crock pot makers *(escudellers)* sent two delegates to Monzón.[26] Druggists *(adroguers)* sent one delegate to request the king's confirmation of their privileges. In addition, they hired Pere Puigvert, who worked for the secretary for the Council of Aragon, Jeroni Gassol, to represent the interests of the druggists before other royal officials.[27] There is no way of knowing how successful these or other master artisans were in securing royal privileges in 1585, but kings regularly granted them.

Occasionally, confraternities sent delegates to the Corts to lobby for royal favors for the city at large. The confraternity of master carpenters, for example, reported that they, along with other confraternities, paid for their own delegates in Monzón to seek royal support for the motu proprio against hoarding.[28] But unlike what had happened a few years earlier, this time master artisans did not organize public meetings of officers from several confraternities in order to secure the king's support for the papal bull.

Master artisans would also seek another major privilege from the king: the restoration of the two consellers for master artisans, which King Ferdinand the Catholic had abolished nearly a century before.[29] To that end, the artistes and the menestrals wanted a privilege from Philip II creating an additional, sixth, conseller. This privilege would allow two master artisans to serve as consellers each year, instead of only one. Master artisans had unsuccessfully requested the additional conseller from Philip II's father, Charles V, during the Corts of 1547.[30] They would try once more in 1585.

However, master artisans faced a major obstacle to requesting royal favors—namely, lack of direct access to the king. As the campaign for the

25. AHCB CC X-49 (LCO 1585–88), fol. 43r: Syndics to Consellers and Committee of Twenty-Four, 9–10 October 1585.

26. José Coroleu é Inglada and José Pella y Forgas, *Las Cortes Catalanas* (Barcelona, 1876), 91.

27. ACA Diversos Col.legi de Droguers i Confiters 1: "Libro I de actas y negocios" (1567–1603), fols. 79–80.

28. AHCB Gremis 37-2 ("Llibre de Consells" 1583–1614): carpenters' council, 25 July 1585.

29. On Ferdinand's privilege of 1493, see Jaume Vicens i Vives, *Ferran II i la ciutat de Barcelona, 1479–1516*, 3 vols. (Barcelona, 1936–37), 2:177–93.

30. *RB*, 1:107.

motu proprio in 1582–84 had demonstrated, artisans could try to see the king, but he would not give them an audience. Master artisans tried to bypass such obstacles, but that was not easy. The example of the college of druggists who hired a royal officer is exceptional. Their records do not indicate how much the druggists paid their man in Monzón, but such well-connected lobbyists were probably too expensive for most confraternities. As that example indicates, master artisans may have sought the aid of Catalans in the royal government, although sources hardly ever detail those efforts. Unable to find the means to reach the king, most artisans had no choice but to rely on the city's official delegates to the Corts.

The prerogative to speak for Barcelona's citizens before the king and the Corts belonged to the city's elite. They were, in the words of the count of Miranda, the viceroy of Catalonia, "the most distinguished and [had] the best reason and discourse" among Barcelona's citizens.[31] As such, they claimed to be the rightful leaders of the Consell de Cent.[32] Officially called the "Council of One Hundred Jurats," the Consell de Cent had in fact one hundred forty-four councilmen, or *jurats,* from the city's four estates. Although jurats and consellers were elected at random, their names pulled from bags containing all candidates to the various offices, the distribution of seats in the council reflected the oligarchy's superiority.[33]

More important, the authority to make proposals before the Consell de Cent lay, for the most part, in the hands of the five consellers; and here too the oligarchy had an advantage, holding the first three consellers, with the fourth going to the merchants and the fifth held alternatively by the artistes and menestrals. Moreover, only men from the first estate could be delegates to the Corts *(síndics de Corts)* and ambassadors.[34] A small group

31. ACA CA llig. 261 no. 34: "Relación de lo q[ue] ha passado acerca el dissetimi[ent]o," n.d. [after January 1586].

32. For an overview of the composition and workings of the Consell de Cent, see Vicens i Vives, *Ferran II,* 1:106–52.

33. The distribution of jurats in the Consell was as follows: honored citizens, knights, doctors of law and medicine (and aristocrats from 1621 on), 48; merchants, 32; artistes, 32; menestrals, 32. Votes and debates in the Consell de Cent were officially secret and therefore not recorded. Occasionally the drafts of Council minutes contain names that might suggest votes; and when there are significant splits, votes might be indicated. Nevertheless, it is usually impossible to know how jurats voted. Vicens Vives guesses that knights, honored citizens, physicians, and jurists were likely to vote with most merchants because members of these two estates often shared family ties. He also argues that master notaries and barber-surgeons, who belonged to the artistes, may have voted with lawyers and physicians out of professional affinities; see Vicens i Vives, *Ferran II,* 1:116.

34. Knights could not represent Barcelona in the Corts because they sat in the noble *braç militar.* The only exception was in the case of a knight who happened to be conseller *en cap;* see Vicens i Vives, *Ferran II,* 2:314.

of men, therefore, represented Barcelona in Monzón. Conseller en cap Jaume Vila—an honored citizen—presided over the syndics from more than thirty Catalan towns in the braç reial. Vila also acted as the first of four syndics, who conducted all negotiations for Barcelona during the Corts.[35] The three other syndics were honored citizens as well: Galceran Desvalls, Miquel Bastida, who had been second conseller, and Miquel Sarrovira, who had also served both as second conseller and as conseller en cap. He had also been the city's chief counsel and was an authority on the Corts's procedures.[36]

In Barcelona, the Consell de Cent supervised its four syndics through a "Committee of Twenty-Four on the Corts" *(consell de vint-i-quatrena de Corts)*. In this committee, which issued instructions to the syndics and drafted proposals for legislation and royal privileges, the city's oligarchy also had a larger number of seats than the other estates.[37] Though votes in the committee were not recorded, its instructions to the syndics tended to relegate master artisans' demands to the lower end of its list of priorities.

The syndics' duty to represent Barcelona seems, in hindsight, nearly impossible to fulfill. And yet everyone from master artisans to the city's oligarchy hoped that these four men would return from the Corts of 1585 with generous royal favors and a long list of accomplishments. With the Corts taking place nearly 175 kilometers from Barcelona, the Committee of Twenty-Four could not always keep close tabs on its four men. The committee sent detailed instructions with numerous items for the syndics to address each day, but the syndics could easily choose how much time and energy to invest in each of those items. Even if the syndics had wanted to wait for orders from Barcelona to arrive before making each and every move, the system of communications made that impractical. Letters sent by horseback courier from Monzón to Barcelona took at least one day and more often two. The Committee of Twenty-Four might take several more days to respond to the syndics' numerous questions and pleas for instructions. Some decisions could not wait that long. Under these circumstances,

35. These four syndics formed the largest delegation in the braç reial. On the procedures to elect Barcelona's syndics, see Ferro, *Dret públic*, 200.

36. AHCB CC II-94 (Delibs. 1584–85), fols. 81r–83r: 25 April 1585. The Corts of 1585 would commission Sarrovira to write *Ceremonial de Corts* (first published in 1599), which became a major work on the Corts's procedures. He served as second conseller in 1563 and as conseller *en cap* in 1572; Bastida was second conseller in 1567; *RB*, 1:48.

37. The composition of the committee was as follows: honored citizens and doctors of law and medicine, 8 jurats; merchants, 6 jurats; artistes, 5 jurats; menestrals, 5 jurats. As members of the braç militar (noble estate), knights and aristocrats could not sit on this committee. For the committee's procedures, see AHCB CC XVI-82 (Corts): "Dietari y breu compendi dels negocis de la xxiiiiª de Corts," 1626.

syndics felt tempted to take matters into their own hands for a variety of reasons, including pressure from royal officers to act quickly,[38] as well as the conviction that they knew what was best for the city.

The four syndics arrived in Monzón in late June and began their mission soon after. On 1 July, they presented a list of petitions to the king. Two days later, the Corts's three braços—clergy, nobility, and towns—met for the first time, which initiated the negotiations over legislation and the resolution of past grievances.[39] The syndics' greatest efforts went to addressing conflicts between Catalan and royal authorities. The syndics sought clarification on a number of disputes over civilian and military jurisdictions; they also opposed the establishment of the royal Council of Italy because it reduced considerably the authority of the Council of Aragon, which until the middle of the sixteenth century had oversight over the affairs of Milan, Naples, and Sicily.[40] The syndics wrote back to Barcelona describing long conversations on the imposition of checks to the authority of the Inquisition and the appointment of Castilians as heads of Catalan monastic orders.[41] Heading the list of royal privileges sought by the syndics was a proposal to establish a system of annual review of candidates to city offices and other measures to prevent abuses by consellers.[42] The new privilege would also allow the appointment of new consellers in case of death or removal from office.[43]

Yet within a few weeks after the start of the Corts, unexpected circumstances seriously affected the syndics' work. By late July, an influenza epidemic had struck Monzón. The town was an ideal place for an epidemic to spread quickly. With few large buildings, Monzón lacked adequate housing for the large numbers of royal servants, guards, ministers, and delegates from three kingdoms. Consequently, the numbers of deaths rose quickly. On 1 August, the Consell de Cent found that syndic Galceran Desvalls had died two days earlier of "acute and continuous fever."[44] It dis-

38. For example, see AHCB CC X-49 (LCO 1585–88), fol. 68: Syndics to Committee of Twenty-Four and Consellers, 13 November 1585.

39. AHCB CC XVI-72 (Corts) Registre de lletres trameses per . . . los Co[n]seller y síndichs, 1563–85: Syndics to Consellers and Committee of Twenty-Four, 7 July 1585.

40. On the creation of the Council of Italy (between 1555 and 1579), see Jon Arrieta Alberdi, *El Consejo Supremo de la Corona de Aragón (1494–1704)* (Zaragoza, 1994), 140–51.

41. AHCB CC II-94 (Delibs. 1584–85), fol. 118v, 120.

42. AHCB CC II-94 (Delibs. 1584–85), fols. 112r–112v; AHCB C VIII-12 (Llibres d'insaculacions), fols. 175r–176v: "Privilegi . . . sobre la forma que se ha tenir en la inseculatió," 27 May 1587.

43. ACA CA llig. 261 no. 34: "Memorial de Barc[elon]a sobre lo de la inseculación," n.d.

44. AHCB CC XVI-72 (Corts) Registre de lletres trameses per . . . los Co[n]seller y síndichs, 1563–85: Syndics to Consellers and Committee of Twenty-Four, 30 July 1585. On the influenza epidemic *(catarro)*, see Antonio de Bofarull y Brocá, *Historia crítica (civil y eclesiástica) de Cataluña*, 9 vols. (Barcelona, 1876–78), 7:200.

patched Jeroni Magarola, a doctor of medicine and former second conseller, to fill Desvalls's vacancy.[45] But by the end of August, Magarola and
the rest of the syndics—who allegedly lived "miserably" in cramped quarters—all had symptoms of influenza.[46] Conseller en cap Jaume Vila feared
for his life, and on 15 September he fled Monzón with his son and two
standard-bearers in search of healthier conditions back in Barcelona. One
of his standard-bearers, Onofre Cho, reported that Vila left Monzón so
abruptly that he did not even take leave of the king or the other Barcelona
syndics.[47]

The Consell de Cent was furious with Vila. A few weeks before, it had rebuked him for allegedly going about Monzón unaccompanied by standard-
bearers, for using side streets rather than the principal road, and for other
behavior that allegedly dishonored Barcelona in the eyes of delegates from
other kingdoms. His unauthorized departure was the last straw. The Consell de Cent dismissed him from his duties as syndic the day after he left
Monzón.[48] Vila's flight left Barcelona with three infirm syndics at the Corts
incapable of coping with all the duties expected of them.[49] They received
letter after letter from Barcelona chastising them for not writing regularly,
to which the syndics fired back complaining that the Committee of Twenty-
Four was taking too long to respond to their letters.[50] The consellers and
Committee of Twenty-Four accused the syndics of being "so busy with your
own business and the claims of private individuals that you forget the affairs of the city."[51] Syndic Sarrovira had been seen with two pot makers from
Barcelona, while Dr. Magarola had reportedly spent time with a carpenter.
These were not innocent encounters. The two master artisans mentioned
were allegedly trying to make the syndics intercede on behalf of their confraternities, probably to secure privileges from the king or other concessions in the Corts. It was alleged that the syndics' shameful behavior

45. AHCB CC II-94 (Delibs. 1584–85), fol. 123v: Consell de Cent, 1 August 1585. Magarola was second conseller in 1579–80; *RB*, 1:49.

46. AHCB CC II-94 (Delibs. 1584–85), fols. 136r–138v: 6 September 1585. For the syndics' lodgings, see Coroleu é Inglada and Pella y Forgas, *Cortes*, 89.

47. AHCB CC II-94 (Delibs. 1584–85), fol. 141: 15 September 1585.

48. Coroleu é Inglada and Pella y Forgas, *Cortes*, 88–90.

49. AHCB CC XVI-72 (Corts) Registre de lletres trameses per . . . los Co[n]seller y
síndichs, 1563–85: Syndics to Consellers and Committee of Twenty-Four, 7 September
1585. Syndic Magarola took up the presidency of the *braç reial*.

50. AHCB CC II-94 (Delibs. 1584–85), fols. 134v–136v: Consell de Cent and Committee of Twenty-Four, 30–31 August 1585.

51. "Que vostres mercés estan tan divisos y ocupats en sobre sos negocis propis é intents
particulars que se obliden dels negocis de la ciutat"; Consellers to Syndics, 4 September
1585, quoted in Coroleu é Inglada and Pella y Forgas, *Cortes*, 93–94 n. 23.

had become the subject of endless gossip in the streets and squares of Monzón.[52]

On 16 September, one day after Vila left Monzón, news arrived that Dr. Magarola had also left the town to recuperate from his illness in the nearby Catalan town of Lleida. The Consell de Cent decided it had had enough of its syndics. It terminated the powers of the three remaining syndics, stripped Vila of his office of conseller en cap, and set up a committee to investigate their actions. But finding new syndics was not easy. The names of six candidates had been suggested before Pere Ferreres, who had been conseller en cap the year before (1583–84), was confirmed as first syndic. Accompanying Ferreres would be three doctors of law: Francesc Saragossa, Montserrat Monfar (a former third conseller), and the honored citizen Lluís Cornet.[53]

The new group of syndics had just arrived in Monzón when they faced another challenge: Philip II had also fallen ill with fever and gout.[54] As the days passed, his condition worsened. There were rumors that the king would suspend the Corts. After four months, Barcelona's delegation might return from Monzón having achieved only a few of the Committee of Twenty-Four's long list of demands.

Who Speaks for the People of Barcelona?

In Barcelona, news of the king's illness prompted the consellers to act quickly in case the Corts were suspended. They convened the Consell de Cent for the afternoon of 28 October to approve new instructions for the syndics. But in an extraordinary move, the council made its approval conditional on the acceptance of a list of major demands. A large group of master artisans, "with powers from their colleges and confraternities," demanded that the syndics seek a royal privilege restoring the sixth conseller because "of the three parts of the people of Barcelona. . . , artistes and menestrals are not just two but far more."[55] The Consell de Cent also ordered the syndics to seek Philip II's support for the papal motu proprio condemning hoarding. In addition, Barcelona's delegation would have to op-

52. Coroleu é Inglada and Pella y Forgas, *Cortes,* 91–93.

53. *DACB,* 5:420 (16 September 1585).

54. AHCB CC X-49 (LCO 1585–88), fols. 40v–45r: Syndics to Committee of Twenty-Four and Consellers, 9–10 October 1585. For the king's illness, see Henry Kamen, *Philip of Spain* (New Haven, 1997), 260.

55. AHCB CC VI-64 (LC 1584–91), fols. 92r–93v: Consellers to King, n.d. [28 October 1585]; AHCB CC II-94 (Delibs. 1584–85), fol. 158v.

pose legislation pending in the Corts requiring merchants to get viceregal licenses to import wheat into the city. Finally, the syndics would have to reject a proposal to lower import tariffs on foreign cloths and to vote in favor of a 50 percent tax on exports of raw silk from Catalonia.

The demands did not stop there. The Consell de Cent appointed a distinguished *artista*, the master barber-surgeon Gaspar Massaguer, to go to Monzón to petition Philip II for the sixth *conseller*.[56] Called by one prominent contemporary "the most skillful of all surgeons in Spain," Massaguer would later hold the chair of surgery at Barcelona's university.[57] By giving him such an important mission, the Consell de Cent reflected its doubts about whether the syndics were able—or perhaps even willing—to win this privilege from the king.

Massaguer and the four syndics had little time left to accomplish so much. Convinced that Monzón was simply too unhealthy, on 30 October Philip II ordered the Corts to conclude their work by the first of December.[58] With only four weeks left, there was a mad rush in the Corts to finish the staggering amount of business. In early November, syndic Ferreres wrote to Barcelona complaining about the slowness with which the Committee of Twenty-Four responded to the syndics' correspondence; and when instructions arrived in Monzón, he added, they had contradictory orders.[59] He confessed feeling "half burnt" from all the negotiations. "God be my witness," he concluded, "and do not blame me because I cannot do anything more."[60]

On 11 November, a religious procession in Barcelona offered thanks to God for the recovery of the king's health.[61] Despite his improvement, Philip II decided to adjourn the Corts shortly and leave Monzón. But for the Corts to end, they first needed to approve the royal subsidy. Time was running out, and it looked as if Barcelona would not be able to secure all of the demands it had hoped for. With that in mind, the Committee of Twenty-Four devised a strategy to gain additional time. It drafted instructions to syndic

56. AHCB CC VI-64 (LC 1584–1591), fols. 95r–95v: Consellers to Syndics, 2 November 1585.

57. Jeroni Pujades, *Dietari de Jeroni Pujades,* ed. Josep Maria Casas Homs (Barcelona, 1975–76), vol. 2: fol. 238v. See also Josep M. Calbet i Camarasa and Jacint Corbella i Corbella, *Diccionari Biogràfic de Metges Catalans,* 2 vols. (Barcelona, 1982–83), 2:127.

58. AHCB CC X-49 (LCO 1585–88), fols. 57v–59v: Syndics to Committee of Twenty-Four, 30 October 1585.

59. AHCB CC X-49 (LCO 1585–88), fol. 56v: Ferreres to Francesc Gamis, 5 November 1585.

60. AHCB CC X-49 (LCO 1585–88), fols. 48r–49v: Ferreres to Francesc Gamis, 5 November 1585.

61. *DACB,* 5:421.

Ferreres to present a formal protest before the Corts stating that he could not vote on the subsidy until he received orders from Barcelona. The protest, known as a dissentiment, required all business in the Corts to halt until the grievance was resolved. Meanwhile, Barcelona's syndics would be able to negotiate more petitions and legislation favorable to the city in return for lifting their dissentiment.

A few days later, the consellers and the Committee of Twenty-Four received surprising news. Philip II had convened the Corts on 5 December in the town of Binéfar, close to Monzón, for a special final session to approve the subsidy. Barcelona's dissentiment should have delayed the vote on the royal subsidy. Instead, and for yet undetermined reasons, the vote took place as scheduled, and the royal subsidy was approved. The Corts of 1585 had come to an end. An angry Consell de Cent tried to reconstruct the confusing last days of the Corts to determine who was to blame for this unwelcome turn of events. Initial inquiries revealed that Barcelona's syndics had presented the dissentiment on 4 December, but for some reason the braç reial had rejected it.[62] Because syndic Ferreres presided over the braç reial, the Committee of Twenty-Four accused him, with the assistance of fellow syndic Francesc Saragossa and former syndic Miquel Sarrovira, of willfully letting the dissentiment fail.[63]

The news of the syndics' outrageous behavior at the Corts provoked indignation and rage that spilled beyond the city council. The count of Miranda, then viceroy of Catalonia, reported that the people in Barcelona had such a bad opinion of Ferreres, Saragossa, and Sarrovira that upon their return to Barcelona, the three men had been warned to stay home for fear of some "insolent act" against them. "The people" were angry, the viceroy wrote, because these syndics had "sold their privileges." Moreover, in the Consell de Cent, "the common people" (*la gente popular*), that is, "the merchants, artistes, and menestrals, who make up one body and form the majority," wanted to punish the syndics for allowing the passage of laws considered harmful to them.[64]

The day after Christmas 1585, the Consell de Cent launched an effort to obtain from the king some of the demands that the syndics failed to win

62. Mònica González Fernández, "Barcelona i la vint-i-quatrena de Corts a les Corts de Montsó de 1585," in *Tercer Congrés d'Història Moderna de Catalunya: Actes*, in special issue of *Pedralbes*, no. 13 (Barcelona, 1993), 1:303.

63. AHCB CC II-95 (Delibs. 1585–86), fols. 18r ff.: Consell de Cent, 26 December 1585.

64. ACA CA llig. 261 no. 34: "Relación de lo q[ue] ha passado acerca el dissetimi[ent]o," n.d. [after January 1586]. The popular resentment apparently did not extend to Gaspar Massaguer, who also failed to win the sixth conseller from Philip II.

at the Corts. The council debated sending a "Committee of Four" *(quatreta)* to the king to protest the dismissal of Barcelona's dissentiment. This committee would consist of one jurat from each of the four estates in the Consell de Cent.[65] On hearing this proposal, honored citizens and knights rose in protest, arguing that such a committee amounted to an embassy and that only members of their estate could act as ambassadors. Unable to overcome these objections, the consellers postponed a final vote. The Consell de Cent reconvened the following day to hold another tense meeting. The presiding third conseller, Josep Dalmau, a doctor of law, refused to call a vote on the Committee of Four to the king. He argued that to do so would violate city privileges, which would go against his oath of office. Unfortunately for Dalmau, he was not in a position to impose his view. Although he could have normally counted on the support of the first and second consellers from his estate, this time he was alone. The Consell de Cent had removed the second conseller, Francesc Saragossa, from office for his role as syndic to the Corts.[66] Conseller en cap Tomàs Pujades was still serving in Rome as the city's ambassador to the papal court. As a result of this exceptional situation, the fourth conseller, Simon Canyet, a merchant, and the fifth conseller, Antoni Roure, a master apothecary, outvoted the other remaining conseller. This allowed the proposal for the Committee of Four to come up for a vote before the Consell de Cent and to be approved.[67]

But the debate was not over yet. Next, the consellers had to appoint the four men who would go to see the king, and that led to yet another confrontation. Normally, each of the consellers would have chosen one member of his own estate, except for the fifth conseller, which appointed both the artista and the menestral. But when asked to nominate someone from his first estate, the third conseller, Dalmau, refused to comply. In an unprecedented move, the Consell de Cent voted to allow the fourth and fifth consellers to make the appointment, which raised loud objections.[68] In view of the situation, the merchant and artisan consellers agreed to adjourn the meeting. For the time being, there would be no delegation to see the king.

A few days later, on 4 January 1586, an investigation into the actions of Barcelona's syndics at the Corts revealed that syndics Ferreres, Saragossa, and Sarrovira had repeatedly disregarded orders from the Consell de Cent

65. AHCB CC II-95 (Delibs. 1585–86), fol. 19.

66. Vacant offices could be filled only by a new election on 30 November. The royal privilege sought by Barcelona in 1585 to reform aspects of the city's government allowed the election of new consellers before election time to avoid these vacancies.

67. AHCB CC II-95 (Delibs. 1585–86), fols. 20v–21r: Consell de Cent, 27 December 1585.

68. AHCB CC II-95 (Delibs. 1585–86), fol. 22v.

and occasionally gone so far as to vote against its instructions.[69] Moreover, the syndics had purposefully let Barcelona's dissentiment against a vote on the royal subsidy fail in order to allow the Corts to conclude. After such startling revelations, the Consell de Cent declared the three syndics ineligible for any city office in the future and stripped Francesc Saragossa of his office as second conseller, to which he had been elected in November 1585. Now was the right time for the fourth and fifth consellers to act on the Committee of Four. Disregarding the protests from the first estate, they appointed Miquel Joan Pol, allegedly the only honored citizen willing to serve.[70] Now the committee could begin its mission, which was to turn around the errors of Barcelona's syndics.

Anger at the syndics' supposed failure as their representatives had led master artisans and merchants to conclude that they themselves could better represent the people of Barcelona before the king. It was a claim based on a narrower definition of "the people" than that held by the city's elite, which argued that the four estates in the Consell de Cent stood for the whole of Barcelona. The Catalan jurist Andreu Bosc summed up this view when he asserted that the Consell de Cent and its committees "are and make up the entire University, Republic, and the people; all the acts deliberated by these councils have as much force as if they had been agreed upon by a meeting of the entire people."[71] In contrast, master artisans, and to a lesser extent merchants as well, saw themselves as the people, and they were therefore entitled to speak for it. This second definition had inspired merchants, artistes, and menestrals in the mid-fifteenth century to form the "Syndicate of the Three Estates and the People," which sent several delegations to Naples to present a number of demands to King Alphonse V. In 1452, the king acknowledged that the syndicate spoke for the people of Barcelona (*"populi civitatis nostre Barchinone"*) when it denounced abuses perpetrated by the city's oligarchy.[72] That master artisans considered them-

69. AHCB CC II-95 (Delibs. 1585–86), fols. 23r–27r: *memorial* by the special committee investigating the syndics, 4 January 1586.

70. ACA CA llig. 261 no. 34: "Relación de lo q[ue] ha passado acerca el dissentimi[ent]o," n.d. [after January 1586]. According to *RB*, 1:113, the Consell de Cent chose a knight *(militar)*. The other three members of the committee were the merchant Francesc Palau, the notary Bartolomé Bofill, and Miquel Esteve (a menestral whose profession is not given).

71. Andreu Bosc, *Sumari, index o epítome dels admirables y nobilíssimis títols de honor de Cathalunya, Rosselló, i Cerdanya* (Perpinyà, 1628; facsimile edition, Barcelona-Sueca, 1974), 430.

72. Privilege by Alphonse V, 14 October 1452, transcribed in Carmen Batlle Gallart, *La crisis social y económica de Barcelona a mediados del siglo XV*, 2 vols. (Barcelona, 1973), 2:429 (appendix 31).

selves better fit to speak for the people had also led to demands for their own consellers. Already in 1386, master artisans argued that "because there are three kinds of people in Barcelona, namely, [honored] citizens, merchants, and menestrals, there should be two consellers from each kind" in order to "have a say in its council and the government. . . of the commonwealth [*la cosa pública*]."[73] This was the same point made by master artisans on 28 October 1585, when they demanded in the Consell de Cent the restoration of the two artisan consellers because "of the three parts of the people of Barcelona. . . , artistes and menestrals are not just two but far more."

It may have seemed natural to think that master artisans would be better fit to represent their own wishes and demands, but there was no proof they would be more effective than their social superiors. The Consell de Cent had sent artisans as "messengers" *(missatgers)* to Philip II before, and they had come back empty-handed: first, in 1582, the notary Nicolau Lentisclà, who went to Lisbon to seek royal support for the papal bull against hoarding; and more recently, in October 1585, the barber-surgeon Gaspar Massaguer, who was sent to Monzón to petition for the sixth conseller. Whether or not this third trial would prove more successful once again depended on the king's willingness to listen.

A Mission to the King

In January 1586, the Consell de Cent's four-man committee, with a list of old and new demands, rushed to the city of Valencia, where Philip II had gone after his long stay at Monzón. Heading the list of demands were the sixth conseller and support for the motu proprio against hoarding.[74] In addition, there was a request for the king to strike a number of laws voted on in the Corts, which allegedly contradicted Barcelona's privileges. One of them prohibited joint meetings of officers from different craft confraternities—such as the ones organized in the early 1580s to request the motu proprio—which apparently prohibited as well the perfectly legal individual meetings of confraternity councils.[75]

73. King Peter IV's privilege, 24 September 1386, transcribed in Batlle Gallart, *Crisis social*, 2:393 (appendix 8).

74. ACA CA llig. 261, no. 34: *consulta*, "Los cabos por q[ue] han supp[lica]do las personas que embió la Ciudad," December 1586.

75. The Consell de Cent also wanted an amendment to a constitution that would allow Catalan cities to impose taxes on imports but that would keep the unpopular viceregal export licenses intact. The city council also sought the repeal of a constitution voted in the 1585 Corts that lowered taxes on the import of foreign cloth, which the syndics had sup-

When Barcelona's delegation arrived at Valencia, Philip II was wrapping up his stay in that kingdom.[76] Nevertheless, the king left on 27 February 1586 without seeing Barcelona's men. The royal entourage slowly made its way back to Castile, and on 26 March it arrived at the imposing palace (also a monastery and a mausoleum) of the Escorial, northwest of Madrid. There, Barcelona's men tried again to meet with the king, but months went by without an answer. In early September, eight months after they had left Barcelona, the delegation had still not seen the king.[77]

Evidently, Philip II did not care to see Barcelona's committee. In general, the king often refused to meet with ambassadors from his various territories, alleging that they were a waste of money. But Barcelona's men were not even officially ambassadors, and granting an audience to Barcelona's men might create a precedent that could lead to other such committees in the future. Nonetheless, the king was not ready to dismiss the four men just yet. The Council of Aragon had warned him that his refusal to see the committee might make Barcelona withhold payments on the royal subsidy. It was proposed that for the moment the delegation could meet with royal ministers. Meanwhile, the new viceroy of Catalonia, Manrique de Lara, should try to collect the royal subsidy in Barcelona.[78]

The outgoing viceroy of Catalonia, the count of Miranda, offered weightier reasons why the king should make an exception and see the committee. Its rebuff would only make Barcelona's "commoners" *(la gente popular)* more stubborn in their demands and send new delegations to the king. Moreover, being "passionate" and "fickle" *(gente desvariada),* they might do and say things that would force the king and his ministers to punish them, which would likely cause further trouble.

Although at first Miranda's assessment of the nature of social conflict in Barcelona seems vague, it was possibly an urgent warning, given the count's forthcoming assignment as viceroy of Naples. A year before, on 9 May 1585, a revolt had erupted in the Italian city during which the "representative of the people" *(eletto)* Giovan Vincenzo Starace was murdered.[79] The son of a rich silk merchant, Starace was held responsible for the sharp rise in the

---

posedly supported in defiance of their instructions; AHCB CC X-49 (LCO 1585–88), fol. 99v: instructions to the syndics, 7 January 1586.

76. For Philip II's stay at Valencia, see Kamen, *Philip of Spain,* 260–61.

77. ACA CA llig. 261 no. 34: *consulta,* 6 September 1586.

78. ACA CA llig. 261 no. 34: *consulta,* "Sobre la audiencia por q[ue] supp[lican] los q[ue] estan aqui por la ciudad de Barc[elon]a," [prior to 6 September] 1586.

79. On the events of 1585, see Rosario Villari, *The Revolt of Naples,* trans. James Newell with John A. Marino (Cambridge, 1993), chap. 2.

price of bread, a rise that was believed to be for his personal gain. After being publicly humiliated by a crowd, he was killed and his body dragged along the streets of the city. The protest culminated in front of the viceroy's palace with the cry "Death to bad government and long live justice!"[80] Starace's death started a campaign by artisans and tradesmen to lower prices and increase popular representation in Naples's city government. Threats of continued disturbances ended only in July with the arrival of Spanish galleons. Authorities prosecuted hundreds and executed thirty-one people during the second half of 1585. On 9 May 1586, the first anniversary of Starace's death, the count of Miranda informed the Consell de Cent that he would leave Barcelona soon for his new post as viceroy of Naples.[81]

There were important similarities and differences between the situations faced by Barcelona and Naples. Among the principal differences was the fact that Barcelona did not have the acutely high prices suffered by Naples at the start of the revolt. In addition, the commoners in Barcelona had greater representation in their city's government than their Neapolitan counterparts.[82] Nevertheless, in both cities, the alleged failure of the representative of the people to act in the interest of the people caused strong reactions. Barcelona's syndics were fortunate enough to avoid Starace's terrible death, but as the count of Miranda had noted, they had been advised to stay home for fear of an ugly incident.[83] The angry response, moreover, led in both cities to calls by the people to be represented by one of their own rather than by gentry or nobles, as well as to "restore" their political representation at the highest levels of the city government (through a second artisan conseller in Barcelona, through the equalization of the distribution of votes of aristocratic and popular representatives in Naples).[84]

From this perspective, Miranda's statements to Philip II may be read as advice on how to prevent the situation in Barcelona from following the tragic course taken by Naples. Miranda believed that the key was not to cave in to commoners' base passions but rather to prevent them from losing the natural hopes and aspirations of all subjects to petition their ruler. According to Miranda, Barcelona's merchants, artistes, and menestrals had supported the committee sent to see the king because "they were the ones

80. Villari, *Revolt*, 26.
81. *DACB*, 5:425.
82. On the limits of popular participation in Naples's city government, see Villari, *Revolt*, 23.
83. ACA CA llig. 261 no. 34: "Relación de lo q[ue] ha passado acerca el dissetimi[ent]o."
84. Villari, *Revolt*, 26.

interested in what [the king] has to revoke and grant" and did not want to entrust such a mission to those who opposed it.[85] "In this city as everywhere else," the count explained, "the noble and leading persons are hated by the people, a hatred born from thinking that the former intend to subject and oppress them." For this reason, Miranda advised the king to make the Barcelona delegation believe that he was willing to listen to their pleas by performing a meaningful gesture. On the king's "public outings," people often approached the monarch individually to give him petitions. Miranda advised the king to let Barcelona's delegation approach him.[86] That way, Miranda concluded, the four men could say they had seen the king, and Philip II could send them back to Barcelona without having granted them a formal audience.

As it turned out, Miranda's scheme proved unnecessary. In September 1586, viceroy Manrique de Lara in Barcelona collected payments on the royal subsidy. Nevertheless, the Council of Aragon urged the king to meet with Barcelona's delegation as a gesture of gratitude.[87] On 17 September, a notarized letter was drafted stating that the king would meet the men only as a special grace that was not to set a precedent.[88] During the brief meeting, Philip II gave the delegation a letter stating that the viceroy in Barcelona would reveal the royal response to their demands. After eight months, the four men could finally return home satisfied that at least they had seen the king.

Philip II's response was disappointing.[89] One by one, he either rejected or refused to take action on virtually all of the artisans' demands. Regarding the sixth conseller, he offered only the vague promise to see to it "in time." The king had disagreed with viceroy Manrique de Lara, who proposed granting not just a sixth conseller for artisans but a seventh one for the city's elite. That way, the viceroy argued, Barcelona "would have a better government and your majesty would deal with people of greater reason and honor; and it would avoid the problem that in case there is a

---

85. "Los mercaderes, artistas y menestrales, deseando meter y tener las manos en todo, dixeron que se avian de elegir de todos los estamentos; pareciendoles quiçá también que, siendo solo ellos los interessados en el punto de lo que dessea q[ue] se revoque y conceda de nuevo, no era bien fiarse de la parcialidad contraria"; ACA CA llig. 261 no. 34: "Relación de lo q[ue] ha passado acerca el dissetimi[ent]o," n.d. [after January 1586].

86. Referring to Philip II, Kamen writes: "He made a rule of being accessible to private petitions while going to or from Sunday mass and deliberately walked slowly, so that people would have a chance to catch up with him"; *Philip of Spain*, 198.

87. ACA CA llig. 261 no. 34: *consulta*, 6 September 1586.

88. ACA CA llig. 261 no. 34: notarized letter by Simón Frigola (vice chancellor of the Council of Aragon), 17 September 1586.

89. *DACB*, 5:466, 525–35 (Philip II's response).

parity of votes, the people, which tends to be riotous, might rebel."[90] The king also did not take any action regarding the motu proprio against hoarding. The Council of Aragon, which until 1584 had strongly encouraged the king to grant this demand, now urged Philip II to categorically reject the motu proprio because it might limit the viceroy's authority in Catalonia and affect ecclesiastic and noble rents. Philip II also refused to alter a number of laws voted in the Corts that allegedly contradicted the city's privileges, claiming that he had already signed them. Of these, the most controversial was the ban on meetings of craft confraternities' officers. The king seemed to side with the opinion of former viceroy Miranda, who welcomed the ban on the grounds that those meetings "might result in many inconveniences, among them that they might take the authority and government belonging solely to the consellers and the Consell [de Cent] as representatives of the entire people." Miranda claimed that without this new law, there might be "many scandals and seditious acts in the city, as has been seen from the experience a few years ago in the case of the motu proprio."[91] In the end, the Committee of Four proved no more successful than Barcelona's syndics to the Corts in winning major demands for master artisans.[92] Nonetheless, there were no reports of threats to the four men or of protests against the king's negative response to the demands of the people of Barcelona. It appeared, therefore, that the count of Miranda was right and that the monarch's simple gesture was all that was needed to ease tensions in the Catalan capital.

Representation and Popular Politics

Despite their failures in 1585–87, master artisans' desire for royal favors was, and would continue to be, central to their political culture. And as

90. ACA CA llig. 261, no. 34: *consulta,* "Los cabos por q[ue] han supp[lica]do las personas que embió la ciudad." Philip II promised to send the privilege reforming the Consell de Cent's elections "soon."

91. ACA CA llig. 261 no. 34: *consulta,* "Los cabos por q[ue] han supp[lica]do las personas que embió la Ciudad de Barc[elon]a después de salidos de Monçón," December 1586; ACA CA llig. 261 no. 34: "Pareçer del visorey y audien[cia]." The king also refused to repeal the constitution lowering taxes on the import of foreign cloth, which was seen as benefiting only the city's craft confraternities. He rejected the city council's claim that the constitution contradicted its authority to establish its own fiscal and economic policies in the city. The viceroy had warned the king that if the city council were given such an authority, craft confraternities would either declare that all foreign goods were of lower quality or immediately insist on raising the taxes on these foreign goods.

92. Two other, less controversial delegations sent by the Consell de Cent to the king in 1587 presented again some of the master artisans' demands with equally disappointing results; *DACB,* 5:477, 480.

long as artisans wanted those favors, they would have to go to the king, who remained the source of privileges. Philip II also gave artisans incentives to seek royal favors. A few craft confraternities won privileges in 1585; and even though he rejected artisans' larger demands, the king left the possibility that he might reconsider some of them "in time." As early modern Spanish political writers pointed out, the wise ruler maintained the promise of reward in order to encourage their subjects to obey the law and serve him.[93]

But the quest for royal favors depended on effective forms of representation, and in this regard Barcelona's master artisans found themselves in the predicament of the vast majority of men and women in early modern Europe. In most cases, the duty to represent subjects before their rulers belonged to intermediaries deemed worthy of the task, who in most cases were members of a political elite. Whether city authorities, royal officers, magistrates, or delegates to representative assemblies, these men were expected to speak to their rulers for the needs, the demands, and the aspiration of subjects at large—be they the people of a city, a kingdom, or a nation. These representatives dominated the exchange of services and favors between subjects and ruler; they usually chose which demands to present and which ones to ignore. Barcelona's artisans responded to this predicament by resorting to some of the means that characterized early modern forms of popular politics. One of those responses was simply to trust that their representatives would carry out their duties and bring them rewards from the monarch. There was little else artisans could do. As Barcelona's syndics to the 1585 Corts realized, if representatives failed in those duties, they might have to face the threat of popular violence. Although the syndics suffered only the humiliation of destitution, other representatives were not as lucky. Starace's murder in Naples was a recent example. Another such incident marked the start of the Comunero Revolt in Castile in 1520, when Rodrigo de Tordesillas, Segovia's delegate (*procurador*) to the Cortes of Castile, was brutally murdered by a mob of wool workers for allegedly selling out the city's interests.[94] The threat of popular violence remained a powerful incentive to representatives, as well as to rulers, to uphold their duties and maintain the trust of the people.[95]

93. José Antonio Maravall, *Teoría del estado en España en el siglo XVII*, 2d ed. (Madrid, 1997), 330–31.

94. Stephen Haliczer, *The Comuneros of Castile: The Forging of a Revolution, 1475–1521* (Madison, Wis., 1981), 3, 162.

95. Barbara B. Diefendorf, *Beneath the Cross: Catholics and Huguenots in Sixteenth-Century Paris* (Oxford, 1991), 27.

Another response was to find alternative routes of access to the ruler. Barcelona's craft confraternities sent delegates to lobby for corporate privileges from the king; or if they had the means, they might hire an advocate with good connections in court. In other parts of Europe, subjects found more dramatic forms of representation. In Germany's Black Forest during the eighteenth century, peasants organized religious pilgrimages to bring petitions to the Habsburg emperors.[96] By doing so, peasants were in effect sidestepping judicial and local intermediaries that stood between them and their ruler. Master artisans took the ideal of the communion between ruler and subjects seriously. They wished to remain close to their king and have the opportunity to offer him gifts and perform for him in public ceremonies. But they also expected that he would express his love for his loyal subjects by listening to their needs and occasionally granting them favors. Clearly, master artisans seemed prepared to accept that their king would not always grant their wishes. But they certainly wished to be heard. The challenge for Philip II and his successors was to figure out how to maintain those aspirations in a monarchy in which fewer and fewer subjects enjoyed the honor of seeing their king.

96. David Martin Luebke, *His Majesty's Rebels: Communities, Factions, and Rural Revolt in the Black Forest, 1725–1745* (Ithaca, 1997).

CHAPTER FOUR

Taking Politics to the Streets

On several occasions between 1588 and 1592, the threat of popular violence in Barcelona brought Catalonia to the brink of a revolt. This was not because popular violence was especially virulent or the number of people involved unusually large. In fact, most riots and other violent acts in Barcelona, as elsewhere, rarely posed more than a temporary challenge to the established order. Popular violence became potentially disastrous at this particular time because it coincided with exceptionally sharp conflicts within Catalonia's political elite. These conflicts pitted the viceroy of Catalonia against the Consell de Cent and at the same time the judges of the royal Audiència against the Catalan Diputació. Each time these disputes reached a climax, popular riots and attacks threatened to escalate to an armed conflict.

To a large extent, this situation was brought on by Catalonia's political elite, which considered it essential to assert its authority in the streets of Barcelona. Although king, viceroy, and consellers refused to admit that popular pressure might influence their decisions, their actions often proved otherwise. They paid attention to rumors, demonstrations, and riots in order to gauge popular sentiments toward specific policies or public actions. The consellers in particular expected the loyalty and obedience of the city's residents. Dressed in their heavy official gowns and accompanied by standard-bearers, the consellers represented Barcelona and its great authority. Their presence during a street disturbance might be enough to restore calm. But just in case that was not enough, the display of the city guard would quickly remind everyone who was in charge. When the Consell de

Cent's bell sounded, the companies of master artisans' confraternities went to city hall to receive orders that came exclusively from the consellers. Nevertheless, allegiance to city officials was not set in stone, and this often showed precisely at times of alarm or uncertainty. More than once during those years, Catalan and royal authorities tried to capture some of that popular support through appeals, threats, and even deceit in order to challenge the consellers' position and perhaps bolster their own.

But whom would "the people" obey? Even when master artisans took their assigned places in the city guard, it was not always possible to maintain absolute discipline in the ranks of what remained a civilian force. During an emergency, lines of communication might fail or the companies might get unclear orders. Many men and women did not take part in the guard, and if they formed a crowd, who knew what they might decide to do? Moreover, artisans had multiple allegiances to the city authorities, their confraternities, the pàtria, and the king. Which of those loyalties prevailed affected how they behaved in the streets, and that in turn proved crucial to the political conflicts taking place in the city.

From a broader perspective, these events in Barcelona reveal the close interrelation between high and popular politics in early modern societies. When faced with irreconcilable differences, contenders within a political elite were tempted to coerce their opponents by deploying armed men or by calling for expressions of public support. But by taking debates that were usually confined to the centers of high politics out into the streets, the protagonists of high politics were in effect allowing a wider audience to feel part of those debates. This situation created many opportunities for popular actions to impact the larger political conflicts. However, the interplay between high and popular was not always explicit. Most rulers and notables indignantly decried any appeal to the vulgar people, and they accused anyone who did so of playing with fire. However, such statements were another form of dissimulation that was characteristic of early modern politics.[1] To find connection between high and popular politics, it is necessary to look closely at the language used and the gestures made, as well as at the kind of actions the participants took.

The conflicts that took place in Barcelona reached a climax in 1588 and then again in 1591. I will describe the two sets of events separately, although they are closely related. The events of 1588 centered on the conflicts between the viceroy and the Consell de Cent over the control of

---

1. Rosario Villari, "Elogio della dissimulazione," in *Elogio della dissimulazione: La lotta politica nel Seicento* (Rome, 1987), 1–48.

wheat supplies in Barcelona and later over the control of the city's guard. At the same time, the judges of the royal Audiència faced off against the Diputació over conflicting claims to be the ultimate interpreters of the law in Catalonia. The events of 1591 focused above all on the renewal of the dispute between the Audiència and the Diputació, which ultimately involved all of the major political figures of Catalonia. Understanding the situation in the streets of Barcelona during these events, including incidents of popular riots and the behavior of the city's guard, reveals the multiple ways in which popular and high politics interacted in early modern societies.

Battle over Wheat

On 22 September 1587, two of Barcelona's consellers made an urgent petition to viceroy Manrique de Lara. Every day, the consellers explained, they heard "many complaints and cries from inhabitants in the present city and principality" regarding the large amounts of wheat, wine, and oil exported from Catalonia "with Your Excellency's licenses." Unless the shipments stopped, the consellers feared "a great want." The nagging problem of high prices brought about by the scarcity of basic goods once more threatened Barcelona. But whereas unscrupulous Catalans and foreign merchants had previously borne most of the blame, now the viceroy shared some of it because of his careless granting of export licenses. Thus the consellers asked Manrique de Lara not to issue any more. Viceroys, however, never liked to take orders from Barcelona, and Manrique de Lara was no exception. "If he wanted," the viceroy replied, "he would give out four thousand"![2]

Given the viceroy's attitude, the Consell de Cent sought the intervention of the king. It was not the first time it complained to Philip II that viceregal licenses caused scarcity. In 1586, the Committee of Four sent to protest the abrupt end of the 1585 Corts raised the matter, but it won no concessions.[3] A year later, in September 1587, the Consell de Cent's emissaries in Madrid presented another plea to end the licenses. Allegedly, the viceroy had allowed the export of 70,000 quarteres (approximately 4,800,000 liters) of wheat, leaving the principality depleted and the poor suffering despite that

2. *DACB*, 5:493.
3. ACA CA llig. 261 no. 34: *consulta*, December 1586: "Los cabos por q[ue] han supp[lica]do las personas que embió la Ciudad de Barc[elon]a después de salidos de Monçón."

year's good crop. The Council of Aragon agreed that the viceroy had given out too many licenses and called for greater restraint. But neither the council nor Philip II asked the viceroy to end them altogether.[4]

The king had reasons to maintain the licenses. Their sale provided a welcome source of revenue to the insufficient viceregal coffers. But how much money was earned from the sale of these licenses is unclear. In 1591, the viceroy of Catalonia charged two Genoese merchants 230 lliures for a license to export wheat.[5] If the same rate applied to the licenses Manrique de Lara supposedly issued to export 70,000 quarteres of wheat in 1587, he could have earned over 8,000 lliures—equivalent to 20 percent of the annual royal revenues in Catalonia.[6] Viceroys were not the only ones profiting from these licenses. Manrique de Lara pointed out that other cities and towns demanded them, and "some prelates and ecclesiastics and many knights" would suffer if he ended all export licenses.[7]

After months of unsuccessful pleas and rising prices, the Consell de Cent decided to act on its own. On 8 January 1588, it considered a proposal to have second conseller Frederic Roig Soler and third conseller Francesc Gamis requisition up to 20,000 quarteres of wheat from ships intending to export the grain. The two consellers would search the principality's coast and take the wheat if necessary by force for a "fair and real price."[8] Allegedly, a fourteenth-century privilege known as *Vi vel gratis* allowed Barcelona to requisition basic goods in times of scarcity.[9] Yet not everyone was entirely convinced of the legality of such a step. As a compromise, the Consell de Cent voted to send Roig Soler first and see what happened.[10]

Soon, the second conseller reported good news back to Barcelona. On 10 January, he captured "much wheat" about to be shipped out by some "Niceans [from Nice] and Frenchmen." The results appeared so promis-

---

4. ACA CA llig. 262 no. 3: *consulta,* 31 October 1587: "Sobre los cabos por q[ue] supp[li]can los síndicos primeros que están aquí por la ciudad de Barch[inon]a." Barcelona's representatives were Bartolomé Bofill and Joan Sala.

5. AHCB C-XX *(Processos),* 12b (1589–99), no. 68. The license went for 5 rals per cafís of grain.

6. According to John H. Elliott, royal revenues for 1634 approached 40,000 lliures; *The Revolt of the Catalans: A Study in the Decline of Spain, 1598–1640* (Cambridge, 1963), 96.

7. *DACB,* 5:506: 7 December 1587.

8. AHCB CC II-97 (Delibs., 1588–89), fols. 31v, 33r: 16 January 1588.

9. Jaime Carrera Pujal, *Historia política y económica de Cataluña: Siglos XVI al XVIII,* 3 vols. (Barcelona, 1946–47), 1:148. The privilege was granted by King Peter IV (1336–87). The Consell de Cent consulted the diputats on its application; AHCB II-97 (Delibs., 1588–89), fol. 23v: 12 January 1588.

10. AHCB CC II-97 (Delibs., 1588–89): 8 January 1588. The dissenting voice was Joan Sauri, who sat on the Committee of Eight on Wheat.

ing that the Consell de Cent ordered third conseller Gamis's immediate departure. Two days later, Roig Soler discovered in the coastal town of Mataró a ship with 670 quarteres (46,900 liters) of wheat bound for Genoa. The second conseller sent the grain to Barcelona instead. When the cargo arrived later that day, three consellers and other city officials went to the port to watch the unloading of the grain. On 18 January, Roig Soler returned to Barcelona while Gamis continued the search. Two days later, Gamis sent to the Catalan capital 3,000 quarteres of wheat belonging to unnamed people with "friends in court." Shortly after, another 500 quarteres belonging to Catalan noble Don Francesc d'Agullana arrived in Barcelona.[11]

On the evening of 28 January, after just over two weeks of requisitioning wheat, Barcelona welcomed back third conseller Gamis with a triumphant entrance. Knights on horseback escorted Gamis to his house. Torches and bonfires lighted the dark streets, where the people of the city offered such a "loud welcome and a thousand blessings that it seemed Palm Sunday."[12]

Requisitions were intended to lower prices, but they quickly raised tensions between the Consell de Cent and the viceroy. Manrique de Lara was "greatly offended" by Roig Soler and Gamis's actions and threatened to prosecute those responsible for the requisitions unless they stopped.[13] However, the Consell de Cent hailed the requisitions as a success: Roig Soler and Gamis had taken more than 12,000 quarteres (800,000 liters) of wheat. Prices had fallen by 5 and 6 sous per quartera. Yet the victory against high prices had been short-lived. The Consell de Cent affirmed that after the return of the consellers to Barcelona, hoarding had resumed. "Wicked and bedeviled men who are not happy without drinking the blood of the poor" had waited for the consellers' return to export "twice as much and more" in "an infinite number of vessels." As a result, prices were again on the rise.[14]

The streets of Barcelona had become the main arena for the battle of wills between the consellers and the viceroy. City authorities clearly wanted to publicize their actions, no doubt to demonstrate the support they enjoyed. They treated each arrival of requisitioned wheat as a major victory

11. *DACB*, 6:3–4, 7, 11. Agullana's wheat was old, but he offered to sell Barcelona 500 *quarteres* of good wheat.

12. *DACB*, 6:13.

13. *DACB*, 6:4–5. See a similar account of the viceroy's actions in BNM MS 2338: anonymous diary, 1577–1628.

14. AHCB CC II-97 (Delibs., 1587–88), fols. 52v–53r: 11 February 1588.

against speculators and hoarders. In that war for fair wheat prices, the second and third consellers had become heroes. Third conseller Gamis's grand entrance on 28 January confirmed him as defender of Barcelona's privileges and savior of the poor. On 9 April, as he presided over the destruction of the place where the recently abolished tax on fresh fish had been collected, overjoyed women fishmongers "held his *gramalla* [the consellers' official gown] and kissed it, saying great benedictions."[15] The widespread support for the consellers and their wheat requisitioning campaign is not surprising. Master artisans had supported the papal motu proprio against hoarders to root out high prices and end the scarcity of bread and other basic goods. By pursuing the new policy of requisitions, the Consell de Cent was at last taking decisive action, not just to make bread cheaper, but to go after those who profited from exploiting the poor.

The Consell de Cent's broad popular support had allowed it to take a defiant stance before the viceroy, but reaching a settlement with him was now harder, if not impossible. Out in the streets, any concessions made to the viceroy could be interpreted as a surrender. This is precisely what happened in February 1588. The Consell de Cent, which on 11 February voted to send second conseller Roig Soler to see Philip II to denounce the viceroy's abuses, on 19 February decided to delay his departure. The delay responded to the hope that the Audiència's chancellor and regent might work out a viable settlement between city and viceroy. However, news that Roig Soler's visit to the king had been put on hold was not well received in the streets of Barcelona. Allegedly, unnamed individuals were "going about talking publicly in squares and on street corners inciting the people."[16] Two days later, negotiations with the viceroy broke off, and the Consell de Cent ordered Roig Soler's immediate departure to Madrid. When he finally left nine days later, "the streets were full of people . . . exceeding the last entrance of his majesty in Barcelona; and all of the people expressed the greatest joy and happiness."[17] The Consell de Cent resumed the requisitioning of grain shortly afterward.

It seemed inevitable that the viceroy would try to punish city officials for their defiance. Back in January, the viceroy had threatened to take action against "the consellers and all those who advise and help them."[18] He had not acted on these threats; city officials had only taken advantage of his pa-

---

15. *DACB*, 6:44.

16. *DACB*, 6:26: 19 February 1588.

17. *DACB*, 6:30. Three days later, the Consell de Cent recalled its emissaries in Madrid—including Roig Soler—and replaced them with conseller *en cap* Galceran de Navel.

18. *DACB*, 6:4–5: 17 January 1588.

tience. On 25 April, there were rumors that the viceroy had arrested master barber-surgeon Gaspar Massaguer. As the man the Consell de Cent had chosen in 1585 to seek Philip II's support for the motu proprio against hoarders, Massaguer was a prominent figure in the city. Moreover, while his arrest was purportedly for a matter unrelated to requisitions, he sat on the "Committee of Eight on Wheat" *(vuitena de forment),* which had proposed the requisitions to the Consell de Cent.[19] The rumor of Massaguer's arrest turned out to be false. Apparently he had decided not to await the viceroy's men and taken refuge in the monastery of Sant Francesc.[20] Yet Massaguer's escape may have been unnecessary, because the viceroy was in no position to confront the city. Just as his frustration with the Consell de Cent's defiant attitude reached a climax, the viceroy had to turn his attention to even more pressing problems involving a delicate dispute between the Audiència appeals court and the Catalan Diputació.

For the time being, Manrique de Lara had to accept defeat in the battle over wheat. Popular support had emboldened the consellers to pursue their requisitions despite the viceroy's objections. But popular support had also pressured city officials, who favored alleviating the needs of city residents over obeying the king's alter ego. With wheat prices temporarily down and a showdown with city officials now unlikely, Barcelona could heave a collective sigh of relief. Nonetheless, the sense of an impending confrontation remained.

"A Storm Taking Shape"

While the consellers and Manrique de Lara disputed over wheat during the fall of 1587, the Audiència and the Diputació were immersed in a conflict that would raise major questions about each institution's authority to interpret Catalan law. At the heart of this conflict was the prominent Catalan noble Don Joan de Queralt. In September 1587, the Diputació ordered his arrest for a series of alleged offenses committed during his term as noble diputat between 1584 and 1587. At first he avoided arrest by appealing to the Audiència. But on 13 May 1588, the diputats decided that it was time to have Queralt imprisoned in the palace of the Diputació.[21] He refused to comply with the order, and as a result a large crowd began to gather in the

19. The reason given for Massaguer's arrest was his involvement in a committee that had supported taking harsh measures against the syndics who represented Barcelona in the 1585 Corts; AHCB CC II-97 (Delibs., 1588–89), fol. 96: 25 April 1588.

20. AHCB CC II-97 (Delibs., 1588–89), fol. 110v: 20 May 1588.

21. ACA G Delibs., vol. 150 (1587–88), fol. 194; *DACB,* 6:50.

Plaça de Sant Jaume. Ferran Fivaller, a canon from Tarragona who held the office of keeper of accounts *(oïdor)* in the Diputació, led a group of ecclesiastics who convinced Queralt to surrender.[22] Describing the incident in his diary, Don Frederic Despalau wrote that "the people were so stirred up" about Queralt that had he resisted the arrest, "it is certain they would have killed him because they hated him."[23] Outraged, the viceroy demanded Queralt's immediate transfer to a royal prison, alleging that the nobleman had a suit pending in the Audiència.

The viceroy's interest in Joan de Queralt's case stemmed in part from the fact that the Catalan noble had assisted the royal cause during the 1585 Corts. Royal officials believed that this action had made his enemies in the Diputació launch an investigation against him.[24] But more importantly, the judges of the Audiència saw the Diputació's actions as a direct challenge to the royal appeal court's claim to be the tribunal of last recourse in Catalonia.[25] Put simply, if Queralt could not appeal to the royal tribunal, this would imply that the Diputació had sole authority to judge its own affairs. This was an opinion shared by key figures within the Diputació, who believed that the body was indeed the ultimate interpreter of law in Catalonia. Accordingly, the Diputació took a number of actions that it considered perfectly legal, but which the judges of the Audiència repeatedly denounced as illegal. Royal and Catalan authorities, therefore, saw in the fate of the former diputat enormous implications for Catalonia's political regime.

Thus by the spring of 1588, just as the viceroy and the consellers were moving toward what seemed an inevitable clash, the conflict over Joan de Queralt was also going in the wrong direction. Reports reaching Madrid at the end of May anxiously described a "storm taking shape" in Barcelona.[26] If a storm were to break out, it would happen in the streets of the city.

In early June, those predictions came true. On the evening of 2 June, the viceroy sent the *veguer,* Don Joan de Comalonga, a royal officer with ju-

22. *Dietaris de la Generalitat de Catalunya,* vol. 3 (1578–1611), ed. Josep Maria Sans i Travé (Barcelona, 1996), 3:217.

23. *Diari,* in *Cavallers i ciutadans a la Catalunya del cinc-cents,* ed. Antoni Simon i Tarrés (Barcelona, 1991), 101.

24. Conde de Chinchón to King, 22 July 1587, transcribed in Carlos Riba, *El Consejo Supremo de Aragón en el reinado de Felipe II* (Valencia, 1914), 131–32.

25. For an excellent discussion of the constitutional issues at stake, see Miquel Pérez Latre, " 'Llevar la corona del cap a sa Magestat': Juntes de Braços i Divuitenes a la Diputació del General de Catalunya (1587–1593)" (licentiate thesis, Universitat de Barcelona, 1994).

26. ACA CA llig. 235 no. 17: *consulta,* 20 May 1588: "Con la carta de don Manriq[ue] de Lara [que falta] sobre el recurso q[ue] interpusieron don Joan de Queralt y Mr. Calvo."

dicial and policing duties, along with his constable *(algutzir)* and three more officers to take Queralt from the Diputació's prison. After several hours, the viceroy's men returned to tell Manrique de Lara that the diputats refused to surrender the Catalan noble. Then at half past one on the morning of 3 June, the viceroy sent his men back to the palace of the Diputació with orders not to leave until they had custody of Queralt. To everyone's surprise, as the royal officers made their way to the Diputació's building, the Consell de Cent's bell started to sound. The consellers, who had gathered in city hall to await news of the events in the Diputació, were "greatly astonished" when they heard the bell. Earlier that day, they had refused a plea from a group of knights to convene the Consell de Cent in order "to avoid gatherings and the commotion of the people." Upset at what seemed a deliberate challenge to their authority, the consellers demanded an explanation from the clock master (a blacksmith) in charge of the bell. He reported that after hearing the bell, he ran to the bell tower and found there a chaplain pulling the bell's rope "because he thought there was bad weather."[27] The clock master removed the bell's rope.

Surprised by the bell, "the people" *(la gent)* had begun to stream into the streets near city hall and around the palace of the Diputació, where royal officers continued to demand Joan de Queralt's surrender. At two in the morning, unidentified "young men" *(mossos)* made "cries" and provoked "confrontations" in the area near the Diputació's building.[28] Second conseller Roig Soler, who had played a prominent part in the wheat requisitioning campaign, went around the city with torches and managed to disperse the crowd. Finally, at four in the morning, the viceroy ordered his men to leave the palace without Queralt, who remained in the custody of the Diputació.[29]

Once more, high politics had spilled out into the streets of Barcelona, and as a result the viceroy had failed to make the Diputació comply with his orders. However, unlike the consellers' carefully orchestrated public ceremonies to build support for its wheat requisitioning policy, the mysterious sounding of the Consell de Cent's bell in the middle of the night had almost led to a chaotic and potentially dangerous situation.

In Barcelona, as elsewhere in Europe, bells served as alarms, whether in the case of a storm—the reason alleged by the chaplain who sounded the Consell de Cent's bell—or of an impending attack on the city.[30] But given

27. *DACB*, 6:58.
28. *DACB*, 6:59.
29. Despalau, *Diari*, 101.
30. On the connection between bells and alarm in a community, see Janine Estèbe's classic work, *Tocsin pour un massacre: La saison des Saint-Barthélemy* (Paris, 1968).

the tensions among viceroy, Consell de Cent, and Diputació, Barcelona's inhabitants could not have missed the connection between the Consell de Cent's bell and the political conflicts taking place. Neither city nor Catalan authorities attempted to investigate who had been responsible for that action. The "chaplain" found in the bell tower by the city's clock master was not identified. The greatest suspicions fell on the supporters of the Diputació who were not happy with the consellers' refusal to sound the bell the night of June 2. Regardless of the identity of the authors of that action, it seems more than likely that it was intended as a show of force against the viceroy, who realized that he could not possibly take on the Diputació with only a few officials and guards.

The viceroy was indignant about the events of June 2–3 and blamed the Consell de Cent and the Diputació for disobedience. But his own belligerent attitude had contributed little to a peaceful resolution of their differences and had done much to create a state of maximum alert. That state of alert in Barcelona continued for weeks. On 17 June, an escort of guards sent by the viceroy to welcome the captain general of the galleys of Spain, Jorge de Padilla, faced loud protests from a crowd in the port that refused to let the captain enter the city. The rioters allegedly came from the Marina, Barcelona's waterfront neighborhood with a high presence of artisans and poor.[31] According to Don Frederic Despalau, the protestors started "a great riot with cries of 'Moors! Alarm!' [*via fora moros*] and 'Treason!'"[32] Cristóbal Pérez de Herrera, Philip II's physician and future author of treatises advocating the reform of charitable institutions in Spain, described the rioters as wool clothiers, weavers, veil makers, mercers, and other Catalan artisans (*oficiales*). The physician believed that they attacked the viceroy's men out of "hatred" toward Manrique de Lara for his opposition to the requisition of wheat. Fearing a disaster, Pérez de Herrera carried in his arms Diego Pérez de Valdivia, an elderly priest at the nearby church of Santa Maria del Mar and the author of various religious treatises. According to the physician, the preacher convinced the crowd to return to order.[33] Second conseller Roig

---

31. On the Marina neighborhood, see James S. Amelang, *Honored Citizens of Barcelona: Patrician Culture and Class Relations, 1490–1714* (Princeton, 1986), 7.

32. Despalau, *Diari*, 102. Padilla was referred to by the title of *adelantado* (once a royal military office) of Castile.

33. Archivo General de Indias (Seville), Indiferentes: *memorial* by Pérez de Herrera, 19 August 1609; Cristóbal Pérez de Herrera, *Amparo de Pobres*, ed. Michel Cavillac (Madrid, 1975), xxix–xxx. I am grateful to Anne J. Cruz for this reference. On Pérez de Herrera's career and works, see Linda Martz, *Poverty and Welfare in Habsburg Spain* (Cambridge, 1983), 88.

Soler arrived at the scene and convinced the protestors to allow the captain in without the viceregal escort.

On 23 June, the eve the feast of St. John the Baptist, artisans from Barcelona's guard led another riot in the Marina neighborhood. This clash occurred after rumors spread that the viceroy had arrested Bernat de Pinós, captain of the wool clothiers' company, who was on watch duty. At the news of his arrest, six hundred men from the guard mutinied and went with their harquebuses to the viceroy's palace to demand their captain's liberation. Only after a number of knights reassured the armed crowd that their captain had not been arrested did the protestors agree to retreat peacefully.[34]

The viceroy could not fail to see in these two incidents in the Marina the extent of the animosity felt toward him in the city and the weakness of his position. Nonetheless, he remained undeterred in his goal to take Don Joan de Queralt from the Diputació and concluded that his only remaining option was to somehow force the consellers to assist him. And so, on 3 July, Manrique de Lara asked the consellers for the assistance of the city guard to retrieve Joan de Queralt from the Diputació's palace. This put the consellers in a bind. They had avoided a direct involvement in the conflict between the Diputació and the viceroy, but at the same time they did not want to openly disobey the viceroy. Fortunately for the consellers, they found a way to delay a response to the viceroy. On the next day, news arrived from Tortosa, a city on Catalonia's southern coast, about an incident involving conseller en cap Galceran de Navel. Tortosa's officers refused to let the conseller, on his way back from an embassy in Madrid, enter the city wearing his official gown or carrying Barcelona's insignia. The reasons for Tortosa's action are not entirely clear. Resentment at the Catalan capital's presumption of superiority in its dealings with other towns in the principality may have played a part. In any event, the Consell de Cent had found an excuse not to act on the viceroy's request for the guard's assistance. On 5 July, it voted to send the guard with four thousand men to Tortosa.[35]

The mobilization of the guard allowed the Consell de Cent to flaunt its might. Under its command were four thousand men, the largest force in the principality. In addition, according to the diary of Frederic Despalau,

---

34. The rumors started after an altercation between Don Galceran d'Armengol, who commanded the guard for the consellers, and a glassmaker (*vidrier*). For unknown reasons, the glassmaker threatened d'Armengol with a knife, which apparently set off the riot. The mutinied men threatened d'Armengol with their harquebuses near the viceroy's palace; see Despalau, *Diari*, 103, and AHCB CC II-97 (Delibs., 1588–89), fol. 122r.

35. *DACB*, 6:70.

"many magnates, nobles, and knights in the city" pledged to send troops. The Llotja (the merchants' guild) and the craft confraternities alone offered at least three thousand men.[36] When Barcelona's force was ready to leave the city on 9 July, it was more than six thousand strong.[37]

Unable to use Barcelona's guard, on 2 August the viceroy ordered Joan de Queralt's capture for a third time. This time, the Audiència's regent, Miquel Cordelles, and the governor, Enric de Cardona, went to the palace of the Diputació accompanied by guards. When they arrived, they found the doors of the building closed, allegedly "to prevent the entrance of a multitude of people in the street who wanted to come in."[38] Once inside, the regent and the governor demanded Queralt's surrender. When this was refused, the viceroy's guard tried unsuccessfully to break into the room where Queralt was. After the strong urging of several clergymen present, Cordelles and Cardona agreed to leave without Queralt.

Frustrated and angry, Manrique de Lara decided to try for the fourth time to get Don Joan de Queralt, this time by going in person. But the Consell de Cent dispatched a group of theologians to convince the viceroy that doing so might lead to a disastrous confrontation. The action posed a "great danger," the clergymen warned, because "Don Joan would not be surrendered except by death or by force."[39] Reluctantly, the viceroy agreed to abandon his plan.

The viceroy had lost in his struggle against the Diputació to a large extent because of public manifestations in the streets. The Diputació could not mobilize the city the way the consellers had done earlier in the year in favor of wheat requisitioning, but it was clear the viceroy enjoyed very little support and inspired a great deal of rancor. Consequently, Catalan authorities felt they could maintain their intransigence toward the viceroy, who had to tread carefully to avoid a commotion in which he would be the greatest loser. By August 1588, the Diputació could even take the offensive against the viceregal administration. On 8 August, it ordered an inventory of the property in the homes of Audiència judges Jaume Mir and Francesc Sans, who had been heavily fined for their involvement in

---

36. Despalau, *Diari*, 108.

37. The guard, however, never left Barcelona, after Tortosa's authorities allowed Barcelona's conseller *en cap* to enter the city with his official gown and insignia; *Llibre de les solemnitats de Barcelona*, ed. Agustí Duran i Sanpere and Josep Sanabre (Barcelona, 1947), 2:120.

38. Cited by Miquel Pérez Latre, "Les torbacions de Catalunya (1585–1593): De les Corts a la suspensió del nou redreç de la Diputació del General," *Afers* 23–24 (1996): 72.

39. Cited by Pérez Latre, "'Llevar la corona,'" 118 n. 6.

Joan de Queralt's case. The Diputació's men entered judge Mir's house without any resistance. However, the viceroy had dispatched guards to prevent the same action in judge Sans's home. Yet the presence of the viceroy's guards had alerted the entire city, and a large crowd surrounded the house. When the Diputació's officers arrived, they could barely move down the street.[40] The viceregal guards hesitated at first, but in light of the situation, they allowed the inventory of the judge's house without further incident.

Unwilling to admit defeat, the viceroy considered undermining public support for the Diputació with two proposals intended to both threaten and appeal to Barcelona's artisans and the poor. The first one called for the transfer of the Audiència to another city in Catalonia. Although the transfer of the royal tribunal would affect everyone in the city, royal authorities recognized that "the poor" of Barcelona would suffer the most because of the great expense and difficulty of seeking appeals.[41] Master artisans would be especially affected, because they repeatedly appealed to the royal judges on a wide range of cases involving their trades. However, Audiència judges considered the viceroy's plan extremely risky and pointed out that they, not Catalan authorities, would be the more likely targets of the wrath of the people of Barcelona. Given the lack of support for his first proposal, the viceroy recommended a second one: that the king grant master artisans' demand for a sixth conseller in exchange for the Consell de Cent's support for the viceroy's efforts to arrest Queralt. However, Philip II rejected the proposal outright without giving any explanation.[42]

It was now clear that the king and his ministers in Madrid had decided that the viceroy's tactics had failed and that it was time to put an end to the whole affair of Don Joan de Queralt. Back in July, the Council of Aragon had wondered whether the viceroy's interest in Queralt's case had more to do with certain Audiència judges' personal grudges than with justice. The council recommended the king to distance himself from the viceroy's actions. Royal justice had been partly compromised by Manrique de Lara's failure, and the best way out of that mire was to seek a negotiated solution.[43]

40. Despalau, *Diari*, 105.

41. ACA CA llig. 266 no. 22: "Pareçer del R[egen]te Quintana," 1588 [after 22 August?]. Miquel Joan Quintana was the Catalan regent of the Council of Aragon.

42. ACA CA llig. 264 no. 128: vice chancellor Frigola and Don Jerónimo Corella to King, 22 August 1588.

43. *Consulta*, 26 July 1588; transcribed in Riba, *Consejo Supremo de Aragón*, 149–50.

Reluctantly, in September 1588, Manrique de Lara had to take part in negotiations between Diputació and royal authorities to find a peaceful resolution to their differences. In November, Joan de Queralt agreed to renounce his appeal to the Audiència.[44] On 7 February 1589, the viceroy and the Diputació agreed to let all of the people go who had been arrested during the course of their dispute. The truce, however, did not address the fundamental issues that had initiated the conflicts between viceroy and Diputació, and these issues would resurface again within a few years. But for now, the open confrontations in Barcelona had come to a peaceful end.

Loyalty and the Defense of Barcelona

The actions by the people of Barcelona during the events of 1587 and 1588 grew out of the people's conviction that the city was under siege. City and Catalan authorities had encouraged that impression. The Consell de Cent had portrayed its policy of grain requisition as a defensive move against the viceroy's abuse of the city's privileges. The Diputació also presented its conflict with the viceroy as a defense of the laws of the land from attacks by the viceroy and royal judges. The sounding of the Consell de Cent's bell—apparently by supporters of the Diputació—as well as the constant rumors and the rhetoric used by city and Catalan officers alike helped to reinforce an atmosphere of defensiveness. For his part, Manrique de Lara's belligerent responses appeared to confirm that a struggle was indeed under way in Barcelona. His threats and the movement of viceregal guards kept the city on watch. The enthusiasm behind Barcelona's mobilization against Tortosa, trumpeted by the consellers as the rightful defense of the city's honor and privileges, seemed the spontaneous reaction of a people who felt they were under siege.

Although in the struggle to defend their city, its privileges, and its institutions, royal authorities seemed the prime enemy, the people of Barcelona never once felt their actions should call into question their loyalty to the king. On the contrary, the Barcelonese, and all Catalans, prided themselves on being "most faithful" (*fidelíssims*) to the monarch and took offense when anyone questioned that loyalty. In an unusually harsh statement read to Manrique de Lara on 4 August 1588, the Consell de Cent made clear just how strongly Catalans resented any hint of infidelity to their king. "The city cannot tolerate anymore . . . that your excellency label, belittle, and reverse the

44. Pérez Latre, "'Llevar la corona,'" 135.

memory of fidelity, which is innate and well-known to all our kings and lords."
Therefore, the statement continued, "we beseech your excellency to cease referring to [Catalans] as either faithful or rebellious." If the city had "suffered
and ignored" the viceroy's remarks, it had been out of respect for his office
and the king's trust in it. However, "Your excellency shall know that if any other
person had spoken thus, on the very spot they had uttered those words they
would have lost their lives and everything they have."[45] According to the
bishop of Barcelona, such sentiments were widespread in the city.[46]

Despite their repeated avowals of loyalty to the king, the events of June
and July 1588 demonstrated that in order to defend their city, the people
of Barcelona were most likely to side with the Consell de Cent. There were
many good reasons for this. The Consell de Cent and its consellers officially
stood for the whole of the city, and a challenge to them meant a challenge
to Barcelona. The fact that there were artisan jurats in the Consell de Cent
and that an artisan was fifth conseller made the ties between the people
and the city's assembly more explicit. The Consell de Cent also controlled
a large number of offices artisans had access to, including tax collector,
standard-bearer, and master of the clock.[47] It also organized public festivities and kept the city supplied with basic goods. All of this helped to foster a sense of dependency on and allegiance to the Consell de Cent.

Artisans in the guard also developed a clear sense of duty to the consellers. When called to defend the city, masters would report to the Consell de Cent to take weapons and receive orders.[48] Thus the first impulse
of many in the city after the sounding of the Consell de Cent's bell on the
night of 2–3 June 1588 was to go to city hall to receive instructions. The
consellers kept the building lighted and its doors open until four in the
morning to reassure the people in the streets that it was just a false alarm.

Given the obedience and loyalty to the consellers and the Consell de
Cent fostered by the guard, it is not surprising that the viceroy had tried to
wrest it away from the city's control. During the 1550s and 1560s, several
viceroys tried to integrate the guard into the military chain of command
that the viceroy headed as "captain general" of Catalonia.[49] But the Con-

45. *DACB*, 6:88.

46. Pérez Latre, "'Llevar la corona,'" 122.

47. An incomplete list of municipal offices for which artisans were eligible is in Appendix 2, section E.

48. BC F. Bon. 73: *Ordres que deu donar y bandos que ha de publicar lo Sr. Conceller en Cap a
cas de rebato o invasión de enemich* [Orders and announcements by the conseller *en cap* in case
of alarm or enemy invasion] (n.p., n.d. [1640?]).

49. See the proposed reform of the guard in AHCB C III-4 (Guerra i política, 1500–99),
doc. 56: "La forma se ha de tenir en lo [de la guerra] de Barcelona" (n.d.). On the viceroy's
duties as captain general, see Víctor Ferro, *El dret públic català: Les institucions a Catalunya
fins al Decret de Nova Planta* (Vic, 1987), 66–71.

sell de Cent insisted that its guard was a civilian force and should therefore remain under the command of the conseller en cap. Ultimately, the consellers won out and maintained direct control over the guard.[50]

The bonds between the artisans in the guard and city authorities were strong, but not perfect. The mutiny in the Marina neighborhood by the wool clothiers' company on the eve of the feast of St. John 1588 had made clear that the consellers' control of the guard could occasionally suffer serious breaks. In addition, street incidents during June and July 1588 demonstrated that in an emergency, the inhabitants of Barcelona were ready to act without direct orders from the Consell de Cent. Certainly, such independent actions were rare; however, they sometimes happened precisely when tensions between viceroy, Consell de Cent, and Diputació reached a critical point. As will be seen later, these spontaneous popular actions at times of heightened political tensions could have grave consequences.

The Consell de Cent wanted to take that popular support for granted, but it could not. The notorious fickleness of the people seemed to make that impossible.[51] In Barcelona as elsewhere, the people might riot for a great variety of reasons: fear of lack of food, an attack against the city or its officials, or as happened on the eve of the feast of St. John, an attack against a company officer.[52]

The potential for popular rioting against Barcelona's authorities underscores the existence of multiple sources of allegiances that might compete with the Consell de Cent. Especially important were loyalties to craft confraternities and to city neighborhoods.[53] The rioters who blocked viceregal guards from entering the city on 17 June were defending both the city and their Marina neighborhood at once. Father Diego Pérez's intervention in that riot revealed the respect felt toward a priest from the nearby church of Santa Maria del Mar. The mutiny of the wool clothiers' company on the eve of the feast of St. John, allegedly caused by rumors that their captain had been arrested, was partly motivated by the desire to defend the confraternity's and the company's honor. There were other examples of

50. For a description of Barcelona's guard, see Agustí Duran i Sanpere, "La defensa de la ciutat," in *Barcelona i la seva història*, 3 vols. (Barcelona, 1972–75), 2:109–23.

51. Christopher Hill, "The Many-Headed Monster in Late Tudor and Early Stuart Political Thinking," in *From the Renaissance to the Counter-Reformation: Essays in Honour of Garrett Mattingly*, ed. Charles Howard Carter (London, 1966), 296.

52. On the subject of riots in Barcelona, see Luis Corteguera, "El motín: ¿Una institución de la política popular en la Barcelona del XVI–XVII?" in *Tercer Congrés d'Història Moderna de Catalunya: Actes*, 2 vols. (Barcelona, 1993), 2:235–41.

53. James S. Amelang, "People of the Ribera: Popular Politics and Neighborhood Identity in Early Modern Barcelona," in *Culture and Identity in Early Modern Europe (1500–1800): Essays in Honor of Natalie Zemon Davis*, ed. Barbara Diefendorf and Carla Hesse (Ann Arbor, 1993), esp. 126–27.

mutinies in the city guard, allegedly in the name of the confraternity's and its company's honor.[54]

Given these multiple allegiances, city, Catalan, and royal authorities found it necessary to coax the support of the people during the summer of 1588. The sounding of the bell on the night of 2–3 June, for instance, appears to have been an attempt by backers of the Diputació to muster popular support despite the consellers' desire to keep the city neutral in that conflict. Likewise, when the viceroy asked the consellers on 3 July to lend him the guard, he wanted to force city authorities to take a stance and to coopt the guard in the viceroy's cause against the Diputació. The Consell de Cent had avoided the viceroy's request by sending the guard to Tortosa. A month later (3 August), when Manrique de Lara again asked for "four or five" companies and the guard's assistance to retrieve Queralt from the Diputació's palace, the Consell de Cent had rejected the viceroy's petition on legal grounds.[55] Manrique de Lara, furious, had taken his revenge by questioning the city's fidelity, which had only weakened his position further.

In the end, the people of Barcelona followed the lead of the Consell de Cent. The consellers' command of the guard and the numerous other ties that bound Barcelona's inhabitants to their city's officials seemed to make that outcome inevitable. One might even conclude that the scenes of chaos when the Consell de Cent's bell sounded on the night of 2 June and during the two riots that followed later that month had only been momentary scares. The allegiance of the people to the consellers seemed unquestionable. Nonetheless, the documentation makes it clear that the consellers could not have prevented angry rioters from taking matters in their own hands, disregarding all calls to order. That did not happen, but it could have. If popular violence had culminated in an attack on one of the viceroy's guards or an Audiència judge, the outcome of the events in 1588 may have been entirely different.

Plague

The truce reached between the Audiència and the Diputació in February 1589 was not likely to last long. The issues at stake were simply too important, and it would not take long for another incident to force all parties to face them again. Nevertheless, the truce would hold for nearly two years because the arrival of the plague submerged all other concerns.

54. AHCB C III-4 (Guerra i política), doc. 81: report on a riot between mercers (*julians*) and hatters over the order of precedence of their flags during a night watch in 1596.

55. Despalau, *Diari,* 105; *DACB,* 6:84–85.

During the spring of 1589, reports of the bubonic plague in France and northern Catalonia reached Barcelona. City officials took preventive measures, but there was a limit to how effectively quarantines and restrictions on trade could ward off disease. Officially, the plague of 1589 in Barcelona began in July.[56] But the truth was that city officials had been trying to keep the first few victims quiet. In towns near Barcelona, precautions were immediately taken as early as June to ward off people and goods that might be infected from coming to the capital. By July, it was impossible to hide the spread of the plague any longer. City authorities now set in motion the limited measures at their disposal to contain the disease and bring about a quick recovery.

The scale of the plague soon proved too much for the traditional measures. The Consell de Cent's official diary testifies to the magnitude of the plague, which not surprisingly seems to have hit the most humble neighborhoods the hardest. Nevertheless, as panic swept the city, all those who could afford to left. In July, the Diputació moved away to Vic while the plague continued in Barcelona. Others followed suit: "Nobility and wealth deserted the city, with no little harm to the people."[57] Manrique de Lara and the Audiència's judges also left not long after that.[58] Fleeing the city, however, did not assure escaping the scourge. Manrique de Lara himself became sick and died, before the end of the year, away from the city that had given him so much trouble.[59]

The number of deaths climbed all through July 1589 and reached its peak between August and September. By 7 January 1590, when the Consell de Cent declared the plague officially over, the death count had reached an astounding 11,723 victims—between a third and a fourth of the city population.[60] Anecdotal estimates give a higher amount—over 22,000 in one case, perhaps reflecting the perceived impact on the city more than the actual number of victims.[61]

Even after the plague was declared over, it took several more months before those residents who had fled Barcelona returned. While most royal officers were away from Barcelona, the Consell de Cent remained virtually

56. José Luis Betrán, *La peste en la Barcelona de los Austrias* (Lleida, 1996).

57. Regarding the Diputació, see Pérez Latre, "'Llevar la corona,'" 150; the quotation comes from the correspondence of the Discalced Carmelites, cited by Pérez Latre (151).

58. ACA CA llig. 266 no. 21: *consulta*, 23 June 1590.

59. ACA CA llig. 266 no. 21: *consulta*, 28 May 1590.

60. Robert S. Smith, "Barcelona 'Bills of Mortality' and Population, 1457–1590," *Journal of Political Economy* 44 (1936): 84–93.

61. According to the memoirs of N. Morató cited in Núria Sales, *Els segles de la decadència (segles XVI–XVIII)*, vol. 4 of *Història de Catalunya*, ed. Pierre Vilar (Barcelona, 1989), 254.

alone in maintaining order in the city for nearly a year. The Consell de Cent took advantage of the absence of royal officers to carry out important actions without bothering to seek royal approval.[62] For instance, it used a galley to carry out more requisitions of grain from ships passing by the Catalan coast. It also imposed a special tax on foreigners, approved the creation of a new city bank, proclaimed its own laws, rejected all titles of honored citizens granted by the king, and even embarked upon the construction of a pier—all without royal approval.

Upon his return to the city in June 1590, Don Enric de Cardona, the governor of Catalonia, was struck by the number of actions the Consell de Cent had taken in the last year. In a letter to the king, he lamented the fact that Barcelona had in effect usurped the royal jurisdiction and therefore had become a virtually independent city.[63] Yet the governor and the rest of the royal government in Catalonia—without a viceroy for a year and a half—could do little more than complain about the Consell de Cent's actions. As had happened in 1587 and 1588 during the Consell de Cent's campaign to requisition wheat, royal officials found that they could do little to stop Barcelona's authorities from acting at will. This was an impression that the consellers also wanted to convey to the rest of the city—namely, that they were willing to do all they could for the good of Barcelona. The Consell de Cent's official diary recorded the presence of its officers throughout the plague, in contrast to those of other institutions, who preferred to flee in order to save their lives. It was a sacrifice Barcelona's authorities must have hoped would be repaid in the future with the continued allegiance of its inhabitants.

Renewal of Crisis

Slowly, during the course of the second half of 1590, life in Barcelona returned, as much as possible, to normal. But that return to normalcy also meant a renewal of tensions between Catalan and royal officials over the very same issues that had generated the bitter conflicts in 1588. The truce of 1589 had not resolved the claims of the Diputació and the Audiència to have the last word in the interpretation of law in Catalonia. Before the end of 1590, that debate would again flare up and lead to another serious political crisis.

62. ACA CA llig. 266 no. 21: *consulta,* 23 June 1590.
63. ACA CA llig. 266 no. 21: *consulta,* 23 June 1590. Cardona stated that the situation was similar in other Catalan towns (which he did not identify).

In late November 1590, royal officers made a number of arrests, including that of two brothers of the new noble diputat Joan Granollachs for their alleged participation in acts of banditry.[64] The Diputació immediately created a committee of eighteen members to investigate the matter, which soon after declared the arrests of the Catalan nobles to be illegal. The committee retaliated by ordering the imprisonment of the royal constable Joan Baptista Sorita in the Diputació's prison for his part in those arrests.

Once more, as in the case of the Diputació's refusal to accept Don Joan de Queralt's appeal to the Audiència, royal authorities saw the Diputació's arrest of the royal constable as a claim to be above the royal tribunal, and in fact, above the king's will. Not surprisingly, in January 1591 the Council of Aragon in Madrid concluded it was necessary to assert the king's authority by punishing the Diputació for its actions. Thus Philip II ordered the arrest of the noble diputat and members of the committee investigating the matter. It was decided, however, to delay execution of the arrests until the arrival in Barcelona of the newly appointed viceroy of Catalonia, Pedro Luis de Borja, marquis of Navarrés, usually referred to by his title of master of the military order of Montesa.[65]

On 11 March, the Master of Montesa was sworn to his office in Barcelona. With the king's orders in hand, the new viceroy was ready to take action. The time for compromise was over, the viceroy insisted; the Diputació had to be punished to avert an even greater confrontation. But acting against the Diputació, Audiència judges warned, was not so easy, and previous attempts had backfired.[66] After two months of indecision, pressure from Madrid finally forced the viceroy to order the arrest of noble diputat Granollachs for the capture of the royal constable Sorita.[67]

On 24 May 1591, the viceroy dispatched several royal officers and eight guards to capture diputat Granollachs. It was noon when the noble diputat made his way across the Carrer de Montcada, a street known for the beautiful residences of Barcelona nobles and merchants. There are conflicting versions of what happened next. According to the Diputació, the viceroy's men assaulted Granollachs while crying "Surrender to the

64. For an excellent and detailed account of the events that followed in 1591–92, see Pérez Latre, "'Llevar la corona,'" chaps. 6–9.

65. Based in the territories of the Crown of Aragon, the Order of Montesa was one of several military orders created during the Reconquista to pursue the Christian crusade against the Arabs in the Iberian Peninsula. In the course of the sixteenth century, the monarchy took control of its rents and of the mastership of the order.

66. ACA CA llig. 266 no. 22: "Pareçer del R[egen]te Quintana," 1588 [after 22 August?].

67. ACA CA llig. 266 no. 26: *consulta*, 16 July 1591.

King," grabbed him, and took away his dagger. The noble diputat insisted that he was on his way to investigate a fraud and commanded the royal officers to accompany him. After half an hour of discussion, the noise had attracted the attention of passersby. Sensing that the situation could easily get out of hand, royal officers let Granollachs go. The royal government, however, insisted that he was released only after a number of men accompanying him brandished their swords and daggers, crying various slogans such as "*Visca la terra!*" (Long live the land!) and "Long live the Generalitat [Diputació]!" and called the royal officers traitors to the land. Concerned that the struggle might incite the watchful crowd that had gathered around them, the royal officers felt it prudent to let the noble diputat go.[68] Granollachs and his companions then went to the palace of the Diputació, which was immediately closed, and armed guards were posted.[69]

The action had been a gross miscalculation on the viceroy's part, which could have had serious consequences if the incident had turned violent— one can only guess how serious. But parallels with a similar event occurring on the same day in the neighboring kingdom of Aragon provide some indication. On the very same day of Granollach's failed arrest in Barcelona, there was a violent protest in Zaragoza against the forced transfer of former royal secretary Antonio Pérez from an Aragonese prison to that of the Inquisition. Unlike Granollach's case, Pérez's directly involved Philip II. As the king's secretary, Pérez had learned about the king's decision in 1578 to murder Juan de Escobedo, secretary to the king's brother Don Juan.[70] Afraid that Pérez might make public the king's participation in the murder plot, Philip II ordered Pérez's arrest. In 1590, after several years' incarceration and aware that his execution was imminent, Pérez fled from his Castilian prison to Zaragoza, where he appealed to the *justicia* of Aragon. Charged with the defense of the laws and liberties of Aragon, the justicia enjoyed the authority to protect Pérez from royal authorities. For this reason, in 1591 Philip II decided to have Pérez tried by the Inquisition's tribunal in Zaragoza. Once the former secretary was in the custody of the Holy Office, his transfer back to Castile would prove much easier. On 24 May, the day after Pérez was transferred to the Inquisition's prison, demonstrators gathered before the house of the marquis of Almenara, the man Philip II wanted as viceroy of Aragon, to denounce the forced arrest.

68. ACA CA llig. 266 no. 26: *consulta,* 30 June 1591; and Pérez Latre, "'Llevar la corona,'" 192.

69. ACA CA llig. 264 no. 83: *consulta,* 6 December 1598.

70. On Escobedo's murder, see Henry Kamen, *Philip of Spain* (New Haven, 1997), 162–67.

The protest soon turned into a riot in which the marquis was fatally wounded.[71]

Despite their coincidence, the events in Barcelona and Zaragoza were unrelated. Nonetheless, royal authorities worried about the possibility that the Catalans might join the Aragonese in a rebellion against Philip II. Several incidents kept that fear alive.[72] On 28 May 1591, Genoese galleys in Barcelona's port, for no apparent reason, opened fire on the city. The attack almost cost the lives of the governor, Cardona, and a small party of royal officials who went to greet the Genoese.[73] The large crowds that had gathered on the wall to see the galleys saw the attack as an affront and sought revenge. For two days, crowds attacked the houses of the Genoese in the city. The quick intervention of the Consell de Cent, however, prevented bloodshed. The next day, 29 May, the Consell de Cent ordered the expulsion of all the Genoese from Barcelona to avoid further disorder.[74] The royal government objected to yet another arbitrary action by the Consell de Cent but did not stop the execution of the ordinance. As it turned out, the Consell de Cent's emergency measures proved effective in restoring order in the city after two days of riots.

The viceroy of Catalonia, who in May supported strong measures against the Diputació, in June advised reconciliation. All care must be taken, he warned, "so that the matter concerning Antonio Pérez is not taken up by the people of the principality [of Catalonia] or that they make demands like those made in the kingdom of Aragon."[75] Clearly, the best solution for Catalonia was to find a negotiated settlement to the differences between viceroy and Diputació. The Consell de Cent assumed the role of negotiator between viceroy and Diputació by proposing a temporary suspension

---

71. For the popular intervention in these riots, see Jesús Gascón Pérez, "Defensa de los fueros y fidelidad a la Monarquía en la rebelión aragonesa de 1591," in *Monarquía, imperio y pueblos en la España moderna*, ed. Pablo Fernández Albaladejo (Alicante, 1997), 459–75; and idem, "El 'vulgo ciego' en la rebelión aragonesa de 1591," *Revista de historia Jerónimo Zurita* 69/70 (1994): 89–103.

72. In June 1591, royal authorities in Catalonia arrested a Flemish servant of Antonio Pérez and whisked him away from the principality in a ship in Barcelona's port. Catalan authorities protested, unsuccessfully, that it was illegal to try anyone arrested in Catalonia outside the principality; ACA CA llig. 266 no. 22: *consulta*, 30 June 1591. A few months later, in November, other men suspected of involvement in the events in Aragon were arrested in Catalonia. The most important of them was Diego de Heredia, a close associate of Pérez, who had tried to reach his Catalan wife's native town of Lleida; ACA CA llig. 266 no. 22: *consulta*, 6 December 1591.

73. AHCB CC IV-22 (Ordinacions 1590–95), fols. 56v–57r; and AHCB CC II-100 (Delibs., 1591–92), fols. 83r–84v.

74. ACA CA llig. 266 no. 22: *consulta*, 30 June 1591.

75. ACA CA llig. 266 no. 22: *consulta*, 30 June 1591.

of the investigation of royal officers. But for a second time, when a negotiated settlement seemed near, the viceroy changed his mind. Accusing the
Diputació of turning its palace into a fort, viceroy Master of Montesa announced that a joint session of the Audiència's three chambers had decided to suspend the tribunal and reconvene it in Perpinyà on 20 August.[76]

The Council of Aragon welcomed the decision to transfer the court as a
means to pressure the Diputació into a speedier resolution of their differences. In the words of the Council of Aragon, "The Diputació worries
greatly that the people will become disorderly once they feel the harm
caused by the absence of the viceroy and the Audiència from that city."[77]
The transfer of the royal tribunal nevertheless posed difficulties for the
royal government, not the least of which was finding a suitable location.
Moving to Perpinyà, which the viceroy could argue had been chosen in
order to better watch the frontier with France, was soon found to be impractical. After dismissing other locations, on 21 August, the viceroy announced the Audiència would reconvene in Tortosa in early September.[78]
The viceroy reversed himself in October and chose Tarragona instead.[79]

While negotiations between viceroy and Diputació moved along, albeit
slowly, events in Zaragoza took a turn for the worse. On 24 September, the
announcement of a second attempt to transfer Antonio Pérez to the Inquisition's prison was preempted by another popular riot that set Philip II's
former secretary free. The king then ordered the army he had been put-
ting together since May to restore order by force. In Zaragoza, the justicia
of Aragon and his supporters declared they would offer military resistance
to the king's army if they entered the kingdom. A revolt in Aragon had been
launched.

There were rumors that the royal army might continue its way to
Barcelona. The Aragonese warned their Catalan neighbors that if the royal
army entered Aragon, "it will not heed border marks, but with the same
design it will enter that principality [Catalonia]."[80] Even the Master of Montesa discussed preparations in case the king chose to punish the Diputació
for its unwillingness to surrender Granollachs.[81] The Consell de Cent and

---

76. Pérez Latre, "'Llevar la corona,'" 214.

77. ACA CA llig. 266 no. 34: *consulta*, 10 August 1591.

78. Lleida was considered unhealthy during the winter. Pérez Latre, "'Llevar la corona,'"
227.

79. ACA CA llig. 266 no. 22: *consulta*, 30 September 1591.

80. Quoted in Xavier Gil Pujol, "Catalunya i Aragó, 1591–1592: Una solidaritat i dos
destins," in *Primer Congrés d'Història Moderna de Catalunya: Actes*, 2 vols. (Barcelona, 1984),
2:129.

the Catalan Diputació, however, issued a long succession of avowals of loyalty to their king.[82] In addition, the Consell de Cent put increased pressure on the Diputació to accept a compromise.[83]

Between late 1591 and early 1592, growing pressures to reach a compromise as soon as possible caused a split within the Diputació and the three braços. On the one hand, a recalcitrant faction led by Granollachs and his supporters among the nobility refused to compromise. On the other hand, another faction led by the president of the Diputació, Girona's bishop Jaume Cassador, concluded that the only resolution to the long-standing dispute lay in turning in Granollachs to royal authorities. On 21 April 1592, the Consell de Cent took the decisive step of agreeing to assist governor Cardona—the provisional head of the viceregal administration after the Master of Montesa's death earlier that month—in capturing Granollachs. Nevertheless, the capture of the noble diputat would not take place. Informed of his imminent arrest, Granollachs escaped from the palace of the Diputació, and with a small group of supporters he took flight from Barcelona. The crisis had come to a peaceful end.

The escape of the noble diputat broke the long impasse between the Diputació and the royal government. With Granollachs gone, advocates of a more conciliatory tone toward the royal government effectively moved the Diputació away from the more ambitious claims to authority it had defended in 1588 and 1591. Although the Catalan institution did not effectively give up its claims to be the final arbiter of its own affairs, at least for now it would not press the point too far. That debate lay in the future.

Revolt Averted

The different paths of Zaragoza and Barcelona underscore the way popular politics could have a major impact on high politics.[84] Although there were important differences in the nature of the conflicts between royal and territorial authorities in each case, the outcomes responded in large measure to differences in the actions of crowds in the capitals of the two king-

81. ACA CA llig. 266 no. 22: *consulta,* 30 September 1591. The viceroy proposed that Philip II order the barons of Catalonia to raise troops against the Diputació.

82. Gil Pujol, "Catalunya i Aragó," 128.

83. ACA CA llig. 266 no. 22: *consulta,* 30 September 1591; ACA CA llig. 265 no. 170: *consulta,* 20 October 1591.

84. For a stimulating comparison between the two cases, see Gil Pujol, "Catalunya i Aragó."

doms. The death of the marquis of Almenara in Zaragoza after 24 May 1591 at the hands of a crowd had no parallel in Barcelona, where no fatalities occurred. Given the magnitude of the riots in the Aragonese capital, Philip II felt compelled to use force to reassert royal authority in the kingdom.

There are several possible explanations why popular actions turned violent in one city and not in the other. First, in the case of Antonio Pérez, orders for his capture on 24 May were announced ahead of time and executed before the public in a central location in the city. In contrast, Granollach's botched arrest was unannounced, and as a result the crowd of witnesses that soon gathered did not seem aware of what was happening. Viceroy Manrique de Lara's attempted capture of Don Joan de Queralt on 2 June 1588 resembled the events in Zaragoza more closely. When the Consell de Cent's bell rang, a large crowd began to gather. However, the viceroy's men never took hold of Queralt. The consellers and the viceroy both expressed great concern at the possibility of that violence might break out in the streets of Barcelona. Even though the viceroy did not go out into the streets, had his guards suffered an attack or a fatality the crisis would have been seriously complicated. There were also important differences in the way Pérez and Granollachs escaped: the former was liberated during the second riots in Zaragoza on 24 September; the latter fled Barcelona with his supporters before the governor arrived to capture him. Once again, the Zaragoza crowd had openly defied the king's orders.

Despite these significant differences in the impact of crowd action, it is striking how close Barcelona came to following the violent path of Zaragoza. The basic context was in many ways the same: in Barcelona (in 1588 and 1591–92) and in Zaragoza, territorial authorities denounced royal actions for allegedly violating the laws, liberties, and privileges of the land. Similarly, in both capitals crises were precipitated by attempts by royal officers to capture prominent figures (Don Joan de Queralt, Joan Granollachs, and Antonio Pérez) under the custody of Catalan or Aragonese authorities. The coincidence of events on 24 May 1591 is all the more surprising. There is no evidence, however, that the royal government consciously planned the arrests of Pérez and Granollachs to take place on the same day.

These similarities highlight how the different fates of the two capitals to some extent depended on the behavior of crowds in their streets. Had any of the numerous violent incidents in Barcelona in 1588 and 1591–92 produced fatalities among royal officers—and it is hard to imagine that there were no deaths on either side—Catalans, despite their repeated claims of loyalty to the crown, might have been headed for an armed confrontation with their king. But even though Barcelona was fortunate enough to avoid Zaragoza's fate, winning over the support of the people remained crucial for the outcomes of the political crises between Consell de Cent, Diputació, and viceroys. In Barcelona, revolt had been averted, but the possibility that popular politics might seriously affect the relations between king and Catalans remained a serious threat for the future.

Ultimately, which allegiance would prove stronger among the people of Barcelona depended on the situation. Multiple, competing allegiances could coexist without any unsustainable contradictions. After all, loyalty to one's confraternity should mean loyalty to city authorities, to a Catalan identity, and to the Spanish monarch. In addition, one does not get the sense that people felt they had a choice in their allegiances. The king as well as the consellers certainly equated allegiance to obedience, and obedience was a matter not of choice but of duty. Nevertheless, it is clear that on occasion the consellers, the diputats, and the viceroy issued different orders, and people had to choose whom to obey. At critical moments in 1588 and 1591, the consellers seemed to command the allegiance of the people. However, that allegiance was not unchallengeable.

CHAPTER FIVE

The Future of Privilege

D uring Philip III's twenty-three-year reign (1598–1621), the Spanish monarchy suffered grave problems often referred to by historians as the "crisis of the seventeenth century."[1] The plagues of
1599–1601 as well as the expulsion of the Moriscos—Christians of Arab
descent—in 1609–11 caused major population losses in Castile and Valencia. Trade and industry slumped in many territories of the monarchy.
The number of poor increased in large cities. Despite Philip III's peaceful
policy abroad, royal finances did not seem capable of recovering from the
financial excesses of his father's many wars.

Catalonia had its share of troubles.[2] Between 1596 and 1598, Philip II's
last war against France had brought destruction to northern Catalonia. The

1. For a recent overview of the crisis of the seventeenth century in the Spanish monarchy, see Alberto Marcos Martín, *España en los siglos XVI, XVII y XVIII: Economía y sociedad*
(Barcelona, 2000), esp. chap. 8. Also helpful are the following works: John Lynch, *The Hispanic World in Crisis and Change, 1598–1700*, 2d ed. rev. (Oxford, 1992); Ciriaco Pérez Bustamante, "La España de Felipe III: La política interior y los problemas internacionales," in
vol. 24 of *Historia de España*, ed. Ramón Menéndez Pidal and José María Jover Zamora, 3d
ed. (Madrid, 1983); and José Manuel Pérez García, "Economía y sociedad," chap. 4 of *La
crisis del siglo XVII*, vol. 6 of *Historia de España*, ed. Antonio Domínguez Ortiz (Barcelona,
1998).

2. Pierre Vilar established the standard interpretation of the crisis of the seventeenth
century in Catalonia; see his *La Catalogne dans l'Espagne moderne*, 3 vols. (Paris, 1962), vol.
1, chap. 3, "Le XVIIe siècle: 1598–1714," 587–633. For recent overviews of the crisis of the
seventeenth century in Catalonia, see Núria Sales, *Els segles de la decadència (segles XVI–XVIII)*,
vol. 4 of *Història de Catalunya*, ed. Pierre Vilar (Barcelona, 1989), esp. chap. 3, and *Crisi in-*

Peace of Vervins, signed in 1598 shortly before the king's death, raised hopes that Philip III's reign might bring peace and prosperity. But by the first decade of the seventeenth century, Catalans reported falling exports, monetary difficulties, and a growing number of poor, as well as persistently worsening banditry in the countryside, which did not make economic recovery any easier. Royal finances in the principality, always insufficient, threatened to paralyze the viceregal administration.

Barcelona, the principality's major economic center, faced especially serious problems. Beginning in the first decade of the seventeenth century, the port's activity declined. The city's wool trades, once the engine of Catalonia's industrial might and employing hundreds of families in Barcelona, suffered hard times. The craft confraternities complained that many master artisans were impoverished and were losing their means of sustaining their families.

The fate of Barcelona's trades was of great importance to all of Catalonia. Were artisans to recover, the city's commerce might pick up and the principality regain its former prosperity. Yet if difficulties persisted, the artisans' craft confraternities might decline and disappear altogether. Such a scenario would mean more than simply an increase in the number of poor masters. Craft confraternities were a fundamental part of the city's social order, and if these institutions disappeared, so would craft ordinances, their charitable activities, and even worse, the authority of master artisans over their women, children, and journeymen. Hindsight shows that the possibility that Barcelona's crafts would fade away was remote. Nevertheless, numerous contemporaries expressed a sincere concern and recommended taking action to avoid such a fate.

The many problems associated with the crisis of the seventeenth century exacerbated what had always been the most basic challenge to Catalonia's political system, which John Elliott has called the struggle between "necessity" and "legality."[3] Occasionally, unusually difficult problems prompted some to argue that it was necessary to ignore certain laws and privileges in order to arrive at a prompt and effective solution. In response to such arguments, others maintained that acting against the law, even tem-

stitucional i canvi social: Segles XVI i XVII, ed. Eva Serra i Puig and Xavier Torres i Sans, vol. 4 of *Història, política, societat i cultura dels Països Catalans* (Barcelona, 1997). Albert García Espuche challenges some long-standing interpretations of the crisis of the seventeenth century in *Un siglo decisivo: Barcelona y Cataluña, 1550–1640* (Madrid, 1998).

3. John H. Elliott, *The Revolt of the Catalans: A Study in the Decline of Spain, 1598–1640* (Cambridge, 1963), 119.

porarily, might threaten the integrity of the legal edifice on which the entire political and social order rested. The growing list of problems in the
early seventeenth century forced everyone in Catalonia—including
Barcelona's artisans—to debate the validity of specific laws, privileges, and
ordinances. In those discussions, the question was not so much whether
rulers and subjects should act legally or whether Catalonia's laws and privileges should be respected but rather which laws and privileges were most
beneficial to the public good. Opponents of one privilege or law might describe it as conducive to "abuse" *(abús)* or "harm" *(dany),* whereas its defenders would counter that its repeal or disregard would constitute a "nov-
elty" *(novetat)* that would lead to even greater harm. This was the language
of the "politics of privilege," which was central to most, if not all, early modern societies.[4]

Barcelona's artisans were familiar with this political language. Masters,
journeymen, and foreigners used it in discussions over how best to resolve
the problems affecting their trades and the city's economy. This will become especially clear later when I examine the important conflicts in the
city's wool trades, which included two unprecedented strikes. All these examples will reveal the importance of privilege in artisans' language and
ideas, as well as in the actions they took to preserve their way of life, professions, and confraternities.

Throughout the reign of Philip III, the so-called crisis of the seventeenth
century threatened to overwhelm craft confraternities, Catalan political institutions, and the relations between Catalans and the Spanish monarchy.
It remains to be seen how all of them tried to cope with those problems
and whether or not it was possible to find solutions that preserved Catalan
laws, liberties, and privileges more or less intact.

---

4. Gail Bossenga, *The Politics of Privilege: Old Regime and Revolution in Lille* (Cambridge,
1991). Aside from Elliott's statement cited above, I have not been able to find an adequate
discussion of the notion of privilege in sixteenth- and seventeenth-century Catalan or Spanish political language. This is an issue that has received far greater attention among scholars of the French Revolution; in addition to Bossenga, see also *The Political Culture of the Old
Regime,* vol. 1 of *The French Revolution and the Creation of Modern Political Culture,* ed. Keith
Michael Baker (Oxford, 1987). Even though he does not use the term "politics of privilege," I have found especially relevant Howell A. Lloyd's article "Constitutionalism" in *The
Cambridge History of Political Thought, 1450–1700,* ed. J. H. Burns with Mark Goldie (Cambridge, 1991), 254–97. For an interesting, if brief, description of the political language
used by early modern Catalan peasants and lords, see Eva Serra, *Pagesos i senyors a la
Catalunya del segle XVII: Baronia de Sentmenat, 1590–1729* (Barcelona, 1988), 53, 79. For a
discussion of Castilian towns' use of privileges to respond to economic problems, see Helen
Nader, *Liberty in Absolutist Spain: The Habsburg Sale of Towns, 1516–1700* (Baltimore, 1990),
esp. chapter 6, "The Economic Pleasures and Perils of Liberty."

Bandits and Taxes

On 20 September 1598, the consellers received a letter from the master barber-surgeon Gaspar Massaguer, Barcelona's delegate in the royal court, reporting Philip II's death and his successor's intention to visit the territories of the Crown of Aragon as soon as possible.[5] Upon learning about the king's death, the Barcelona priest and historian Jaume Ramon Vila (1570–1638) reviewed in his diary the events during the last decade of his reign: the tense confrontation among the Consell de Cent, the Diputació, and viceroys between 1588 and 1592; the royal army's invasion of the kingdom of Aragon; and the recently concluded war between the Spanish and French monarchies. Vila concluded that the memory of the old king merited an especially harsh epitaph: A "most Catholic and prudent" monarch, "but with respect to the privileges, liberties, articles and acts of Corts, usages and customs, proclamations and *fueros* [liberties] of the entire Crown of Aragon, the king who most contradicted them."[6]

In contrast to the last years of Philip II's reign, Catalans hoped their new king would rule over a time of lasting peace, prosperity, and improved relations with the monarchy. Such was the mood in which Barcelona welcomed Philip III when he arrived on 14 May 1599. This was his second visit to the city; the first had taken place in 1585, when he was nine years old. Fourteen years later, he returned as king, just married to Margaret of Austria in Valencia—not a happy reminder to the city because Barcelona had initially expected to host the royal wedding, and as the consellers told Philip III, the change of venue had produced such sadness that some "thought they would die of the pain."[7] Nevertheless, the city did its best to put on great festivities for the new monarch, undoubtedly hoping to endear itself to him.

The efforts paid off. On the tenth day of celebrations, the king's Catalan secretary, Pedro de Franqueza, announced that his majesty had agreed

5. AHCB CC X-57 (LCO, 1598–99), fol. 87: Massaguer to Consellers, 20 September 1598.

6. AHCB MS B-100: diary of Jaume Ramon Vila (for 1596–1601), 204. On this author, see Josep Maria Roca, *Discursos llegits en la Real Academia de Buenas Letras de Barcelona en la solemne recepció pública de Joseph Ma. Roca el dia 20 de maig de 1918: En Jaume Ramon Vila heraldista catalá de començaments del segle XVIIé* (Barcelona, 1918); and Mar Batlle, *Patriotisme i modernitat a La fi del Comte d'Urgell* (Barcelona, 1999), appendix 3.

7. *DACB*, 7:389. Thomas Platter reported that the king had chosen Valencia because Barcelona would welcome him only as count of Barcelona; *Journal of a Younger Brother: The Life of Thomas Platter as a Medical Student in Montpellier at the Close of the Sixteenth Century*, trans. Seán Jennett (London, 1963), 202.

to convene the Corts in the city.[8] This was welcome news for several reasons. The Corts had not been held in Catalonia's capital since 1563. But in addition, Catalans and their king had to tackle a staggering list of issues that had accumulated in the years since the last Corts of Monzón in 1585.[9] Highest on the Catalan list of priorities were the need to address the serious conflicts that had taken place between 1588 and 1592, numerous complaints against the officials of the Inquisition, and the construction of four galleys to protect the principality's coast. Of course, Catalans of all social levels longed for their share of royal gifts and privileges. The most pressing concerns for the royal government involved replenishing the desperately low royal coffers in Catalonia and reforming the royal justice system. It was perhaps an overly ambitious agenda that would have required long hours of discussions and more likely another royal visit in the not too distant future. But Philip III was eager to return to Castile as soon as possible, and nobody could predict when the Corts would meet next.

The Corts of 1599 would address an avalanche of topics in the record time of two months, making it one of the shortest meetings ever. On 3 August, a few days after the conclusion of the Corts, the consellers reported its achievements before a full meeting of the Consell de Cent. The list was impressive.[10] The Corts had approved a generous royal subsidy—in fact, the largest ever—and reforms in the Audiència, as well as funding for the city's main hospital. Philip III had granted numerous honors, including the creation of an unprecedented number of nobles and honored citizens.[11] As we will see later, master artisans also had their share of honors in the form of craft confraternity privileges.

Despite the consellers' positive response, time would reveal the failure of the Corts of 1599 to resolve fully two major issues having to do with the future of Catalan privileges: the problem of banditry and the precarious state of royal finances in the principality.[12] Both issues would dominate the relations between Catalonia and the Spanish monarchy for the rest of

---

8. *DACB*, 7:205–6.

9. See Ernesto Belenguer Cebriá, "Un balance de las relaciones entre la corte y el país: Los *greuges* de 1599 en Cataluña," *Estudis* 13 (1987): 99–130; Elliott, *Revolt of the Catalans*, 49–50.

10. AHCB CC II-108 (Delibs. 1598–99), fols. 161v–163r.

11. James S. Amelang, *Honored Citizens of Barcelona: Patrician Culture and Class Relations, 1490–1714* (Princeton, 1986), 40, 65; Joan Lluís Palos, *Catalunya a l'imperi dels Àustria: La pràctica de govern (segles XVI i XVII)* (Lleida, 1994), 53.

12. For a discussion of the legal and political implications of the Corts of 1599, see Ernest Belenguer i Cebrià, "La legislació político-judicial de les Corts de 1599 a Catalunya," *Pedralbes* 7 (1987): 9–28.

Philip III's reign and would have long-lasting adverse implications for the relations between Catalans and the royal monarchy.

Complaints about the bandits in Catalonia's countryside went back for centuries, but between the second half of the sixteenth century and the early part of the seventeenth their numbers and actions increased significantly.[13] Poverty in the countryside was partly to blame for driving people to a life of banditry. Equally important were the long-standing feuds between two factions known as the *nyerros* and the *cadells*. Named after groups of Catalan nobles and their followers, since the 1580s these two factions had taken part in armed attacks, robberies, and vendettas throughout the countryside. By the early seventeenth century, nyerros and cadells had acquired extensive networks of allies in local, Catalan, and royal institutions capable of protecting friends and relatives involved in banditry.[14] There was a broad consensus that the problem of banditry required immediate and effective action, but specific remedies proposed often led to sharp debates.

In the aftermath of the 1599 Corts, a political crisis erupted over the monarchy's efforts to stamp out banditry and Catalan officials' concern about the illegality of those efforts. Differences arose over the printing of the legislation approved at the Corts of 1599, which contained a number of constitutions that numerous Catalan officials insisted had been added without parliamentary approval.[15] Two of them involved matters of public order. One restricted the number of weapons Catalan nobles and their servants could carry. A second one forbade them the use of short-barreled firearms known as *pedrenyals,* named for their flintlock mechanism. Bandits allegedly liked small pedrenyals because they could hide their weapons more easily—for example, under their capes. For this reason, the Corts of 1585 had declared the pedrenyal "useless for war, treacherous, false, evil, and unworthy of the very name of firearm."[16]

As a result of these differences, more than a year and a half after the conclusion of the Corts of 1599 its legislation remained unpublished, which, according to the judges of the Audiència, resulted in "great harms" to the entire principality. The king denounced opponents of publication as "friends of novelties," and the viceroy blamed them for preventing Cat-

---

13. Xavier Torres i Sans, *Els bandolers (s. XVI–XVII)* (Vic, 1991), esp. 37–42.

14. For an excellent discussion of this subject, see Xavier Torres i Sans, *Nyerros i cadells: Bàndols i bandolerisme a la Catalunya moderna (1590–1640)* (Barcelona, 1993).

15. *Dietaris de la Generalitat de Catalunya,* vol. 3 (1578–1611), ed. Josep Maria Sans i Travé (Barcelona, 1996), 3:776–77. On the events that followed, see Elliott, *Revolt of the Catalans,* 50–51.

16. Text of 1585 constitution quoted by Torres, *Bandolers,* 173.

alonia from "enjoying the benefit of these laws."[17] The publication of the Corts's legislation evenly split the Diputació, with its six chief officers standing at opposite sides of the debate. The ecclesiastic diputat and oïdor, together with the town oïdor, advocated publication with a disclaimer about the disputed constitutions, but the noble diputat and oïdor, along with the town diputat, refused to go along.

Tired of what he considered nothing more than "unbridled obstinacy," an impatient duke of Feria, the viceroy of Catalonia, announced on 14 July 1601 that if the laws were not published within three days, he would mete out exemplary punishment against those who stubbornly refused to obey their king's will.[18] Don Joan de Vilanova, Andreu Reart, and Don Josep de Castellbell—the two diputats and the oïdor who were opposed to publication—responded to the viceroy with their own strong words: any action against them would infringe on royal privileges, constitutions, and other "rights of the land." The viceroy had no basis for challenging their "innate fidelity and love for the king," especially when it was illegal to publish the five constitutions not voted by the Corts and which for that reason violated previous constitutions and privileges.[19] The royal judges counseling the viceroy were themselves divided over the legality of arresting the Diputació's officers, and despite the duke of Feria's wish to act, his deadline passed without any action taken.[20]

Early in 1602, after learning of his appointment as viceroy of Sicily, the duke of Feria decided it was time to end the debate before he left his post in Barcelona. On 2 March—more than eight months after his threat of immediate action—the viceroy ordered the arrests of the diputat Joan de Vilanova and the oïdor Josep de Castellbell for their opposition to the publication of the 1599 constitutions. The viceroy's order faced a barrage of criticism. He was accused of causing "irreparable harms and prejudices" and trampling over Catalan laws and privileges. Even royal judges admitted the arrests were legally questionable.[21] The Barcelona lawyer Jeroni Pujades went even further and privately described the viceroy as a tyrant. The

17. *Dietaris de la Generalitat*, 3:385 (Audiència's statement), 386–87 (Philip III's statements).

18. Viceroy to Diputats, 12 July 1601, in *Dietaris de la Generalitat*, 3:402.

19. *Dietaris de la Generalitat*, 3:403–4.

20. *Dietari de Jeroni Pujades*, ed. Josep Maria Casas Homs, 4 vols. (Barcelona, 1975–76), 1:157.

21. *Dietaris de la Generalitat*, 3:423. Pujades pointed out that the Audiència judge Antoni Oliba, who had opposed the arrests back in July 1601, had died the following October, leaving "no one to be watchdog [*qui lladràs*] of the *pàtria*, or better said, of justice." But Judge Bonet expressed his misgivings after the arrests, thus provoking the viceroy's rage; Pujades, *Dietari*, 1:174.

duke, Pujades wrote in his diary, looked at the two arrested officers from the prison window, and "like another Nero," shouted: "Take their daggers and swords and imprison them!"[22] The duke of Feria's departure to Sicily made possible a compromise between the Diputació and the new viceroy, the archbishop of Tarragona, Joan Terés. And so in July 1602, the two Diputació officers left prison. The Diputació agreed that all the 1599 constitutions could be printed, along with a statement from the viceroy promising that the contested ones would not be applied until the matter was fully resolved at a later time.[23]

That dispute, however, had done nothing to address the problem of banditry, which in some respects had worsened. Pujades's diary describes an alarming number of robberies and murders in and around Barcelona, where "not even three days pass without there being robberies, deaths, or mutilations."[24] In April 1603 he reported that more than three hundred people had been killed with pedrenyals within a year. He himself had luckily escaped an attack, but it was a very close call: in September 1602, as he was riding his horse accompanied by a servant in the fields just beyond Barcelona's Portal Nou, a man dressed in shepherd's cape and black hat pointed a pedrenyal at him. Pujades and his servant escaped unharmed, but he did not report the incident to the authorities because "there is no justice, and I do not know where to seek it except to thank God who guarded me." In fact, he blamed the situation on the very officials charged with delivering justice. The Audiència judges, Pujades argued, had done all they could to delay the application of laws voted at the 1599 Corts in order to protect their allies among the nyerros and cadells factions, which were involved in countless incidents of banditry.[25]

The royal government's response to the continuing problem of banditry revived the struggle between legality and necessity. Since 1560 viceroys had issued at least half a dozen proclamations limiting or banning the use of pedrenyals, even though such prohibitions failed to curb crime, just as viceregal proclamations against hoarding had failed to lower grain prices in the late sixteenth century.[26] In 1599 the duke of Feria had issued another proclamation against the firearm, and during the second half of 1602 royal officials sought to enforce it. They arrested and severely punished nu-

22. Pujades, *Dietari*, 1:175. The oïdor Andreu Reart escaped arrest because he was away in his native city of Perpinyà.

23. *Dietaris de la Generalitat*, 3:429 (6 July 1602).

24. Pujades, *Dietari*, 1:205.

25. Pujades, *Dietari*, 201 (attack on Pujades), 212.

26. Torres, *Bandolers*, 173.

merous individuals—commoners and nobles, laymen and ecclesiastics—
for carrying pedrenyals. A peasant and a wool weaver were sent to the galleys. One nobleman was sentenced to seven years of exile in Italy.[27] Catalan nobles and diputats insisted that these actions violated noble privileges,
violated Catalan constitutions, and threatened "the liberty of the pàtria."
They alleged that royal proclamations could not prohibit those firearms
that were not explicitly banned by Catalan constitutions.[28] Nevertheless, in
April, July, and August 1603, royal officials issued more of these proclamations against pedrenyals, insisting that they were necessary to prevent
criminal acts and violated no constitution.[29] But these repeated declarations were a constant reminder of the proclamations' ineffectiveness and
occasioned renewed Catalan complaints of illegality.

Faced by the continuing inability to resolve what was an extremely complex problem, royal and Catalan authorities occasionally managed to agree
to coordinate their forces in what were known as *unions* of armed men.
Often celebrated with laudatory poems, these *unions* gave the impression
that something was being done to restore order: "Of robbers and murderers / Catalonia had her fill / But upon hearing of the *Unió,* / They all fled
the land."[30] In August 1605 Pujades described in his diary the success of
his cousin, Audiència judge Francesc Mitjavila, in leading a unió for the
area near the town of Vic, which particularly suffered from banditry. After
only two or three months, Pujades wrote, his cousin left Vic in a state of
"great peace."[31] In November 1605 Barcelona's Consell de Cent agreed to
take part of a unió for the first time since 1565. But like the viceregal
proclamations against pedrenyals, the *unions* did not prove effective in the
long run. As if to underscore the failure of all of these efforts, bandits repeatedly carried out spectacular attacks. Among them, Perot Rocaguinarda
(or Roca Guinarda), whom Cervantes incorporated in the adventures of
Don Quijote and Sancho Panza, had an especially active career murdering
and robbing with a band of as many as one hundred companions. Pujades
recounted that in January 1610, Rocaguinarda dared to climb the belfry
at the castle of Montcada to sound an alarm against himself.[32] In 1612 and
1613, bandits carried out major robberies on the silver route between
Seville and Genoa, which went across Catalonia.[33] Time and again, reports

---

27. *Dietaris de la Generalitat,* 3:440, 444.
28. Pujades, *Dietari,* 1:214 (6 November 1602).
29. Pujades, *Dietari,* 1:256–57, 292; *Dietaris de la Generalitat,* 3:460, 808.
30. Quoted by Torres in *Bandolers,* 171.
31. Pujades, *Dietari,* 1:395 (3 August 1605).
32. Pujades, *Dietari,* 2:140.

insisted that robbers had the protection of Catalan lords, who would not allow royal officials to enter their jurisdictions to capture the criminals.

Despite the escalation of criminal acts, royal authorities felt that responding strictly by the book would cause "great delays" and "[obstruct] the good administration of justice."[34] The argument that Catalans had too many privileges and liberties that encouraged licentiousness and weakened royal authority dated to well before the seventeenth century. Yet the royal government seemed convinced that the eradication of banditry would require occasionally illicit actions. This was clearly the point made in a letter to Philip III written by the marquis of Almazán after his appointment as viceroy of Catalonia in 1616: "When I arrive at Barcelona, I shall put the entire Principality in the galleys. . . . And as regards the *fueros* and constitutions of this principality, Your Majesty must please not be surprised if I trample on some of them which stand in the way of the administration of justice."[35]

Almazán's determination to stamp out banditry resulted in a few impressive victories, but they did not put an end to the problem. His campaign led to the execution of more than ninety men and the destruction of castles and houses of suspected bandits and their protectors. Yet, after a lull of a few years, the activities of bandits continued into the 1630s and 1640s, well after Philip III's reign.

By 1616 the basic terms in the debate over the problem of banditry in the principality had been set. On the one hand, the monarchy led those who insisted on the "necessity" to restore order by acting forcefully and without too many scruples about legality. On the other hand, the Diputació and the noble braç denounced the arbitrariness of the actions of royal officials, which "abused" the privileges and laws of Catalonia. The Consell de Cent and officials in other Catalan towns, concerned about restoring order, occasionally took a more ambivalent position toward the use of a heavy hand against bandits.[36]

Catalans and the monarchy used the same terms in their debate over a second and possibly more serious issue, namely, the dire state of royal finances in the principality. In this second debate, the monarchy stood once more on the side of "necessity," whereas the Consell de Cent now stood clearly on the side of legality. The economic situation of the early seven-

33. Elliott, *Revolt of the Catalans,* 110–11.
34. The statements are those of by the marquis of Almazán in 1614 and the duke of Albuquerque in 1616, quoted in Torres, *Bandolers,* 161.
35. Elliott, *Revolt of the Catalans,* 118.
36. Torres, *Bandolers,* 183.

teenth century could only make more difficult finding a way to bolster what John Elliott has described as the "exceptionally precarious" fiscal foundations of the royal government.[37] The problem had less to do with the economic conditions than with the fact that the king had an "exceptionally small" patrimony.[38] In 1609 the Council of Finance had earmarked taxes collected in Castile to pay for the defenses in Catalonia, which were in a desperate situation.[39] By 1616 royal finances were in such a desperate state that the crown owed 38,825 lliures in arrears of mercès, the treasury was empty, and the frontier defenses were hopelessly neglected.[40]

Royal officials argued for the necessity to implement new policies to halt the impending crisis in royal finances in Catalonia. Since at least the late sixteenth century, they had argued that the king's patrimony had been depleted by towns and cities that did not pay the king what was known as the *quint*—that is, a fifth of their revenues.[41] Over the course of centuries, towns and cities had secured privileges exempting them from this payment. However, in some cases, the collection of the quint had simply lapsed for any number of reasons. The decline in royal revenues had been a problem throughout the sixteenth century, but it was during Philip III's reign that royal officials decided to correct this problem by again collecting the quint from those municipalities that could not produce a privilege of exemption. During the Corts of 1599, the royal government agreed to forgive anything owed up to that year as long as payments began.

In 1606, the monarchy created two new offices to deal with conflicts arising from the collection of the quint.[42] Various towns began to pay the quint, but one city refused to comply: Barcelona. Catalonia's capital insisted that the fact that it had not paid in centuries was evidence of its exemption from such an onerous demand. Nonetheless, when required by royal officers, the city could not produce a privilege explicitly stating that exemption. For royal officers, to allow Barcelona to disregard the king's au-

---

37. Elliott, *Revolt of the Catalans,* 92.

38. Ibid., 94.

39. Bernat Hernández, "Un assaig de reforma del sistema fisco-financer de la monarquia a Catalunya: L'impost del quint sobre les imposicions locals, 1580–1640," *Manuscrits* 14 (1996): 300.

40. Elliott, *Revolt of the Catalans,* 138.

41. Hernández, "Assaig de reforma," 300–301. More specifically, the quint was the price paid to the monarchy for the privilege of establishing and collecting taxes, which was first introduced in the reign of Ferdinand I (1412–16). The *quint* was not exclusively paid by towns. Royal officers also expected it from the Llotja (merchants' guild) of Perpinyà and that of Barcelona.

42. Hernández, "Assaig de reforma," 302–3.

thority would only encourage others to follow suit. In addition, to be able to collect the quint from Catalonia's largest and richest city would have gone a long way toward redressing royal finances. But in Barcelona, the demands of royal officers would be repeatedly denounced as a disregard of its privileges.

At the same time that the duke of Almazán launched his often brutal offensive against banditry, his officials made preparations to collect Barcelona's share of the quint. In 1617, they began to gather information on taxes collected in the city in order to calculate how much Barcelona owed the king.[43] Barcelona allegedly owed no less than 300,000 lliures, an enormous sum, far greater than all of the city's revenues.[44] However, in order to determine the exact amount, it was necessary that the city turn in its tax accounts. Viceroy Almazán left that task to his successor, the duke of Alcalá, who in August 1620 decided it was time to act. He ordered city officials to surrender the accounts of all its taxes collected since 1599. After continued delays, in October 1621 city officials received an order to turn in those accounts within thirty days or incur a large fine. Instead, the Consell de Cent denounced the viceroy's action as "a new and extraordinary thing, and contrary to the well-known right of the city and to the liberties and freedoms this city has received."[45] But just as a showdown between the viceroy and city officials appeared inevitable, fate intervened in Barcelona's favor. Philip III had died back in March 1621, and on 3 November 1621 the new king, Philip IV, ordered Alcalá to halt his proceedings against the city, declaring that the viceroy had "exceeded his order."[46]

This latest compromise deferred to the future a final determination of Barcelona's share of the quint. Alcalá's inflexible position had done little to remedy royal finances and much to embitter the monarchy's relations with the city of Barcelona. As in the case of banditry, the insufficiency of royal finances in Catalonia remained a constant problem that would outlast Philip III's reign.

The debates over banditry and the quint underscored the crucial question that would have to be addressed before Catalonia's growing problems could be solved: Who should determine which privileges and laws should stand and which ones should not? The monarchy and Catalan institutions had different answers. To the Diputació, the Corts remained the place

---

43. Royal officials' initial investigations involved the revenues from the *imperiatge* tax collected by the Llotja, or merchants' guild of Barcelona; Hernández, "Assaig de reforma," 315.

44. Elliott, *Revolt of the Catalans,* 146.

45. Quoted in Hernández, "Assaig de reforma," 315.

46. Elliott, *Revolt of the Catalans,* 150.

where they could discuss those questions with their monarch. But such meetings took time, and as problems seemed to worsen, royal authorities had little inclination for the seemingly slow Catalan political system. Sometimes the monarchy would decide to take actions regardless of the legal constraints, but at other times it seemed willing to respect Catalan laws and privileges, in part because of the strong opposition from Catalan authorities. However, although Catalan authorities were especially concerned about protecting those laws and privileges that directly affected the balance of power between the principality and the monarchy, they did not universally defend all laws and privileges. Catalans too could feel at times the urge to act quickly and to disregard legal barriers that they thought allowed problems or abuses to persist.

This was precisely the case with the problems affecting Barcelona's economy and artisans. The difficulties experienced by the city's trades generated debates between city officers and artisans, between masters and artisans who were not masters, between Catalan and foreign artisans and merchants. Although the specific issues did not always affect the relations between Catalonia and the Spanish monarchy, even seemingly minor conflicts hinged on the question of how to determine which privileges and laws should remain in place and which ones should not.

Artisans, Privileges, and Economic Crisis

The Corts of 1599 proved relatively good to Barcelona's master artisans, despite a few major disappointments. They once again failed to win the reinstatement of the sixth conseller. The king agreed only to allow his viceroy to discuss this and other proposals with city officials in the future.[47] Moreover, the king granted a privilege limiting master artisans' input in the appointment of extraordinary committees in the Consell de Cent.[48] However, Philip III granted a privilege that allowed fifteen new menestral candidates eligibility for the office of fifth conseller. Masters from thirteen different craft confraternities, some of which had never before been eligible for this office, now had the potential to become a conseller.[49] The king also granted numerous royal privileges that reaffirmed previous trade ordinances and

---

47. AHCB CC II-108 (Delibs. 1598–99), fol. 162v.

48. Shoemakers and furriers wanted lower excises on the imports of leather to Catalonia, which the Corts approved; Jaime Carrera Pujal, *Historia política y económica de Cataluña: Siglos XVI al XVIII*, 3 vols. (Barcelona, 1946–47), 1:359.

49. For a list of confraternities with new candidates, see AHCB C VIII-12 (Llibres d'insaculacions): "Llibreta de inseculacions" (1594–1657).

privileges, although occasionally artisans slipped in a few new ordinances. This is precisely what master wool clothiers did; their privilege confirmed old ordinances and a few new ones.[50] Jug or jar makers *(gerrers)* and wool weavers also secured royal approval for new ordinances.[51] In addition, tanners, masons, silk mercers *(passamaners)*, and blacksmiths won privileges confirming previous ordinances.[52] Even journeymen carpenters *(joves i fadrins fusters)* obtained the privilege to form a confraternity—something master carpenters did not welcome, although the fact that they too won a royal privilege may have eased the bad news.[53]

Artisans' determination in 1599 to win royal privileges probably responded less to specific concerns about economic conditions than to their long-held belief that privileges were essential for the protection of their confraternities and trades. Privileges and trade ordinances stipulated the reason for a trade's existence, its aims, and how it should function. Thus privileges and ordinances gave artisans legal recognition of their professional life and identity. From a more practical point of view, privileges and ordinances established areas of competence over one or several trades—everything from who could exercise the trade to technical details about the products made or services offered by the trade. It is not surprising, then, that Barcelona's artisans took advantage of the extraordinary visit of their king to secure protection for their ordinances and privileges.

The value of privileges would become clear during the years after the Corts of 1599, as continuing economic changes and temporary crises would at times appear to threaten the future of many artisans' trades. The devastating plague that killed so many throughout the kingdom of Castile between 1599 and 1601 spared Catalonia. Nevertheless, in the first three decades of the seventeenth century, the principality suffered from periodic subsistence crises, commercial stagnation, and monetary uncertainty. During the winter of 1602 and 1603, extremely cold winds blowing from the coast ruined olive and orange crops and destroyed pastures, killing many cattle as a result.[54] In

50. AHCB Gremis 26-1 ("Llibre de privilegis" 1599): wool clothiers' book of privileges.

51. Antonio de Capmany y de Montpalau, *Memorias históricas sobre la marina, comercio y artes de la antigua ciudad de Barcelona*, ed. Emilio Giralt and Carmen Batlle (Barcelona, 1961–63), 1:499, 523.

52. AHCB Gremis 35-34 ("Tresllats de plets" 1681–83), fol. 3r: memorandum on the tanners' legal suits. For the other craft confraternities, see Capmany y de Montpalau, *Memorias históricas*, 1:582, 538, 555.

53. For the journeymen carpenters' privilege, see AHCB Gremis 37-2 ("Llibre de consells" 1583–1614), fol. 84r: master carpenters' book of councils. For master carpenters' privileges, see Capmany y de Montpalau, *Memorias históricas*, 1:542.

54. BUB MS 115, Sevillà, "Historia General del Principado de Cataluña . . . 1598–1640," 13v.

January 1603, many people fell ill and died in Barcelona, and in the following September, Pujades said an "infinite number of people" died of diarrhea,
fever, and other illnesses.[55] A year later, in August 1604, many more people
died from fevers in Barcelona and throughout the rest of the principality.[56]
That December 1604, many women blamed the shortage of grain in
Barcelona on the irresponsible speculation of the fifth conseller. A crowd of
four thousand destroyed much of the conseller's house and tried to burn
it.[57] The bad weather once more affected crops in 1605, as reported in the
city's diary: "This month of April has been very dry and the winds have really damaged crops; and in Barcelona there have been many tragic deaths."[58]
Catalans suffered from high wheat and olive oil prices, famine, and illnesses
for several more years.[59]

Barcelona's volume of trade also appeared to decline sharply. In 1603,
the city reported losses from the farming of its tax on tonnage of ships entering Barcelona, known as the *dret d'ancoratge*.[60] The Diputació's own taxes
on imports and exports collected in the port of Barcelona, perhaps the
largest source of fiscal wealth in Catalonia, fell considerably around 1603.[61]
By 1605–6, the *dret d'imperiatge*, an ad valorem tax on ships collected by
the Llotja, or merchants' guild, had also fallen considerably in relation to
the 1580s.[62] Taxes collected by the city on imports and exports and known
simply as the "city tax," or *dret de duanes*, which had steadily risen in the
1590s, fell sharply around 1609.[63] These measures are not perfect indica-
tors of a weakening economy because they do not account for the fluctu-
ations in currency over these years. But other sources confirm the gloomy
condition of Barcelona's economy.

In 1615, the Audiència of Barcelona drafted a memorandum that
reported a reduction in Catalan exports to only three items: dried fruits,
iron, and wool cloth. However, even though Catalan cloth had been one

55. Pujades, *Dietari*, 1:239, 294.

56. Pujades, *Dietari*, 1:374–75.

57. *DACB*, 8:146–47; Pujades, *Dietari*, 1:382–83.

58. *DACB*, 8:183.

59. Pujades, *Dietari*, 2:49, 52 (1607), 67 (1608); see also Vilar, *Catalogne*, 1:599.

60. Carrera Pujal, *Historia política*, 1:362; Vilar, *Catalogne*, 1:589.

61. Elliott, *Revolt of the Catalans*, appendix 3, table 1, 564.

62. Robert S. Smith, *The Spanish Guild Merchant: A History of the Consulado, 1250–1700*
(Durham, N.C., 1940), 140. Unfortunately, the only sums recorded between 1587 and 1644
are the ones for 1605–6.

63. The *dret de duanes* had been established in 1592 as part of yet another attempt to reform the city's fiscal administration; Carrera Pujal, *Historia política*, 1:364–65 and Vilar,
Catalogne, 1:589.

of the principality's major exports since the late Middle Ages, the memorandum was pessimistic about its future: "Those who used to practice it in Catalonia have been left in great poverty, this which used to be the means that provided the most money to this province."[64] These problems continued through the 1620s, a period of economic recession not just in Barcelona but throughout Catalonia, which especially affected the wool industry.[65]

Many of Barcelona's masters were concerned about the decline of their trades. Master artisans in general responded to the economic problems by asserting their privileges before what they denounced as the harms and abuses of journeymen and foreign artisans and merchants.

Artisans who had the title of master enjoyed important privileges. Only masters could set up shop, trade, or conduct the activities that were exclusive to the profession.[66] The title of master was granted after an aspirant completed a period of apprenticeship (usually four years), passed an examination, and paid a number of fees. Once the examination requirement was completed, the new master was admitted as a confrere, had the right to participate in the confraternity's administration, and benefited from the various forms of assistance it provided to its members.

Master artisans and city and royal authorities looked on journeymen's organizations with suspicion. In 1525, after disturbances in Barcelona, the Consell de Cent forbade journeymen's confraternities for the "benefit, tranquillity, and peace" of the city.[67] Worship of journeymen's patron saints was not abolished but was taken over by the masters' confraternities. Despite the 1525 ordinance, between the late sixteenth and early seventeenth centuries journeymen wool clothiers, shoemakers, masons, carpenters, and gardeners *(hortolans)* established confraternities. These journeymen confraternities often met separately from their masters and celebrated their own religious activities, although they had no authority over trade matters

---

64. AHCB CC XV-3 (Diversorum), fol. 157: "Difficultats ultimament donades contra la nova licencia de fabricar moneda q[ue] demana la ciutat de Barcelona" (n.d. [1617]). See also Carrera Pujal, *Historia política*, 1:365–66, and Vilar, *Catalogne*, 1:589.

65. Sales, *Segles de la decadència*, 300–301.

66. In the fifteenth century, journeymen could sometimes take part in the religious activities of the masters' confraternities as devotional confreres; Pierre Bonnassie, *La organización del trabajo en Barcelona a fines del siglo XV* (Barcelona, 1975), 36–37. In the early seventeenth century, journeymen wool clothiers stated that some masters' confraternities admitted journeymen and offered them benefits; BC MS 501: [Gabriel?] Berart and [Francesc?] Congost, *Molt illustres, magnifichs, y savis senyors* (1623 [sic 1632?]) (memorandum from the officers of the confraternity of journeymen wool clothiers to the consellers).

67. AHCB CC II-47 (Delibs. 1523–25), fol. 50v: Consell de Cent, 18 August 1525.

and might still be subject to their masters' authority.[68] During the course of the 1599 Corts, a few journeymen confraternities had managed to secure royal privileges for their organizations. These allowed journeymen confraternities to have chapels dedicated to their patron saints, to conduct religious activities, and to perform acts of charity, such as providing assistance during burials. In the 1620s concerns about economic conditions rekindled masters' wish to ban journeymen confraternities, and in 1629 the Consell de Cent approved an ordinance disbanding them "because of the many harms they cause to the common good."[69] Although it is not possible to determine who made these proposals, it seems fair to assume that they came from the master artisan representatives in the city council. But despite the ordinance, journeymen confraternities did not disappear altogether from Barcelona.[70]

The economic problems of the early seventeenth century also convinced masters of the necessity to seek additional restrictions on the activities of foreign artisans and merchants, who caused "great harms" to Barcelona's artisan men and women.[71] In this effort, masters secured the support of the Consell de Cent. In October 1629, the same year the Consell de Cent approved an ordinance to disband journeymen confraternities, it also approved an ordinance barring Frenchmen from becoming officers in any craft confraternity or college. A month later, a second ordinance prohibited French masters from participating at all in any craft confraternity. In addition, the ability of foreign artisans to become masters was severely restricted. Measures against foreign workers were not new. In 1590, the Consell de Cent abolished the confraternity of foreign stevedores *(traginers de mar)*.[72] In 1596 cotton and linen weavers obtained a royal privilege excluding foreigners as officers in their confraternity.[73] The 1626 ordinances

68. Wool clothier journeymen defended the right to have their own confraternity on the grounds that theirs was a strictly religious organization that did not address craft matters; BC MS 501: memorandum by the officers of the confraternity of journeymen wool clothiers to the consellers. The Confraternity of Journeymen Shoemakers even had to pay a fifth of its revenues to the masters' confraternity; AHCB Gremis 1-92 ("Llibre de consells" 1613–24): shoemakers' council, 31 August 1618.

69. Carrera Pujal, *Historia política*, 2:175–76.

70. Examples of conflicts between journeymen and masters included the masons, tailors, wool clothiers, and notaries; *RB*, vol. 5, chap. 93.

71. BC F. Bon, 5151: *Advertiments ab los quals se mostra esser molt vtil, y convenient al be publich de tot lo Principat de Cathalunya y Comptats de Rosello, y Cerdanya, lo prohibir vestir, y clasar de tota sort de Robes fabricades fora Regne* (n.p., n.d.) [1619–1630].

72. Carrera Pujal, *Historia política*, 2:161.

73. José Ventalló Vintró, *Historia de la industria lanera catalana* (Tarrasa, 1904), 77. According to Capmany y de Montpalau, the Consell de Cent requested this privilege; *Memorias históricas*, 1:484.

of the silk shopkeepers' confraternity *(botiguers de teles)* forbade masters from accepting foreign apprentices.[74] Most craft confraternities, however, simply charged substantially higher fees for examining foreigners as a means of discouraging them from becoming masters.[75]

The limitations on and exclusion of foreigners in Barcelona's trades mostly affected Frenchmen who had come to live and work in the city. Since the late fifteenth century, many French natives had migrated to Catalonia, and they continued to do so into the 1620s, making up between 10 and 20 percent of Catalonia's male population between 1570 and 1620.[76] Many settled in Catalan coastal towns,[77] but there were important concentrations in Barcelona as well. Between 1611 and 1615, 40 percent of the inhabitants of the Barcelona parish of Sant Just i Pastor not born in the city was French.[78] In 1637 the French made up more than a tenth of Barcelona's population.[79] At that time, nearly half (44.46 percent) of the French in Catalonia worked as artisans in smaller trades.[80] But they were also in larger trades. Between 1599 and 1630, 11 out of the 232 new master shoemakers in Barcelona were French. Between 1620 and 1636, 10 out of a total of 56 licensed cobblers in Barcelona were Frenchmen.[81]

The 1629 ordinances coincided with the last waves of immigrants from south and southwestern France.[82] Their precise impact is unknown, but it appears that many soon concluded that the ordinances unfairly harmed French masters, who in some cases had lived for many years in Barcelona and married Catalan women. And so in 1631 a compromise was reached

74. Carrera Pujal, *Historia política,* 2:173.

75. Before 1618, Catalan shoemakers paid 8 lliures and foreigners 16 lliures; after 1618, 16 lliures 4 sous and 25 lliures, respectively; see AHCB Gremis 1-2 ("Llibre de promenia" 1612); 1-3 ("Llibre de promenia" 1615); 1-92 ("Llibre de consells" 1613–24), fol. 103r. The average price of shoes remained 8 sous in the early seventeenth century, so that a foreigner had to sell sixty-three pairs in 1618 to make up the examination fees.

76. Jorge Nadal and Emilio Giralt, *La population catalane de 1553 à 1717: L'immigration française et les autres facteurs de son développement* ([Paris], 1960), 62.

77. Nadal and Giralt, *Population catalane,* 144–52; Vilar, *Catalogne,* 1:528; García Espuche, *Siglo decisivo,* 63.

78. Antoni Simon and Jordi Andreu, "Evolució demogràfica (segles XVI i XVII)," in *Història de Barcelona,* ed. Jaume Sobrequés i Callicó, 8 vols. (Barcelona, 1991–97), 4:156, figure 16.

79. Enric Moreu-Rey, *Els immigrants francesos a Barcelona (segles XVI al XVII)* (Barcelona, 1959), 19.

80. Emilio Giralt Raventós, "La colonia mercantil francesa de Barcelona a mediados del siglo XVII," *Estudios de Historia Moderna* 6 (1956): 220. For the list of trades of Frenchmen, see Moreu-Rey, *Els immigrants francesos,* 20.

81. AHCB Gremis 1-92 ("Llibre de consells" 1613–24) and AHCB Gremis 1-93 ("Llibre de consells" 1625–36).

82. Giralt Raventós, "Colonia mercantil francesa," 222.

whereby the Consell abolished the 1629 ordinances but barred confraternities from admitting French apprentices in the future.[83]

Journeymen and foreign artisans could do little to counter the discriminatory actions of masters. The same may be said about women artisans, who not only remained excluded from masters' confraternities but apparently could never even consider organizing their own craft confraternities, as did journeymen.[84] Confronting the alleged abuses of foreign merchants, however, was a far more difficult problem for master artisans.

Resentment against foreign merchants, and particularly against the Genoese, was not new in Barcelona—as demonstrated by their expulsion from the city in 1591. The economic problems of the seventeenth century renewed the belief that behind Barcelona's troubles lay the abusive practices of foreigners. In 1585 the master shoemakers, skinners, and tanners were all rich, but now "all three are poor," explained the shoemakers' confraternity in 1620. The culprits were Genoese hoarders, who would buy up all the leather from the slaughterhouses, leaving none for Catalan artisans to work with. In fact, all foreign merchants, the shoemakers continued, lived like the swallow: in good times they made their nests in Catalonia, but after growing fat and raising their children, they left the country, taking their money and leaving behind only trash in their houses.[85]

It is not surprising, therefore, that master shoemakers along with many other Barcelona master confraternities fully supported an ordinance approved on 1 June 1620 by the Consell de Cent to curb the activities of foreign merchants by imposing a 10 percent tax on their imports to the city. Foreign merchants quickly responded by challenging the ordinance's legality before the Audiència. They also commissioned the eloquent Catalan lawyer Francesc Soler to write a long pamphlet denouncing the illegality of the ordinance. According to Soler, throughout Catalonia's history ordinances against foreigners had been based on false arguments of necessity—whether the threat of treason or the danger of war—not on legal grounds. The latest ordinance, Soler continued, trampled over Catalan constitutions and asserted powers such as the authority to declare who was

83. The two ordinances limiting Frenchmen's participation were dated 6 October and 8 November 1629; *RB,* 5:228. The ordinance repealing the two earlier ones dates from 15 October 1631; AHCB Gremis 4-2 ("Llibre de les ordinacio[n]s . . . dels julians," seventeenth century): mercers' book of ordinances. For other examples of discrimination against Frenchmen in other Catalan towns, see García Espuche, *Siglo decisivo,* 64–68.

84. Marta Vicente, "Images and Realities of Work: Women and Guilds in Early Modern Barcelona," in *Spanish Women in the Golden Age,* ed. Magdalena S. Sánchez and Alain Saint-Saëns (Westport, Conn., 1996), 127–39.

85. AHCB Gremis 1-92, fols. 230–34: 7 August 1620.

a foreigner, which belonged exclusively to the king.[86] Soler and foreign merchants were not the only ones to question the legality of the ordinance. On 7 July 1620, the diputats submitted to the Consell de Cent a memorandum listing the constitutions and privileges violated by the ordinance.[87]

Faced with such strong opposition, in September 1620 the Consell de Cent decided to amend the ordinance. Supporters of the ordinance insisted that the 10 percent tax was necessary not only to tackle the grave fiscal and economic problems faced by the city, but also to prevent future abuses. The ordinance would take strong action to thwart "a thousand sudden misfortunes," just as viceroy Almazán's aggressive campaign had dealt a powerful blow to bandits only four years before.[88]

Nevertheless, in March 1621 the Audiència judge Joan Magarola sided with foreign merchants and ordered the city to suspend the ordinance until the tribunal issued a final decision. The following month a special committee of the Consell de Cent recommended the ordinance's revocation.[89]

The economic problems of the early seventeenth century demonstrate how the position of Catalans on the legality / necessity divide could shift. This time, it was not royal officials but master artisans and city officials who argued for the necessity of forceful actions that did not always conform with the laws and privileges of Catalonia. Yet if master artisans generally agreed on the need to confront journeymen, foreign artisans, and merchants, their agreement could quickly vanish when the contenders were other master artisans with the resources and privileges of their own craft confraternities.

Politics of Privilege

During the 1599 Corts, representatives from the Llotja denounced the decline in the export of woolens. According to the merchants, woolens made in the city and in the rest of Catalonia were "very inferior, bad, and hardly lasted, and most of them are counterfeit."[90] They faulted artisans for making fabrics of low quality, insisting that "fitters [*aparelladors*] do not

86. BC F. Bon. 8-VI-37: *Memorial de Francesch Soler* (Barcelona, 1620).

87. AHCB CC II-129 (Delibs. 1619–20): memorandum bound between fols. 104 and 105.

88. BC F. Bon. 9063: Narcís Peralta, *Memorial en Favor de la Ordinacion hecha por la ciudad de Barcelona* (Barcelona, 1620), fol. 80.

89. AHCB CC II-130 (Delibs. 1620–21): memorandum bound between fols. 60 and 61.

90. AHCB CC II-108 (Delibs. 1598–99), fols. 304v–305r: Committee of Twenty-Four, 22 June 1599. For an overview of the events of 1600 and 1626, see Valentín Vázquez de Prada and Pere Molas, "La indústria llanera a Barcelona: Segles XVI–XVII," in Pere Molas, *Economia i societat al segle XVIII* (Barcelona, 1975), 143–59.

fit them well, weavers do not weave them well, millers do not make them sturdy, dyers do not dye them well, shearers [*baixadors*] do not shear them well; as a result, out of one hundred fabrics, not even ten come out well made and as they ought." With the support of Barcelona's syndics, the Corts approved regulations enforcing the proper length of woolens.[91]

While merchants sought legislation to correct what they believed were the problems in the wool industry, wool clothiers and weavers each sought and won royal privileges. One of the wool clothiers' ordinances, confirmed by the 1599 privilege, allowed clothiers to establish the wages of any weavers they hired without the permission of the weavers' confraternity.[92] Clothiers wanted to pay lower wages than those dictated by the weavers' confraternity. Naturally, weavers were not pleased.

In February 1600, citing a 1386 privilege granted to their confraternity by King Peter IV, the weavers imposed a fee on wool clothiers for every piece of cloth commissioned to a master weaver.[93] The clothiers complained to the consellers, declaring the weavers' fee an illegal new tax.[94] The Consell de Cent agreed with the clothiers that the weavers' new fee was "prohibited by constitutions of Catalonia as well as by royal privileges." The weavers' action, the city council stated, had resulted in "a great harm to all of the inhabitants of Barcelona."[95] On 29 February 1600, the Consell de Cent ordered the weavers to annul the new fee, fined them five hundred lliures, and barred their confraternity officers from eligibility for city office.[96] Rather than succumb, the weavers' confraternity appealed to the Audiència.[97] Moreover, weavers refused to work for clothiers.[98] As historian Pierre Vilar points out, weavers had effectively declared a strike against clothiers.[99]

On 8 March the Consell de Cent responded to the weavers' bold defiance by allowing clothiers to hire anyone to weave until master weavers returned to work and suspended their appeal in the royal court. Realizing the severity of these measures, on 14 March weavers agreed to rescind the new fees imposed on clothiers.[100]

91. Carrera Pujal, *Historia política*, 1:358.

92. AHCB Gremis 26-1 ("Llibre de privilegis" 1599), fol. 13r.

93. Carrera Pujal, *Historia política*, 2:162.

94. Jaime Carrera Pujal, *Aspectos de la vida gremial barcelonesa en los siglos XVIII y XIX* (Madrid, 1949), 8.

95. AHCB CC II-109 (Delibs. 1599–1600), fols. 48r–49v: 29 February 1600.

96. AHCB CC II-109 (Delibs. 1599–1600), fols. 48r–49v.

97. Carrera Pujal, *Aspectos*, 8.

98. AHCB CC II-109 (Delibs. 1599–1600), fols. 53v–55r.

99. Vilar, *Catalogne*, 1:595.

100. *RB*, 5:222.

In September 1626 both trades were again at odds over weavers' salaries. The weavers' confraternity now accused clothiers of paying lower salaries to some weavers. In response, the weavers' confraternity ordered each member to bring every piece of cloth he made for any clothier to the weavers' treasurer. The treasurer would then pay each weaver's salary according to the established fees and collect that money, in cash, from the clothier.[101] Master weavers working for a clothier who refused to comply with the new procedures had two options: pay a fine of three lliures or refuse to work for that clothier.

Faced with a second strike, the clothiers denounced the weavers' actions to the Consell de Cent, which ordered the weavers to reverse their decision and return to work for the clothiers. On 4 September 1626, after the weavers' confraternity unanimously refused to obey, the Consell de Cent annulled the weavers' latest order, had their confraternity officials imprisoned, and threatened to punish any weaver who did not go back to work. The viceroy also took part in the dispute, requiring clothiers to pay weavers' salaries in cash, and in return he set free the weavers' officers. But in early October the weavers' confraternity appealed to the Audiència. In addition, it appeared that most master weavers remained unwilling to work for the clothiers. The Consell de Cent now decided to reinstate the 1600 ordinance that allowed clothiers to have anyone they wished weave for them until the weavers agreed to work again. The final outcome of the conflict remains unclear, but in all likelihood the weavers eventually had no choice but to suspend their appeal before the Audiència and to accept the compromise imposed on them by the viceroy.

To Pierre Vilar, the decades-long conflict between weavers and clothiers represented the struggle between two "forms of distribution of labor." To Vilar, the conflict was between the weavers' "medieval, corporate" practices and the clothiers' capitalist ones.[102] Accordingly, the Consell de Cent, dominated by mercantile, capitalist interests, sided with the clothiers against trade restrictions.

Unfortunately, unless more evidence is presented in support of such a claim, it is difficult to agree with this conclusion. In that struggle, the Consell de Cent tried to mediate a solution that would prevent disruptions to the industry. Although in 1600 and 1626 it sided with the clothiers against the weavers' strikes, the Consell de Cent did not really seek to undermine

101. The weavers' actions were first reported before the Consell de Cent on 4 September; Vilar, *Catalogne*, 1:597n.
102. Vilar, *Catalogne*, 1:598.

the craft system—a system that, in any case, survived until the early nineteenth century.[103] The city ordinances that allowed clothiers to hire anyone to weave were powerful blows against the weavers' confraternity. Nevertheless, they appear to have been temporary measures intended to force weavers back to work and, just as important, to make them desist from appealing to the Audiència.

Moreover, on other occasions, the Consell de Cent acted against the clothiers and in favor of the weavers, especially on the important issue of access to raw wool. In 1614 a city ordinance prohibited the export of raw wool from Barcelona; essentially, its purpose was to avoid giving work to spinners or weavers living outside the city. The ordinance was in response to pleas by weavers and so-called poor clothiers, who claimed that "a few wealthy clothiers" benefited at the expense of many other artisans.[104] If the export of raw wool were left unchecked, weavers and poor clothiers argued, those few wealthy wool clothiers would eventually monopolize the city's wool textile industry.

In its dealings with both weavers and clothiers, the Consell de Cent's overriding principle was to assert its supreme authority to determine which confraternity ordinances and privileges should stand and which should not. The Consell de Cent took harsh steps against the weavers in 1600 and 1626 to punish a craft confraternity that had decided openly to defy city authorities by appealing to the Audiència. Likewise, on 6 May 1594 the Consell de Cent had suspended all of the clothiers' ordinances after they appealed to the Audiència.[105]

In Barcelona, the Consell de Cent, and more specifically, the consellers, cited a privilege granted by Ferdinand the Catholic on 5 April 1509 allowing them to determine which artisans' privileges were for the common good of the city.[106] The Consell de Cent estimated that the letter of the privilege was explicit: the Consell was to be the sole judge over craft confraternity issues.[107] Since then, all kings had confirmed the privilege. As re-

103. On the abolition of guilds in the early nineteenth century, see Pedro Molas Ribalta, *Los gremios barceloneses del siglo XVIII* (Madrid, 1970), 547–53.

104. Nonetheless, the ordinance may not have been put into effect at the time. Weavers and poor clothiers complained in 1619 about exports of raw wool by clothiers. According to the clothiers, the 1614 ordinance was not applied until 1622, when the city government ordered that raw wool leaving the city be confiscated at the city gates (see AHCB Gremis General, Paraires: wool clothiers' memorandum to the Consell de Cent, n.d. [1627?].

105. *RB*, 5:222.

106. Transcribed in Jaume Vicens i Vives, *Ferran II i la ciutat de Barcelona, 1479–1516*, 3 vols. (Barcelona, 1936–37), vol. 3, doc. 212.

107. Víctor Ferro, *El dret públic català: Les institucions a Catalunya fins al Decret de Nova Planta* (Vic, 1987), 167.

cently as October 1598, the consellers had asked for confirmation of this interpretation, and a judgment by Diego Clavero, regent of the Council of Aragon, in January 1605 sided with the city.[108] Nevertheless, the issue was far from settled.

As the conflicts between wool weavers and clothiers demonstrated, masters would dare to question the Consell's claims. Master artisans followed a careful strategy based on legal interpretations of the nature of privileges. Essentially, that strategy consisted of exploiting what appeared to be a significant implication of the Consell de Cent's power—namely, that it could override the king's prerogative to grant privileges. For example, the tailors complained that the consellers had wrongly revoked their 1599 privilege by issuing an ordinance favorable to the furriers. The furriers declared that the tailors' privilege had been obtained without the knowledge of city authorities and was therefore invalid. Yet in a text drafted by their lawyer, the tailors declared that if the city could revoke royal privileges, the king would have in fact renounced "the power to grant privileges to the confraternities of this city whenever he considered it convenient, and if that were so, he would cease to be king."[109] On the basis of this interpretation, artisans challenged the Consell's authority to override their confraternity privileges by appealing to the Audiència of Barcelona, which claimed to be the court of first instance in cases involving the scope and application of royal privileges.[110] The Consell de Cent considered such appeals to be illegal because it insisted that matters pertaining to all city trades fell under its exclusive jurisdiction, which was based on King Ferdinand's privilege. Nevertheless, and despite important royal declarations prohibiting them, appeals from master artisans to royal judges did not stop. In 1602 masons and wool clothiers sued the city before the Audiència.[111] In 1607 it was the cottoners *(cotoners)* and apothecaries against the city; in 1608 the bakers; in 1611 curriers and tanners; linen and cotton weavers and cottoners again in 1613; potters *(gerrers)* and wool clothiers in 1614; wool and silk dyers in 1615; the confraternity of brokers *(corredors d'orella)* in 1618; and so on.[112] In 1601,

108. *DACB,* 7:153 (1598); *RB,* 5:275 (1605).

109. For this argument, see BC F. Bon. 5414: [Francesc?] Congost, *Discurs per la Confraria dels Sastres acerca del recors interposat per los proms dela Confraria dels Pellers* [address by the tailors' confraternity regarding the appeal of the officers of the frippers' confraternity] (n.p., n.d. [1627?]), fol. 113r. The address was made to the consellers.

110. On the Audiència's claim to review royal privileges, see Ferro, *Dret públic,* 112–13.

111. Masons and wool clothiers were banned from city offices. Clothiers renounced their case on 16 December 1602; *RB,* 1:176.

112. *RB,* 5:224–25.

1611, and 1619 master tanners and curriers appealed to the royal tribunal against the city and won each time.[113]

The Audiència and the Consell de Cent cared about these appeals by artisans for an important reason: they established precedents for answering the question of who should determine which privileges should stand and which ones should not. The Consell de Cent feared what it might mean to allow the Audiència to become the final arbiter of artisans' privileges. For instance, the royal court might want to determine which of Barcelona's privileges should stand and which ones should give way to the needs of the monarchy in matters such as commercial policy or the payment of the quint. Likewise, for royal judges, allowing the consellers to override any privileges, even if only those belonging to artisans, might limit the king's power to grant privileges or undermine the royal tribunal's claim to interpret all privileges.

Ultimately, the disputes over master craft confraternities' privileges were one more context in which Catalans and their monarch struggled over the principles of legality and necessity. Neither side had a clear-cut position in that struggle, but rather shifted positions depending on the issues at hand. In the debates over banditry and the king's financial difficulties, royal authorities were squarely on the side of necessity and Catalan authorities on the side of legality. However, this was not always the case. Although Barcelona and other Catalan towns denounced the arbitrariness of royal demands for the quint, sometimes they could be less hostile to the idea of applying strong medicine to cure the problem of banditry. Likewise, confronted with serious economic difficulties, the Consell de Cent underscored the necessity to establish legislation that critics declared contrary to Catalan laws or to craft confraternity privileges. Similarly, craft confraternities sometimes called for swift action and other times insisted on the inviolability of their privileges. Even the royal government sometimes came down on the side of legality, when the Audiència defended masters' privileges against actions that the Consell de Cent claimed had been taken for the good of the city.

If the legality/necessity divide appears permeable, it is in part because this dichotomy was more rhetorical than real. Even ardent critics of Catalans' excessive freedom did not argue that a good and just government could exist outside of legality. To disregard the law would have made any viceroy or monarch a tyrant. Arguments for the necessity to disregard or abrogate laws and privileges insisted all along on their legality.

113. AHCB Gremis 35-34 ("Tresllats de plets" 1681–83): memorandum on the tanners' suits.

In the end the problems of Philip III's reign, although unprecedented in their magnitude, revolved around an old but fundamental question: Who in Catalonia could determine which laws were to be maintained and which ones needed to be superseded? This question was at the heart of the conflicts between the royal government and the Diputació over the publication of the 1599 constitutions or between the Audiència and the Consell de Cent over who had the power to determine which craft confraternity privileges could stand and which ones could not. This was also the issue confronted by the Diputació and the Audiència in 1588 and 1591 in the cases of Joan de Queralt and Granollachs. When Philip III died in March 1621, this thorny matter remained unsolved. Reaffirming the Audiència's claim as the ultimate legal authority in the principality would become one of the defining issues of Philip IV's reign.

CHAPTER SIX

Demand for Justice

Philip IV began his reign in 1621 with the determination to reform the royal justice system because justice was essential for good government. His program included a series of investigations called *visitas* intended to rid tribunals of bad judges and to expedite the notoriously slow flow of cases. For Barcelona's artisans, such reforms were long overdue. Over the course of the sixteenth century, master artisans, and occasionally journeymen, had increasingly become dependent on their ability to appeal to the royal Audiència in Barcelona to defend and enforce their privileges. Long delays by overworked and understaffed judges meant that cases dragged on, sometimes for years, and many craft confraternities could not afford the price of justice. The success or failure of Philip IV's reforms, therefore, could determine the fate of many artisans, their professions, and their means of making a living.

By examining artisans' motivations for and use of appeals before the Audiència of Barcelona, it is possible to open a window into their notions of justice. At its most basic, artisans believed that justice lay at the heart of the relationship between rulers and subjects, and without justice there could not be good government; for this reason, they had high expectations of those officials charged with the duty to dispense justice. Artisans saw justice not as a gift but as something they could demand, and if one court did not satisfy that demand, they would seek it in another.

From a broader perspective, artisans' appeals to the Audiència pointed to two important problems in the relations between Catalans and their king. The first problem involved the Consell de Cent's authority over the

FIGURE 5 Philip IV flanked by four continents. From Virgilio Malvezzi, *Sucesos principales de la monarquía de España en el año de mil i seiscientos i treinta i nueve* (Madrid, 1640). Courtesy of the Kenneth Spencer Research Library, University of Kansas.

city's craft confraternities, which Barcelona's officials insisted belonged exclusively to the Consell. The second problem involved the royal tribunal's ability to meet artisans' demand for justice. The possibility of presenting appeals to royal judges meant that artisans could look to the king's officers as a source of justice. But what if the monarchy chose not to admit such appeals? And even if they were accepted, what if conditions in the Audiència of Barcelona were such that the judges took an excessively long time to make their final pronouncements? To understand the significance of such problems, one must first determine how much artisans relied on the royal court.

Artisans and the Audiència

Master artisans' craft confraternities appealed to the Audiència to defend their corporate privileges from competing confraternities or the Consell de Cent.[1] The Confraternity of Master Tanners and Curriers *(blanquers i assaonadors)* provides a clear example. In 1552, the Consell de Cent approved an ordinance that curtailed the confraternity's authority over the leather trade. Its masters appealed to the Audiència. The royal judges ruled in favor of the masters and declared the city ordinance invalid.[2] In 1574, more suits and appeals invalidated a similar city ordinance. And again in 1601, 1611, and 1619, master tanners-curriers appealed to the royal tribunal in suits against the city and won each time.[3] Only in 1684, after the Consell de Cent disbanded the confraternity for appealing to the Audiència, did the master tanners and curriers finally give in to the city.

Throughout the sixteenth and seventeenth centuries, other Barcelona artisans also took great risks in order to appeal to royal justice.[4] The Consell de Cent repeatedly protested such appeals, insisting that the Audiència had no jurisdiction over cases involving artisan professional craft confraternities and colleges.[5] The Consell de Cent threatened to bar artisans from municipal office and to abolish their craft confraternities if they took

1. Parts of this chapter appeared in "The Painter Who Lost His Hat: Artisans and Justice in Early Modern Barcelona," *Sixteenth Century Journal* 29 (1998): 1021–40.

2. AHCB Gremis 35-90 ("Llibre d'ordinacions" 1422–1710): tanners' book of ordinances. Their dispute began in 1552, after the Consell de Cent annulled a fifteenth-century ordinance that required every person buying or selling leather in Barcelona to report it to the tanners' confraternity.

3. In 1601, the Consell de Cent defended the refusal of four individuals—most likely leather tax farmers—to inform the tanners' confraternity of their leather imports. The four men claimed that the 1574 ordinance, which exempted anyone who was not a master tanner from reporting purchases of leather, had not been repealed and remained in force. The Consell de Cent asserted that King Ferdinand's privilege of 1506 allowed it to repeal any ordinance whenever it deemed necessary. The Audiència apparently ruled against the city council in 1603. For the 1611 ordinance, see AHCB CC II-120 (Delibs. 1610–11), fol. 278. For the 30 August 1619 ordinance, see *RB*, 5:225. The ordinances of 1611, 1616, and 1619 are described in Jaime Carrera Pujal, *Historia política y económica de Cataluña: Siglos XVI al XVIII*, 3 vols. (Barcelona, 1946–47), 2:163–65, 169–70.

4. Numerous examples in Carrera Pujal, *Historia política*, vol. 1, and *RB*, esp. vol. 5, chap. 93.

5. Barcelona cited Ferdinand the Catholic's 5 April 1509 privilege, transcribed in Jaume Vicens i Vives, *Ferran II i la ciutat de Barcelona, 1479–1516*, 3 vols. (Barcelona, 1936–37),

the city to court, sanctions that were enforced against the tanners-curriers in 1684.[6] In addition, appeals were expensive. The artisans going to court had to pay fees to lawyers, notaries, confraternity officers, and judges, which could soon consume the incomes of better-off artisan corporations such as the tanners-curriers and the shoemakers.[7] But even the much poorer cobblers and journeymen shoemakers mustered the necessary resources to appeal to the Audiència.[8] Despite artisans' lack of money and resources, and despite the threats of the Consell de Cent, artisans continued appealing to the Audiència all through the sixteenth and seventeenth centuries.

Michael Sonenscher has shown how French journeymen in the late eighteenth century became familiar with their system of justice by going to court.[9] Similarly, Barcelona artisans appealing to the royal Audiència gained firsthand experience of judges, lawyers, and judicial institutions. Those who appealed to the Audiència developed a professional relationship with lawyers, some of whom were renowned jurists. In the early seventeenth century, master shoemakers, who had one of the largest confraternities in Barcelona, hired several distinguished lawyers who eventually became Audiència judges, including Drs. Felip Vinyes, Joan Pere Fontanella (author of several legal treatises), and Miquel Carreras.[10] There might even be personal ties. Antoni Mohet, a professor of law from Flanders, described himself as a friend of master painter Guerau Vilagran.[11]

Although the precise nature of the interaction among artisans, lawyers, and judges remains unclear, elite concepts of justice were not entirely alien to artisans. When lawyers spoke on behalf of artisans in court or in legal briefs, they did not necessarily reflect their clients' ideas. Nonetheless, confraternity officers were very familiar with the general thrust of the lawyers'

---

appendix doc. no. 212; Carrera Pujal, *Historia política,* 2:153 (Charles V's 1537 privilege); *RB,* 5:275 (1605 ruling by Diego Clavero, regent of the Council of Aragon).

6. Likewise, in July 1582, the Consell de Cent disbanded the master masons' confraternity for eight years; *RB,* 5:221.

7. AHCB Gremis 1-92 ("Llibre de consells" 1613–24): meetings of the confraternity of master shoemakers, fols. 116 (8 February 1619), 126 (6 April 1620).

8. See the Audiència's inventory in ACA. The confraternity of cobblers (*ataconadors*) and journeymen shoemakers brought master shoemakers to court in 1630 and 1631; AHCB Gremis 1-93 ("Llibre de consells" 1613–24), fols. 131, 150.

9. Michael Sonenscher, "Journeymen, the Courts, and the French Trades, 1781–91," *Past and Present* 114 (February 1987): 85.

10. AHCB Gremis 1-92 ("Llibre de consells" 1613–24), fols. 29v, 35r (Carreras); AHCB Gremis 1-7 ("Llibre de rebudes i dates" 1625–36), fol. 36 (Fontanella); AHCB Gremis 1-6 ("Llibre de promenia" 1622), fol. 35r (Vinyes).

11. ACA CA llig. 273 no. 37: "Copia autentica informationis contra mag[nifi]cum Michaele Carreres Judicum regie" (1624).

arguments used in court; and those arguments centered above all on the defense of their confraternities' privileges, which, as I showed in the previous chapter, were essential to artisans' professional lives.

Artisans, not just their lawyers, did much to defend their privileges. Confraternity officers kept copies of privileges, ordinances, lawyers' arguments, and judges' decisions in their corporate archives as ammunition for court battles.[12] These came in handy not only during Audiència appeals but also as part of the regular business of the trade. Officers of masters' confraternities and colleges acted as judges over disputes in their trades. In this sense, James Farr's conclusions about Dijon artisans apply as well to Barcelona: "Craftsmen . . . had some familiarity with the law and were willing to exploit it to their advantage."[13]

Barcelona artisans' demands for royal justice reflected a broader trend in Catalonia. The total number of civil cases brought before the Audiència reached its highest point in 1603, with 1,593 cases. After that, the number of cases declined, but not by much: 1,290 in 1630 and 1,239 in 1631.[14] Although the documentation does not indicate how many of these cases involved artisans, appeals by master artisans—and occasionally journeymen—were not rare. Another piece of evidence indicates the widespread recognition by royal authorities that demand for appeals to the Audiència came from a large cross section of Barcelona's population. Between the late sixteenth century and the first half of the seventeenth century, Spanish kings threatened to take the Audiència away from the city to force its inhabitants to submit to royal will. In 1588, Philip II and his ministers considered the possible effect of taking such action, convinced that the poor and the powerless in Barcelona would miss the Audiència the most.[15] This proposed action never took place, largely out of concern that the judges' departure might trigger riots in the streets. In 1591, the king agreed to order the court's transfer from Barcelona despite reports that there was "great worry about the people becoming disorderly once they feel the harm caused by the absence of the viceroy and the Audiència."[16] Although the Audiència's removal was not the only issue at stake, there is no doubt that

12. Surviving documentation from craft confraternity archives forms the core of the Gremis section in AHCB.

13. James Farr, *Hands of Honor: Artisans and Their World in Dijon, 1550–1650* (Ithaca, 1988), 212.

14. James S. Amelang, "Barristers and Judges in Early Modern Barcelona: The Rise of a Legal Elite," *American Historical Review* 89 (1984): 1271 (table 3) and 1276.

15. ACA CA llig. 266 no. 22: Miquel Joan Quintana (Catalan regent of the Council of Aragon) to King, [after 22 August] 1588.

16. ACA CA llig. 266 no. 34: *consulta,* 10 August 1591.

Barcelona made concessions to the royal government in order to bring back the royal court. Philip IV used the same threat to transfer the Audiència again in 1622 to force Barcelona to make political compromises— and this would not be the last time this king made this threat.[17]

Contemporary sources indicate that the threat to remove the Audiència from Barcelona carried considerable weight in the city because of the desire of many of its people to have close access to justice, and among those people were artisans. If artisans and journeymen had perceived the high court as inherently contrary to their interests, they would not have invested the considerable time and money it took to appeal. Artisans' repeated appeals depended on the public confidence in judges. If judges were perceived as being unfair, the credibility of the justice system would suffer. This was what master painter Guerau Vilagran implied when he accused judge Carreras of being an "evil magistrate" and asserted the need for King Philip IV to dismiss him.[18] Vilagran wrote to the king accusing the judge of using excessive force and of dishonoring him during a brawl near Barcelona in 1624. In saying that "God would be greatly served" by getting rid of a bad judge such as Carreras, Vilagran recalled the well-established belief that judges who failed to perform their duties properly would incur divine wrath. After all, dispensing justice was no ordinary task. Indeed, Spanish writers of the period described the duties of a judge as "a sacred trust."[19]

Although we lack statements such as Vilagran's from other Barcelona artisans about the divine nature of justice, there is evidence that the concept was widespread. Paul Freedman has argued that Catalan peasants were familiar with notions of "Christian justice" drawn from the Bible.[20] The image of God presiding at the Last Judgment had a long tradition in Catholic iconography, a tradition reflected in Spanish *autos-de-fe*.[21] The quasi-ecclesiastic attire of judges was also a reminder to everyone of the solemnity of their duties.

Catholics and Protestants in sixteenth- and seventeenth-century Europe widely acknowledged the sacred nature of delivering justice, of which they

---

17. John H. Elliott, *The Revolt of the Catalans: A Study in the Decline of Spain, 1598–1640* (Cambridge, 1963), 156.

18. For Vilagran's case, see Corteguera, "The Painter Who Lost His Hat."

19. Richard L. Kagan, *Lawsuits and Litigants in Castile, 1500–1700* (Chapel Hill, 1981), 182.

20. Paul Freedman, "The German and Catalan Peasant Revolts," *American Historical Review* 98 (February 1993): 50, 53–54.

21. Maureen Flynn, "Mimesis of the Last Judgment: The Spanish *Auto de fe*," *Sixteenth Century Journal* 22 (1991): 281–88.

found ample evidence in the Bible. For example, the renowned French jurist Jean de Coras quoted from the Book of Deuteronomy to describe judges as a vehicle for divine justice: "Judgment is a thing of God; and the judge is His minister and attorney, who is not allowed to give away that which is God's."[22] Joan Pau Xammar, a distinguished Catalan lawyer from the seventeenth century, cited Proverbs 8:15 to declare that God was the source of justice: "By me kings reign, and princes decree justice."[23] The Spaniard Alejo Salgado Correa's 1566 *Rule of Judges* asserts that in order to uphold such a serious duty, every judge has "to live very prudently [and be] warned that if he wishes [not] to fall from divine grace, he not consent to any sin that might be a disservice to God."[24] An English manual for justices of the peace warned that the worst thing a judge could do was to allow the wicked to go unpunished and the just to suffer injustice; and to underscore the warning, the anonymous author used an epigraph from Proverbs 17:15: "He that justifieth the wicked, and he that condemneth the just: even they both are abomination to the Lord."[25]

"Evil Judges" and the "Bad Administration" of Royal Justice

The sacred nature of justice and the threat of God's punishment were at the heart of a popular story that began circulating in Catalonia in the 1620s. In 1620, Friar Joan de Canet related the tale of a peasant from northern Catalonia named Pere Porter who had allegedly visited hell some years before. Porter reported seeing several Audiència judges there who had died shortly before; he described their punishments for alleged sins while in office.[26] Regardless of whether Porter made up his story for some undetermined purpose or honestly believed he had been to hell, he still offered a scathing critique of abuses in the Catalan justice system and a warning to bad judges who persisted in their evil ways.

Porter's story became popular because it struck a chord at a time when the royal justice system in Spain faced increasing criticism for its numerous problems.[27] Although the king had agreed in 1599 to conduct a *visita,*

---

22. Jean de Coras, *Discours des parties et office d'un bon et entier juge* (Lyon, 1605), 43.

23. Joan Pau Xammar, *De officio iudicis, et advocati liber unus* (Barcelona, 1639); quoted in Víctor Ferro, *El dret públic català: Les institucions a Catalunya fins al Decret de Nova Planta* (Vic, 1987), 289 n. 1.

24. Alejo Salgado Correa, *Libro nombrado regimiento de jueces* (Seville, 1556), 4, quoted in Kagan, *Lawsuits,* 182.

25. *A manuell, or a justice of peace his vade-mecum* (Cambridge, 1641).

26. *Viatge a l'infern d'en Pere Porter,* ed. Josep Maria Pons i Guri (Barcelona, 1999).

27. Kagan, *Lawsuits,* 212–35.

or review, of Barcelona's Audiència every six years, in 1624 there were complaints that a decade had gone by since the last one.[28] In 1624, the same year in which master painter Vilagran accused judge Carreras of being an "evil magistrate," there were revelations of serious problems in the Barcelona tribunal. A December 1624 memorandum by the Council of Aragon outlined excessive delays in the Audiència's handling of cases. The same document also complained that numerous cases were never dispatched.[29] It explained that Philip IV frequently made matters worse by issuing letters allowing some cases to be tried before others that had been waiting longer for a hearing. Judges were told to dispatch cases within a "competent time," but they had too much work and too few resources. More money, rather than more orders, might have alleviated these problems. But the Council of Aragon insisted there was not even enough money for "ordinary obligations." Low salaries kept good candidates away from the high court's offices, which fell on men of "lesser abilities." Although the memorandum did not admit any injustices, it concluded that in Catalonia, justice was *desauctorizadissima*—without authority.[30]

Artisans may not have known the details of these problems in the royal justice system in Catalonia, but they were aware that something was wrong. The delays, which resulted in higher costs and lengthy trials, affected everyone who appealed to the Audiència, including master artisans. Although complaints about the slowness of the tribunal were not new, in the 1620s there was a sense of urgency.[31]

Correcting the "bad administration" of justice was a major concern to the royal government and elicited much public discussion in the 1620s. In 1623, Jerónimo de Zeballos's influential *Royal Art for the Good Government of Kings, Princes, and Their Subjects* explained the nature of the problem: Every "republic . . . goes into *declinación* [decline] either by bad government . . . or by natural causes that proceed from time itself."[32] Bad government, however, could be cured through reform, beginning by rooting

28. Elliott, *Revolt of the Catalans*, 89.
29. ACA CA llig. 273 no. 2: *consulta*, 20 December 1624.
30. ACA CA llig. 273 no. 21: *consulta*, 8 August 1626.
31. The 1585 Catalan Corts approved the creation of the Audiència's Third Chamber to solve the long-standing problem of delays in the tribunal's civil and criminal chambers; Amelang, "Barristers and Judges," 1276. Allegations that insufficient salaries restricted the choice of good candidates for offices in the royal justice system date from at least the mid-sixteenth century; for examples, see Xavier Torres i Sans, *Els bandolers (s. XVI–XVII)* (Vic, 1991), 163, 175.
32. Jerónimo de Zeballos, *Arte real para el buen govierno de los reyes, y príncipes, y de sus vasallos* (Toledo, 1623), 4; quoted in J. H. Elliott, "Self-Perception and Decline in Early Seventeenth-

out all those responsible for abusing the government of the monarchy. Such a theory lay behind the determination of the count-duke of Olivares, Philip IV's chief minister, to restore good government in order to set Spain on the course of renewed greatness. Beginning in 1621, Olivares launched the monarchy on a crusade of reform. In a memorandum to Philip IV written between 1624 and 1629, Olivares argued, "The remaining business in these kingdoms comes down to concern for *justice and its good administration,* preserving equity among Your Majesty's subjects, and keeping them dependent on you" (my emphasis).[33]

In the early 1600s, "projectors" or *arbitrista* showered the court with every imaginable proposed project or advice—serious as well as ludicrous—on how to correct the mounting problems of the monarchy in order to prevent its decline.[34] Jean Vilar, who studied the character of the arbitrista in late-sixteenth- and seventeenth-century Spanish literature, shows that many of these projectors were "men of little standing."[35] We know of at least one Barcelona artisan who was an arbitrista. Pau Pedrola, a master mercer, wrote two pamphlets in the 1620s to local authorities on how to fix a variety of problems.[36] In 1632, Pedrola wrote to a secretary of the king of Spain with a proposal for a lottery to solve the royal fiscal problems.[37] Pedrola, like other arbitristas, assumed he had a duty to address his rulers on matters concerning the common good of the monarchy. It was the same sense of duty that moved a peasant to stand before Philip IV during a Corpus Christi procession to warn the king that "everybody fools the king. Sir, this monarchy is coming to an end, and whoever doesn't remedy it will burn in hell."[38]

Century Spain," in *Spain and Its World, 1500–1700: Selected Essays* (New Haven, 1989), 249.

33. Quoted in J. H. Elliott, *The Count-Duke of Olivares: The Statesman in an Age of Decline* (New Haven, 1986), 201.

34. Elliott, "Self-Perception," 234; Pierre Vilar, "The Age of Don Quixote," trans. Richard Morris, in *Essays in European Economic History,* ed. Peter Earle (Oxford, 1974), 100–113.

35. Jean Vilar Berrogain, *Literatura y economía: La figura satírica del arbitrista en el Siglo de Oro* (Madrid, 1973), 37.

36. BC F. Bon. 6558: [Pau Pedrola], *Molt illustres senyors diputats* (Barcelona, 1626); and BC F. Bon. 5409: Pau Pedrola, *Memorial de arbitres* (Barcelona, 1628).

37. ACA CA llig. 503: Pedrola to Juan Lorenzo de Villanueva (secretary of Catalonia in the Council of Aragon), 24 August 1632.

38. José Pellicer de Tovar, *Avisos históricos,* in Antonio Valladares, *Semanario erudito* (Madrid, 1790), quoted in María de Jesús de Agreda, *Cartas de la Venerable Madre Sor María de Ágreda y del Señor Rey Felipe IV,* ed. Francisco Silvela, 2 vols. (Madrid, 1885–86), 1:43. For examples of visionaries of humble background who warned their kings of dangers to the Spanish monarchy, see Richard L. Kagan, *Lucrecia's Dreams: Politics and Prophecy in Sixteenth-Century Spain* (Berkeley, 1990).

The king, as the source of earthly justice, seemed the only one left who could correct the bad administration of the royal justice system. As the friar Alonso de Castrillo explained, the king was the source of justice on earth.[39] The king was *vicedios*—"God's lieutenant."[40] Parallels between the king and God were commonly reinforced through ritual, art, and literature. In his play *Valor, fortuna y lealtad* (Valor, Fortune, and Loyalty), Lope de Vega, one of the most popular playwrights of early-seventeenth-century Spain, had one peasant explain to another the status of the monarch. Of course the king is a man, "yet a man made god [*endiosado*]: a king is God on earth."[41] God was commonly described as the "king of heaven," who had a court full of saintly favorites who might act as advocates for human beings to plead for mercy, favors, and justice.[42]

It has been customary to see such claims of the divine character of Spanish monarchs as encouraging a widening distance between king and subject. But an increasingly "invisible" king still remained someone subjects felt they could appeal to for justice. Although Barcelona artisans got to see less of their kings during the course of the sixteenth and seventeenth centuries, they looked up to the monarchs as they did to God and hoped to obtain from them "graces" (mercès) such as privileges for their confraternities. Likewise, just as all Christians could plead for divine justice, so too could the king's subjects appeal to royal justice. In the 1620s, the Welsh courtier James Howell was struck by the dignified style with which these demands for justice were made:

> Here it is not the style to claw and compliment with the king, or idolize him by "Sacred Sovereign" and "Most Excellent Majesty." But the Spaniard, when he petitions to his King, gives him no other character but "Sir," and so relating his business, at the end doth ask and demand justice of him.[43]

39. J. A. Fernández-Santamaria, *The State, War, and Peace: Spanish Political Thought in the Renaissance, 1516–1559* (Cambridge, 1977), 29.

40. Carmelo Lisón Tolosana, "Realeza," in *La imagen del rey (monarquía, realeza y poder ritual en la Casa de los Austrias)* (Madrid, 1991); José Antonio Maravall, *Teoría del estado en España en el siglo XVII*, 2d ed. (Madrid, 1997), 197–99. For examples in France and England, see *Cambridge History of Political Thought, 1450–1700*, ed. J. H. Burns with Mark Goldie (Cambridge, 1991), 80, 180.

41. Quoted in Antonio Feros, " 'Vicedioses, pero humanos': El drama del Rey," *Cuadernos de Historia Moderna* 14 (1993): 111.

42. For numerous examples of parallels made between earthly and heavenly courts, see María de Jesús de Agreda, *Cartas de Sor María de Jesús de Ágreda y de Felipe IV*, ed. Carlos Seco Serrano, vols. 108–9 of *Biblioteca de Autores Españoles* (Madrid, 1958).

43. R. A. Stradling, *Philip IV and the Government of Spain, 1621–1665* (Cambridge, 1988), 14.

Despite this, to Roman Catholics, who were perhaps more used to seeing their God as a human Christ, the humanity of the king did not necessarily imply that he was less divine.

This vision of kingship has been termed "naïve monarchism," which inspired artisans and peasants throughout Europe to seek their rulers' intervention to remedy wrongs.[44] Naïve or not, such principles shaped the attitudes of subjects toward their rulers and offered a standard against which to evaluate the monarchy. In the end, of course, it is difficult to say whether painter Vilagran, mercer Pedrola, peasant Porter, and their contemporaries were ingenuous enough to expect their rulers to measure up to the ideals of kingship or whether they simply manipulated the rhetoric with the hope of winning something for themselves.

Artisans' Justice

Was Barcelona's master artisans' notion of justice "popular"? For several decades, historians have maintained that popular conceptions of justice informed various aspects of early modern popular culture. Most have concluded that artisans and peasants had a sense of "social justice." For instance, George Rudé argues that popular riots showed a "rough-and-ready kind of 'natural justice' " as well as a "traditional 'leveling' instinct" that moved the poor to seek an "elementary social justice."[45] E. P. Thompson's notion of a "just price" assumes a form of economic justice that also inspired riots.[46] But popular justice also had a more negative side. All over Europe, peasants and artisans believed in the myth of the just king, "a Solomon-figure, the judge seated on his throne, the father of his people, described with adjectives like 'just,' 'wise,' and 'merciful.'"[47] This belief allegedly responded to a naïve conception of justice that perpetuated the subjection of the popular classes by the dominant classes.[48]

Behind these arguments lie several assumptions about the difference between popular and elite ideas about justice. First, popular justice had to be

---

44. David Martin Luebke, *His Majesty's Rebels: Communities, Factions, and Rural Revolt in the Black Forest, 1725–1745* (Ithaca, 1997), 172–73.

45. George Rudé, *The Crowd in History: A Study of Popular Disturbances in France and England, 1730–1848* (New York, 1964), 6, 224.

46. E. P. Thompson, "The Moral Economy of the English Crowd in the Eighteenth Century," in *Customs in Common: Studies in Traditional Popular Culture* (New York, 1993), 185–258.

47. Peter Burke, *Popular Culture in Early Modern Europe* (London, 1978), 151.

48. E. J. Hobsbawm, *Primitive Rebels: Studies in Archaic Forms of Social Movement in the Nineteenth and Twentieth Centuries* (1959; reprint, New York, 1965), 120.

different from the more sophisticated interpretations of justice held by jurists, political writers, or scholars. The latter often based their definitions of justice on written sources not readily available to the general public. In contrast, artisans and peasants drew their notions of fairness or injustice from customs and experience.[49] Second, it has long been assumed that law, justice, and judicial systems in general were stacked against those who were "dominated" and contributed to their domination.[50] Popular justice relied instead on usually violent extrajudicial and extralegal means, such as riot or revolt.[51] Participation by the "dominated" in formal justice systems therefore represented the imposition of a "hegemonic" definition of justice.

More recent work has dispelled or revised some of these assumptions. Although it is fair to state that judicial systems tended not to favor peasant and artisan men and women, there were notable exceptions. Master artisans and even journeymen who hired lawyers and went to courts of law sometimes succeeded in defending their interests.[52] Artisans occasionally used the courts to exploit divisions among the "dominant classes." For instance, city, noble, and royal authorities sometimes engaged in jurisdictional battles that resulted in benefits for artisans and peasants.[53] Likewise, the myth of the just king could challenge, rather than reaffirm, the subjection of artisans and peasants.[54] Declaring that the king was always just could be a strategy to challenge government policies and even to terminate allegiance to the ruler: A just king would not allow his ministers to take unjust actions, and if he did, he ought not to be king.[55]

49. George Rudé, *Ideology and Popular Protest*, reprint, with a foreword by Harvey J. Kaye (Chapel Hill, 1995), 22. For the connection between experience and "social justice," see Barrington Moore Jr., *Social Origins of Dictatorship and Democracy* (Boston, 1966), and Moore's *Injustice: The Social Bases of Obedience and Revolt* (White Plains, N.Y., 1978), 5–15, 23–25.

50. For example, see Pedro L. Lorenzo Cadarso, *Los conflictos populares en Castilla (siglos XVI–XVII)* (Madrid, 1996), 158–65.

51. Yves-Marie Bercé, *History of Peasant Revolts: The Social Origins of Rebellion in Early Modern France*, trans. Amanda Whitmore (Ithaca, 1990), 219; Michel Foucault, "On Popular Justice: A Discussion with Maoists," in *Power/Knowledge: Selected Interviews and Other Writings*, ed. Colin Gordon (New York, 1980), 1–36. J. S. Bromley has argued that pirates had their own "freebooter justice"; see his "Outlaws at Sea, 1660–1720: Liberty, Equality, and Fraternity among the Caribbean Freebooters," in *History from Below: Studies in Popular Protest and Popular Ideology*, ed. Frederick Krantz (Oxford, 1988), 315.

52. Sonenscher, "Journeymen," 77–109.

53. Farr, *Hands of Honor*, 32–35, 50–55; Carlo Poni, "Norms and Disputes: The Shoemakers' Guild in Eighteenth-Century Bologna," *Past and Present* 123 (May 1989): 80–108.

54. James C. Scott, *Weapons of the Weak: Everyday Forms of Peasant Resistance* (New Haven, 1985), 333.

55. See, for instance, David Martin Luebke, "Of Emperors and the Queen of Heaven: The Seditious Uses of 'Naive Monarchism' and Marian Veneration in Early Modern Germany," *Past and Present* 154 (February 1997): 71–106.

Barcelona artisans conceived of justice in ways that challenge long-standing descriptions of popular justice. These artisans expected the system of royal justice to work to their advantage. Those expectations were based not on naïve trust in royal judges or the king but on the fact that artisans won cases. These appeals further suggest that artisan conceptions of justice were not strictly social or economic. Artisans shared basic assumptions about justice with their erudite contemporaries. The distinction between popular and elite notions of justice is hardly clear-cut.

Do these examples from Barcelona artisans' ideas and actions confirm the existence of "popular justice"? An answer depends on what is meant by "popular." On the one hand, if "popular" means belonging to the *poble menut* —the *menu peuple,* or "little people," of Barcelona—the answer is yes. It is clear that artisans had developed notions of justice that inspired some of their actions. Yet those actions did not have to be extrajudicial or violent. Artisans regularly appealed for and expected justice. Money spent on lawyers, notarial work, and court fees and the time consumed in litigation indicate that artisans were willing to undergo considerable financial and political risks to get the justice they felt they deserved.

Although appeals to the Audiència were especially important to artisans for the defense of their craft confraternities' privileges, artisans also sought justice in other tribunals. In the tribunal of Barcelona's *veguer,* a lower royal court that handled small civil claims and some minor criminal offenses, artisan men and women of modest means sought justice for fairly minor matters.[56] Artisans did not rely exclusively on courts to obtain justice. In the case of confraternity officers, we find artisans delivering justice to members of their own trades. It is likely that there were other, informal methods by which artisans sought justice, perhaps by going to the parish priest or to neighbors, about which we still know very little. In this context, resorting to violence as a means to secure justice appears to have resulted from a breakdown of the formal and informal systems of justice.[57]

On the other hand, artisans' ideas about justice were not necessarily popular in the sense that they were distinct from elite conceptions of justice. Rather, popular and elite ideas of justice shared a core of assumptions that were neither inherently popular nor elite. This common ground included the very assumption that there was such a thing as justice. In addition, it was widely recognized that justice should emanate from the monarch, that

56. The papers of the *veguer*'s court are in AHCB. There were also other tribunals, such as ecclesiastical courts, which I have not investigated.

57. According to Sonenscher, "The 'typical form of protest' in the eighteenth-century trades was neither the food riot nor the strike, but . . . the lawsuit" ("Journeymen," 90).

there was a divine connection to justice (such as the belief that God was a judge). There were also widely shared assumptions about standards of fairness and the actions of those charged with the duty to dispense justice on earth. At their most basic, these assumptions were part of a commonsense feeling about justice that might often require little or no explanation, although they might equally serve as starting points for highly complex works by jurists.[58] Artisans may have shaped their ideas about justice through contact with institutions and people representing Barcelona's legal and political elite of lawyers and judges.

Artisans' daily struggle for justice in early modern Barcelona forced them to appeal to institutions and arguments dominated by men belonging to different professional and social backgrounds. Theirs was not, however, a struggle between popular and elite notions of politics: It was about artisans' demand for justice.

Justice and the Crown

Having royal justice as a recourse was important to artisans for several reasons. The preservation of their craft confraternities' privileges depended on their being able to present appeals before the Audiència judges. But if they could not appeal, artisans would lose one important means of countering challenges to their privileges. And if they could not defend their privileges, artisans' craft confraternities, their trades, and even their livelihoods could be at risk.

From the 1620s on, two circumstances made artisans' demand for justice increasingly difficult. On the one hand, as their economic situation worsened, artisans faced a more difficult task of paying for their court trials. On the other hand, the reform of the royal justice system did not resolve the most pressing problems in the Audiència, which in turn made cases take longer and cost more to artisans.

None of these changes in artisans' access to royal justice happened overnight. All through the seventeenth century, craft confraternities continued to appeal to royal judges, even if sustaining those appeals seemed more difficult. In the end, however, artisans found their positions weakened, and the privileges they had once used to defend their interests were less reliable than they had once been.

58. For the notion of "common sense," see Thompson, *Customs in Common*, 10. Thompson has been influenced by Antonio Gramsci's use of this term; see Gramsci's *Selections from the Prison Notebooks of Antonio Gramsci*, ed. and trans. Quentin Hoare and Geoffrey Nowell Smith (New York, 1971), 323, 325–26.

In 1640, Diego Saavedra Fajardo wrote: "The center of justice makes the circumference of the crown. The latter would not be necessary if one could live without the former."[59] Even when the king had already become an unfamiliar figure who rarely visited the Catalan capital, at least he had remained for many the ultimate source of justice. In his absence, royal judges had provided a court of appeal. As access to royal justice became more difficult, one of the principal bonds between Barcelona's artisans and the Spanish monarchy loosened.

59. "Del centro de la justicia se sacó la circunferencia de la Corona. No fuera necesaria ésta, si se pudiera bivir sin aquélla"; Diego Saavedra Fajardo, *Idea de un principe politico christiano representada en cien empresas* (Munich, 1640), 124 (*empresa* 8).

CHAPTER SEVEN

Refusing to Fight

King Philip IV paired the reform of justice to restore good government with the pursuit of war to restore the Spanish monarchy's reputation abroad. Thus in 1621, the same year he rose to power, the king renewed the war between the Spanish monarchy and the Dutch republic after their twelve-year truce expired. Not long after, the monarchy became involved in conflicts in the Holy Roman Empire, in Italy, and, by the middle of the 1630s, in France. For the count-duke of Olivares, success in these wars depended on the participation of all the king's subjects in a "union of arms." Yet throughout the Spanish Habsburg lands, the ministers' program faced strong opposition. In the 1630s, riots in the Basque Country and Portugal protested heavy taxes; Naples complained of excessive royal demands; and Castilians of all social backgrounds resisted the king's repeated demands for soldiers and money.

Catalans also rejected royal demands to increase the principality's share of the monarchy's war effort, and in Barcelona that opposition was not limited to city and Catalan authorities. When asked by royal officials to contribute soldiers and money, Barcelona's master artisans responded with little more than symbolic gestures. Volunteers were hard to find in the city, and those who agreed to fight demanded fair payment for their service. Suspicions that officials were breaking laws or disregarding privileges would lead to a variety of forms of resistance that included protests, desertion, and—only rarely—riots.

Popular resistance to military service in Barcelona became a highly divisive issue for Catalans and their king because each side saw it as a serious deviation from the expected relations between subjects and rulers. To Olivares, to the viceroys of Catalonia, and to their subordinates, resistance was nothing more than disobedience, which went against everything that defined a good and loyal subject. In contrast, Catalans insisted that they had made many generous sacrifices and that the insatiable demand of royal ministers and officers threatened to bring misery to the principality and to violate the laws and privileges of the pàtria. Nevertheless, Barcelonese, Catalan, and royal authorities all agreed that enlisted men had to comply with orders to fight, and they all considered riots and desertion to be criminal actions worthy of exemplary punishment.

However, on closer examination, it is clear that popular forms of resistance in Barcelona were also shaped by the inhabitants' understanding of the relations between subjects and rulers. Resistance to military service was not a sign of disloyalty or disobedience. In the war against France, Catalan soldiers would demonstrate great courage, which was inspired by their love for their pàtria and loyalty to their king. As Ruth MacKay has found in the case of popular resistance to military levies in Castile, the decision of Barcelona artisans and ordinary Catalans to riot, to desert, or simply to disobey orders responded in most cases to popular understanding of their duties as subjects, as well as to the expectation that the ruler should recognize their service with rewards.[1]

War

When France declared war on the Spanish monarchy in May 1635, Catalans could expect to see hostilities in the principality. During the last conflict between 1595 and 1598, Catalonia's long frontier with France had made it a major battleground. Control of the passes along the Pyrenees was crucial for any invasion by either side. Catalans had been fortunate: the peace treaty ending that war in 1598 had held the longest of any in more than a century. Yet recently that official peace had become a mirage. The Spanish Habsburg and French Bourbon dynasties had been indirectly at war with each other since 1627 in Italy and in the Holy Roman Empire.[2] For Catalans, the renewal of war in 1635 now brought those hostilities home. The decision to move from proxy war to all-out conflict also un-

---

1. Ruth MacKay, *The Limits of Royal Authority: Resistance and Obedience in Seventeenth-Century Castile* (Cambridge, 1999), chap. 4.

2. On the relations between France and Spain leading to 1635, see J. H. Elliott, *Richelieu and Olivares* (Cambridge, 1984); *The Thirty Years' War,* ed. Geoffrey Parker (London, 1987).

derscored the fact that the struggle between the two powers had reached a turning point. For the count-duke of Olivares, the war against France was over supremacy in Europe. "To my mind," he wrote to the king,

> this will lose everything irremediably or be the salvation of the ship. Here go religion, king, kingdom, nation, everything, and, if our strength is sufficient, let us die in the attempt. Better to die, and more just, than to fall under the dominion of others, and most of all of heretics, as I consider the French to be. Either all is lost, or else Castile will be head of the world, as it is already head of Your Majesty's Monarchy.[3]

In late 1635, preparations began for a triple invasion of France the following spring from the north, east, and south. The southern forces would consist of an army of 40,000 soldiers advancing from Catalonia under the command of the king himself.[4] Italians, Walloons, and Spaniards arrived in Catalonia and prepared to fight. But by January 1636, the Catalan campaign was scrapped for lack of money and men. The royal government blamed Catalans for a persistent lack of cooperation. In May 1635, the king had asked the Consell de Cent for 60,000 ducats (99,000 lliures) and 2,000 men, but he got less than half of the amount of money requested and no soldiers. Barcelona gave a "donation" of 40,000 lliures.[5] Again in March 1636, a royal request for 3,000 to 4,000 soldiers for six months from Barcelona failed.[6] Other towns and nobles followed suit.

Royal officers tried every imaginable incentive to recruit soldiers. According to the duke of Cardona, the viceroy of Catalonia, anyone who served would be exempt from billeting troops.[7] As a result, the only troops royal officers managed to recruit in 1636 were criminals whose death sentences were commuted for military service or (if the condemned had sufficient means) the offer of soldiers. One proposal included the offer of remission of court sentences—even to people found guilty by the Inquisition—in exchange for going to war.[8] These incentives, however,

---

3. Memorial of 14 June 1634, quoted in John H. Elliott, *The Revolt of the Catalans: A Study in the Decline of Spain, 1598–1640* (Cambridge, 1963), 310.

4. Memorial of 14 June 1634, quoted in Elliott, *Revolt of the Catalans*, 309.

5. Ibid., 301, 303; 1 ducat = 1.65 Catalan lliures.

6. Ibid., 318.

7. AGS GM leg. 1174: Cardona to King, 22 August 1636. On recruitment procedures in Spain, see I. A. A. Thompson, *War and Government in Habsburg Spain, 1560–1620* (London, 1976), chap. 4.

8. ACA CA llig. 235 no. 19: Bayetolá to Jerónimo de Villanueva, 12 July 1636.

had little effect. Offers of soldiers amounted to a mere 800 men, and officers complained that there were few prospects of finding any more soldiers
in the near future. Unless the king came in person, said a recruiter, it was
"totally impossible" to enlist more soldiers.[9] But once they reached the
front, these men deserted the army, along with other foreign mercenaries
hired by the king. Soldiers "fle[d] in the hundreds," reported Don Juan de
Benavides, inspector-general of the royal army.[10] The Neapolitan Lelio
Brancaccio, marquis of Montesilvano and captain general of the cavalry,
was outraged that troops "fle[d] continuously"—even after receiving their
pay![11]

In 1637, Olivares's war plans in Catalonia fared better, although they
came nothing close to his expectations. On 13 June 1637, Philip IV declared a general mobilization on the basis of the medieval usage *Princeps
namque,* which allowed the king to call for the assistance of his subjects
against enemy attack.[12] Viceroy Cardona received instructions to recruit
6,000 Catalans, paid for by towns and the nobility, to launch an attack on
France. However, the Diputació declared the mobilization invalid because
it required the presence of the king in Catalonia. And so, when Spanish
troops besieged the French fort of Leucata on 29 August 1637, only the
towns of Girona, Empúries, Olot, Santa Pau, and Peralada sent men. On 7
September, Barcelona promised 500 soldiers within three months. The
company cost Barcelona 11,000 lliures.[13] But twenty days later, the French
broke the Spanish siege and recovered Leucata before any of the Barcelona
men arrived. In Olivares's eyes, the 1637 campaign had ended with only a
halfhearted contribution by Catalans to the war.[14]

Frustrated by the royal demands and incapable of changing Catalan attitudes, the duke of Cardona resigned his office of viceroy in February
1638, less than five months after the humiliating defeat at Leucata.
Olivares concluded that the only way to make Catalans fight was to pro-

9. ACA CA llig. 235 no. 19: Bayetolá to Jerónimo de Villanueva, 28 June 1636.
10. AGS GM leg. 1174: Benavides to Fernando Ruiz de Contreras, 3 August 1636.
Fernando de Fonseca Ruiz de Contreras, marquis de la Lapilla, was secretary of the Council of War and of the Junta de Ejecución. The Junta de Ejecución, which in 1636 became
the principal body in the monarchy for the administration of war, met in Olivares's offices;
see MacKay, *Limits,* 28–29.
11. AGS GM leg. 1180: Montesilvano to Ruiz de Contreras, 8 October 1636.
12. Elliott, *Revolt of the Catalans,* 324.
13. Ibid., 333.
14. The Diputació said 3,000 Catalans served; Eva Serra i Puig, "Notes sobre l'esforç
català a la campanya de Salses: Juliol 1639, gener 1640," in *Homenatge al Doctor Sebastià García Martínez,* 3 vols. (Valencia, 1988), 2:8 n. 4.

voke a French attack on the principality during the summer of 1638; he hoped this might at last compel Catalans to defend their land. But when the prince of Condé led his French troops across the Pyrenees in July 1638, he marched through Basque country rather than Catalonia, laying siege to the fortress of Fuenterrabía. With the war far away, Catalans felt little desire to contribute. Catalans also refused to form an army of 10,000 to 12,000 soldiers, proposed by the new viceroy, the count of Santa Coloma, to defend the principality in case of a French invasion.[15] When Spanish troops broke the French siege on 27 September, Catalans had managed to avoid making any contribution.

Why did Catalans refuse to fight in the war against France? Poverty was one major reason. In many cases, soldiers claimed they could not afford to go to the front because their families needed them. In the Rosselló, the main area of fighting, small, isolated villages in the Pyrenees valleys were poor and chronically deficient in basic food and military supplies. What Rosselló had in plenty were bandits, who crisscrossed the frontier, attacking villages and stealing cattle.[16] Moreover, since 1626, troops billeted on the frontier had exhausted the area's meager economy with additional demands.[17] Food for soldiers had to be transported at considerable expense. Soldiers could not even find decent quarters. The fort of Salses, for instance, was described as "a grave for soldiers," where sixty out of one hundred men were sick from the cold wind, "and the remainder," explained one officer, "are good for nothing."[18] Those who could not stay in forts camped out in the open. Report after report complained that the soldiers faced soaking rains, cold winds, and disease. The army lacked medical facilities, and the sick died in droves. "The main cause of the undoing of soldiers," reported one officer, "was the lack of a hospital."[19]

The rest of Catalonia also considered itself too poor to contribute much. Towns, nobles, and even the city of Barcelona insisted they could not possibly fulfill the onerous demands from Madrid. Falling tax revenues and contemporary accounts confirm a rather grim picture of the Catalan economy in the early seventeenth century.[20] Even royal ministers admitted the

---

15. Elliott, *Revolt of the Catalans*, 334. For a biography of Santa Coloma, see Pere Català i Roca, *El virrei comte de Santa Coloma* (Barcelona, 1988).

16. AGS GM leg. 1262: Francesc Pasqual i de Cadell to Santa Coloma, 22 August 1639.

17. Serra, "Notes sobre l'esforç català," 22–24.

18. AGS GM leg. 1180: Montesilvano to King (?), 1 October 1636.

19. AGS GM leg. 1174: Benavides to Ruiz de Contreras, 13 August 1636.

20. Elliott, *Revolt of the Catalans*, 339.

principality was "so needy and exhausted" that it was impossible to expect much from it.[21] But poverty was clearly not the sole reason for Catalans' refusal to go to war.

Catalan resistance to the king's war demands was based on laws that prevented committing men and money to anything other than the defense of the principality. The Barcelona city guard, for instance, by law could not serve outside city territory except under imminent threat of an attack. In addition, recruitment remained voluntary: when towns sought men to go to war, they would need to recruit volunteers, so they had to sway them, usually with monetary incentives. Even where lords could demand service from vassals, it appears that recruitment still remained voluntary, as suggested in this letter by the duke of Cardona to the count of Santa Coloma, his successor as viceroy:

> Your Highness knows as well as I the efforts I made with my vassals and the pressures and threats that were used; and that no other means, whether through justice or any other way, were found except that they voluntarily chose to follow. . . . It had to be done like this because all the ministers his majesty has in this principality could find no other way to force them.[22]

The royal government, of course, saw matters differently. Jerónimo de Villanueva, protonotary of the Council of Aragon, told a Catalan ambassador in Madrid:

> It is a fine thing to call self-defense against French invasions a "service," . . . look how you people defend your constitutions . . . and refuse to go to war beyond the frontier. . . . No, sir, payment for fortifications is a matter not of grace but of justice.[23]

It would be a mistake to forget that it was not just Catalan authorities who did not want to take part in what was essentially the king's war; most of those asked to take up arms did not care for it either. Royal officers failed to enlist volunteers despite their offer that anyone who served would be exempt from billeting. Whether such widespread opposition to military service responded in any way to the reasons expressed by the Catalan ruling classes remains a mystery.

---

21. ACA CA llig. 235 no. 19: Bayetolá to King, 4 October 1636.
22. ACA CA llig. 283 no. 33: Cardona to Santa Coloma, 2 June 1638.
23. Quoted in Elliott, *Revolt of the Catalans,* 336.

Barcelona's Artisans and the War

As far as Barcelona's artisans were concerned, their attitudes to fighting for the king had little to do with obedience or allegiance to their monarch. That was never in question. Instead, the cause of popular resistance was as protonotary Villanueva had stated: Catalans saw their military duties as service. If the king expected his subjects to serve him, they expected a reward from him commensurate with their efforts.

In March 1635, the governor of Catalonia began preparations for a levy of Barcelona men by ordering all colleges and craft confraternities to report the number of journeymen and assistants in their trades, whether or not they lived with their masters.[24] Such a measure was necessary to recruit journeymen, who did not usually serve in the masters' companies. The consellers protested this intervention in the affairs of the city guard, but this only made royal officers more determined to disregard city authorities and appeal directly to Barcelona's master artisans.

Popular reactions in Barcelona to demands for assistance in the war ranged from apathy to strong opposition, depending on the means used to demand such assistance. In October 1635, royal officials appeared before several craft confraternities in an effort to elicit assistance for the war effort. But the response was cold. The few individual donations made amounted to very little. On 22 October, Lluís Ramon, legal counsel (*assessor*) to the governor, asked the mercers' craft confraternity, in the name of Philip IV, to offer some "charity" to help the king in his wars. The confraternity answered that it did not have any money. After a second visit on 2 November, the confraternity asked individual members for voluntary contributions. But when this raised little money, the confraternity finally agreed to give the modest sum of 20 lliures—or the cost of a master examination.[25] It was a respectable sum for a small confraternity, but it was obviously insufficient for the king's military aspirations.

If pleas for charity produced little, the use of force only made matters worse for royal recruiters. For instance, on 12 June 1636, rumor had it that Joan Agustí Forés had tricked six reapers (*segadors*) into enlisting and that he held them by force in his house until they were shipped to Italy.[26] A group of reapers went to the recruiter's house to protest the illegal action,

24. *RB* 5:231 (5 and 7 March 1635).

25. AHCB Gremis 4-13 ("Llibre dels consells de la confraria dels mercers botig[ue]rs de teles" 1626–49), fols. 99–100.

26. Miquel Parets, *De los muchos sucesos dignos de memoria que han ocurrido en Barcelona y otros lugares de Cataluña*, in *MHE*, vols. 20–25 (Madrid, 1888–93), 20:99–101.

but armed men sent by the governor turned them away. After the governor's men left, five hundred *segadors* returned to Forés's house. When someone inside threw a brick that killed or nearly killed a demonstrator, the enraged crowd stormed and sacked the house.[27] Forés escaped to a nearby church and was incarcerated to protect him from the rioters.[28]

A second reason for Catalans' refusal to fight was the popular perception that behind royal demands was some secret, sinister plan. It was rumored that recruits would be shipped abroad to Italy—or even worse, confined to the royal galleys. Regardless of official assurances to the contrary, Catalans refused to serve. Matías de Bayetolá, secretary of the Council of Aragon and charged with recruiting soldiers, ascribed Catalans' refusal to fight to their "aversion" to and "abhorrence" of fighting abroad, noting that Catalans were "bedeviled about trying to take their soldiers away from the province."[29] Even when the levies had supposedly rid Catalonia of "vermin" *(sabandijas),* Bayetolá explained, popular resentment of the levies was so great that no one dared to recruit soldiers "publicly."[30]

Two weeks after the riot against Forés, rumors of forced conscription incited a second riot in Barcelona.[31] Juan, a twenty-eight-year-old man from Berga, a village northwest of Barcelona, enlisted for 12 lliures cash and a salary of 2 rals a day. The recruiter then took Juan to the house of the inspector *(veedor).* On their way there, Juan said he needed to relieve himself and went over to the gallows across from the city's fish market. Nearby, a man sitting in front of the customhouse told Juan: "Where are you going? They're fooling you! They'll put you in the drassanes and you'll never leave."[32] Juan allegedly answered: "I don't care if they fool me." Then two boys aged sixteen or seventeen also warned Juan that he was being fooled and began to throw stones. Soon a crowd of about sixty men and women surrounded Juan and the recruiter. A man in the crowd pulled Juan away,

27. ACA CA llig. 220 no. 65: Aleix de Marimon to King, 3 July 1636. Marimon was governor of Catalonia and provisionally in charge of the royal government in Catalonia, awaiting the appointment of a viceroy.

28. On Forés's arrest, see Elliott, *Revolt of the Catalans,* 318–19.

29. ACA CA llig. 235 no. 19: Bayetolá to Juan Lorenzo de Villanueva, 12 July 1636.

30. ACA CA llig. 235 no. 19: Bayetolá to Juan Jerónimo de Villanueva, 5 July 1636.

31. ACA CA llig. 220 no. 65: testimony before investigation of incidents, 8 July 1636.

32. Miquel Vendrell, the soldier in the royal navy who recruited Juan, identified the man sitting before the customhouse as Jaume Pi. There is a Jaume Pi who was a merchant and son-in-law of Dr. Joan Francesc Rossell, a prominent political figure in Barcelona. Pi, along with Rossell's son, Pere Joan, and two other men were arrested during serious incidents in Barcelona on 16 June 1634; see Elliott, *Revolt of the Catalans,* 297.

telling him not to go with the recruiter because he was a traitor who sold his brother's flesh. They were taken to a tavern, where the recruiter suffered insults and more accusations of treason; he was accused of having "sold human blood" and of taking recruits by force to the shipyard. The harassed recruiter ran away and Juan disappeared.

As a result of these riots, royal efforts to enlist men in Barcelona came to a halt. No one dared recruit soldiers publicly. The royal government tried to circumvent that problem by pressuring towns and lords to do the recruiting. Although municipal institutions provided most Catalans with the first line of resistance to military service, towns were not immune to royal pressure. Even the Consell de Cent, which resisted most demands for men and money between 1636 and 1638, occasionally found it necessary to make a contribution. In 1639, the royal government exerted even greater pressure with its most drastic measure to date. After French troops invaded Rosselló and easily captured the fortress of Opol on 10 June 1639, viceroy Santa Coloma declared a *sometent general,* or general alarm. Commoners who did not enlist faced ten years in the galleys, whereas knights would suffer exile or death. The viceroy had even wanted to declare all objectors traitors, but royal magistrates dissuaded him.[33] Catalan towns promised 2,000 soldiers.[34] By 11 July, 5,000 Catalans arrived at the passes separating Rosselló from the rest of Catalonia; another 2,500 Catalans joined the 8,000 troops from other nations assigned to relieve the besieged fortress of Salses.[35]

If the royal government thought it had finally figured out a way to circumvent popular opposition to military service, it had merely fostered new forms of resistance. The royal government discovered the problem after disaster struck. On 19 July 1639, French forces took the strategic fortress of Salses, which threatened to overrun the eastern Rosselló and end Olivares's dream of Spanish greatness. At the Council of State of 1 August, ministers discussed reports that questioned Catalans' commitment of soldiers. Instead of 7,500 men, Don Cristóbal de Benavente said, the actual number of Catalan soldiers did not reach 7,000.[36] A few days later, viceroy Santa Coloma announced even more disturbing news: of the 10,000 men with which he entered Rosselló, there were only 8,000 left—in other words, 2,000 men had fled! Royal ministers in Madrid called for the use of force

33. AGS GM leg. 1289: Santa Coloma to King, 24 June 1639.
34. AGS GM leg. 1289: Santa Coloma to Olivares, 27 June 1639.
35. Elliott, *Revolt of the Catalans,* 365.
36. AGS GM leg. 1262: statement by Don Cristóbal de Benavente in Junta de Estado, 1 August 1639.

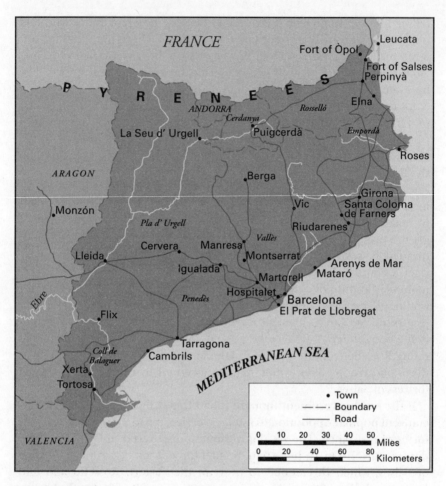

MAP 2. Catalonia

as the only way to stop Catalan unruliness. "Punishment . . . is the most effective means to correct the desertions," explained the marquis of Mirabel,
"because fear of it will do much to prevent them."[37]

After days of nonstop thunderstorms in late September 1639, the viceroy
wrote that if the rains and the winds continued, "many will fall sick and
leave en masse."[38] On 29 September, the commander of Spanish troops in
Rosselló, Felipe Spínola, second marquis of los Balbases, informed the king

37. AGS GM leg. 1262: Junta Grande, 10 August 1639.
38. AGS GM leg. 1263: Santa Coloma to King, 26 September 1639.

that Catalans "leave extremely fast each hour" and calculated the losses at about 3,000.[39] In early October, he warned the king of the imminent danger of the collapse of the entire Spanish army: "Never in my life since serving your majesty have I seen the undoing of more people than at present."[40] In November, out of 11,237 men, 9,091 Catalan soldiers were missing. The Barcelona company of 700 was reduced to 136 men.[41]

Although army officers and royal ministers complained that mass desertions reflected Catalan unwillingness to serve their king, the problem was more complex than royal authorities wanted to admit. The huge losses just cited were, of course, not solely due to desertion. Inaccurate accounting, underreporting of casualties, and above all disease explained many of the losses. The marquis of los Balbases told Olivares that some officers went so far as to hide the real number of deaths. Nevertheless, Balbases admitted some of the disappearances were probably casualties from combat and disease.[42] One royal officer alone granted 1,200 sick leaves for lack of hospital facilities in Rosselló. In fact, everyone pointed to the fear of dying from disease as the main reason for the high number of desertions. Likewise, unpaid salaries—which army officers pocketed—moved others to flee.

But disease and unpaid salary were universal reasons for desertion— which leads me to another important point: Catalans were hardly alone among deserters. Don Pedro Girón marched with a company *(tercio)* from Tolosa (in the Basque country) to Aragon. He started the long march with 1,011 men, and after one day, traveling six leagues, he lost 415 of them. The next day, he lost another 200. On the way from Tolosa to Pamplona, recruits from the province of Alava left; thereafter, Castilians, Andalusians, and Galicians followed suit; finally, 200 noble *hidalgos* refused to go on such a long journey because they were not volunteers. Allegedly, word got around that they were headed for Italy, and soldiers insisted that even if their heads were chopped off, they would not go. All Girón was left with were a few good men. But, as he added in a postscript to a letter, "after writing this, my company sergeant informed me that tonight twenty-two men and a squadron corporal have left—all people I trusted."[43]

39. AGS GM leg. 1261: Balbases to King, 23 September 1639.

40. Ironically, Balbases's father, the famous commander Ambrosio Spínola, first marquis of los Balbases, witnessed an even greater loss during the failed siege of Bergen-op-Zoom, in the Netherlands, in 1622: 9,000 soldiers, of which 1,900 may have deserted; see M. S. Anderson, *War and Society in Europe of the Old Regime, 1618–1789* (New York, 1988), 41.

41. Elliott, *Revolt of the Catalans,* 381–82.

42. AGS GM leg. 1262: Balbases to Olivares, 23 September 1639.

43. AGS GM leg. 1261: Pedro Girón to Ruiz de Contreras, 12 October 1639.

Even when it begins to seem as if no one was left in the Spanish army, there were men fighting, including some Catalans. Not everyone refused to go to war, but those who went charged a heavy price. Catalans must have been tempted by increasingly better offers to volunteers. In 1636, Juan (the man from Berga whose own recruitment led to a riot in Barcelona) enlisted for one payment of 12 lliures and a salary of 2 rals a day, or about 6 escuts monthly. He should have waited. In June 1639, some towns were paying between 7.5 and 9 escuts monthly.[44] By July 1639, Barcelona offered the king seven hundred volunteers for three months. By September, the same men demanded a hefty price for staying beyond their time: a raise of 3 rals per day, and 4 rals to the sick.[45] Even those who did not want to fight paid generously for replacements. The Barcelona master mercers, who in 1635 could hardly come up with 20 lliures for the king's wars, on 27 December 1639 voted to take a loan to offer 25 lliures to any master or son of a master and 15 lliures to any journeyman who went to Salses. On top of that, the Consell de Cent would add 25 lliures, and the merchants' guild also offered a supplement.[46] And yet only three mercers volunteered.[47]

The timing of the mercers' vote is important. Just four days before, on 23 December, the royal government outbid everyone in one of the most desperate moves of the war. Under orders from the king, viceroy Santa Coloma offered the following rewards to anyone from Barcelona who fought in Salses: titles of master to journeymen, registration in the city's gentry roll to master artisans and merchants, knighthood to the Barcelona gentry, and to knights, titles of nobility. The Consell de Cent condemned such an outrageous offer; but a riot on 27 December forced it to send the city guard to the front immediately under the command of the conseller en cap. The riot has been interpreted as reflecting the popularity of the king's offer, but new evidence raises some doubt. Several masters' confraternities promised journeymen the title of mastership before the royal decree. Moreover, masters approved the order, suggesting they still preferred journeymen to go in their place.[48] Although one might think that jour-

---

44. AGS MG leg. 1289: Santa Coloma to Olivares, 27 June 1639.

45. AGS GM leg. 1262: Junta Grande, 9 September 1639.

46. For Barcelona's payment, see Serra, "Notes sobre l'esforç català," 11.

47. AHCB Gremis 4-13 ("Llibre dels consells de la confraria dels mercers botig[ue]rs de teles" 1626–49), fol. 175.

48. On the 27 December riot, see Elliott, *Revolt of the Catalans,* 383. On 27 December, the master mercers' confraternity offered significant incentives to masters, sons of masters (25 lliures), and journeymen (15 lliures). Even on 28 December, when news reached some master mercers that the Consell de Cent would issue a call to go to the front, their confraternity sent a delegation to urge Barcelona's consellers not to comply with those orders; see

neymen would rush to take advantage of this opportunity, their numbers appear to be small. And I have not found a single case of a master from Barcelona who demanded the title of merchant or honored citizen for his services in Salses. But perhaps they did not live to do so. By the time French troops in Salses surrendered on 6 January 1640, between 4,000 and 10,000 Catalans—including a quarter of the nobility—had died of disease and wounds.[49] It represented an enormous human and financial loss that hardly altered the course of the war.

"A Thousand Prizes and Honors"

In Catalonia, Castile, and everywhere else, resistance to military service often stemmed from such mundane concerns as the cost of giving up work to fight or the fear of dying in combat or from disease. Other times, choosing to fight or not became a matter of weighing service against reward. Catalans also expressed serious concern about royal abuses of Catalonia's laws and privileges. These privileges secured a fair share of rewards by making it illegal to force Catalans to serve against their will. Laws and privileges also ensured that military service would be well paid in salaries and in "a thousand prizes and honors."[50]

In short, the great variety of forms of resistance by ordinary Catalans were informed by popular political ideas. Barcelona artisans saw their military duties as one more aspect of their relationship with the monarch, which depended on the exchange of gifts for services. Master artisans wanted to serve their king, but in return they expected titles or other honors. Contrary to the statements of a number of royal officials, this respect for privileges was not an excuse to avoid serving the king. For the majority of Catalans, loyalty to the king was not in conflict with loyalty to the pàtria, because to serve one was to serve the other. However, serving the king should not require going against their privileges and the laws of the pàtria; such a requirement would undermine the fundamental pact that bound ruler and subject—and that also made good government policy. In this sense, what MacKay has concluded about Castilians' loyalty is also true for Catalans—namely, that "loyalty was not unconditional, that their duty was derived from a pact, and that such a pact ennobled them all."[51]

AHCB Gremis 4-13: ("Llibre dels consells de la confraria dels mercers botig[ue]rs de teles" 1626–49), fols. 170, 174.

49. Elliott, *Revolt of the Catalans,* 384.
50. BC F. Bon. 6129: Fareal Guseno, *Salsas recuperada* (Barcelona, 1640).
51. MacKay, *Limits,* 177.

CHAPTER EIGHT

The Monster Unbound

On 7 June 1640, the viceroy of Catalonia, the count of Santa Coloma, lay dead on a beach near Barcelona's port with stab wounds inflicted by a sailor and a reaper *(segador)*. By Christmas of that year, crowds of agricultural workers and people from the city had also fatally stabbed, shot, or defenestrated five judges from the Audiència of Barcelona. In January 1641, Catalans severed their allegiance to the Spanish monarchy and elected France's Louis XIII as their new king.

The unprecedented popular violence in Barcelona beginning in the spring of 1640 was a response to the presence of royal troops billeted throughout the principality after the victory over France in Salses in January of that year. Accusations of abuses by royal troops against Catalan towns and villages had exacerbated tensions between Catalan and royal authorities and sparked a peasant uprising against the king's soldiers. Barcelona did not suffer any attacks by royal troops and did not billet any soldiers; yet the demonstrations and riots in the city reflected the widespread anger, especially at the viceroy and the judges of the Audiència for letting such abuses elsewhere in Catalonia go unpunished.

Although the violence was a response to immediate concerns about the royal troops in Catalonia, long-standing notions of justice, the duties of rulers and judges, and the need to defend the pàtria shaped the choice of actions and language of the crowds that took part in those events. In other words, the motivations behind the murders of prominent royal officers in Barcelona in 1640 were above all political. Rebels claimed to be defenders of the land, determined to punish the viceroy and his judges as traitors as well as to force the king to reverse his policies.

The events in Barcelona at the start of the Catalan Revolt of 1640 underscore how popular politics could have a major impact on high politics. The revolt marked a culmination in the legal and political relations between Catalonia and the Spanish monarchy, and it is important to remember that to a large extent it came about as a result of popular violence in the streets of Barcelona. Although it is not possible to demonstrate that the crowds that perpetrated a good deal of the attacks intended a break between Catalan and royal authorities, it was their actions that ultimately convinced both sides that armed confrontation would be inevitable. For this reason, it is all the more important to try to decipher the meaning of popular violence and its connection to what would become the most serious political crisis in the Spanish monarchy in the seventeenth century.

A review of the violence in Barcelona between June and December 1640 reveals two important aspects of popular politics and its relation to political history. First, even in the extreme circumstances of a revolt, popular political actions in Barcelona were consistent with patterns of popular politics in the city that went back for decades. Riots used language, actions, and ideas that were part of the popular political culture of the city. At the same time, the extreme violence and open defiance of royal authorities reveal the radical possibilities of that political culture, which were in many ways new and had a transforming impact on politics in the city and beyond. Second, despite the unwillingness of Barcelonese, Catalan, and royal authorities, popular politics became a driving force in the relations between Catalans and their king. Publicly, all these authorities denounced the armed attacks, the riots, and the murders as criminal acts that were detrimental to peace and order. However, behind those statements one often senses an ambivalent response toward popular violence. Barcelonese, Catalan, and royal authorities recognized that the abuses perpetrated by royal troops and a number of royal officials were legitimate reasons for the widespread anger throughout Catalonia. More important, authorities in Barcelona and Madrid used that anger to fault each other for contributing to the general state of lawlessness that bred the rebellion. In other words, both sides rejected the violence and at the same time used it to further their own positions without ever truly caring to find out the possible motivations of those perpetrating the violence.

"A New War"

After the Pyrrhic victory at Salses on 6 January 1640, Spanish royal authorities faced a major problem: finding a way to support the army in Catalonia until the renewal of hostilities against France in the spring.[1] The viceroy, Santa Coloma, received orders from Madrid to quarter the army south of the Rosselló, which had suffered greatly as a result of the fighting in 1639 and could not possibly fulfill all the troops' needs. Yet despite the viceroy's determination to please his king, the plan faced enormous legal and practical obstacles. Laws and privileges strictly limited Catalans' contribution to the support of the army. Moreover, royal authorities in Catalonia admitted that the principality did not have the economic resources to bear the enormous cost of feeding and lodging the troops. Many Catalans also feared the violence of rowdy troops abusing the locals and sacking their properties. Clashes between civilians and the military took place in the early months of 1640, and efforts to restrain both parties were often late and ineffective.

The billeting of the king's army became a political test. Royal ministers in Madrid and Barcelona insisted Catalonia simply had to comply with the needs of their king. To Catalan authorities, the demands seemed excessive and illegal. On 19 February 1640, the Barcelona knight Francesc Joan de Vergós, a jurat in the Consell de Cent, convinced the assembly to cancel the annual carnival celebrations to demonstrate the city's displeasure with the royal policies. Another jurat, the merchant Lleonard Serra, drafted a proposal by which the Consell de Cent declared a state of mourning to protest the billeting. Meanwhile, the diputats convened a meeting of the braços, which decried the billeting as illegal. In Madrid, the Council of Aragon deemed Vergós's and Serra's actions "detestable" because they sought to inflame popular opinion and foster an uprising.[2]

The royal government responded with extraordinarily harsh measures of its own that would inflame tensions in the city even more. It ordered the immediate commencement of billeting in Catalonia, a levy of six thousand Catalans, and the arrest of the jurats Vergós and Serra, along with that of one or more diputats. The arrest of a diputat would presumably instill "greater respect for justice and greater fear among the people."[3] Concerns that the arrests might trigger popular disorders were brushed aside, and on 10 March royal officials imprisoned the two jurats. A week later, on 18 March, at seven in the evening, the royal constable (*algutzir*) Miquel Joan

---

1. The following discussion is based on John H. Elliott, *The Revolt of the Catalans: A Study in the Decline of Spain, 1598–1640* (Cambridge, 1963), chaps. 14–15; and Eva Serra, "1640: Una revolució política: La implicació de les institucions," in *La revolució catalana de 1640* (Barcelona, 1991), 3–65.

2. ACA CA llig. 285 no. 7: *consulta,* 27 February 1640.

3. ACA CA llig. 394: Santa Coloma to King, 15 March 1640.

Monrodón arrested the noble diputat Francesc de Tamarit. Upon learning of the arrest, the *braços* and the cathedral chapter sent out calls that same evening for emergency meetings. The Consell de Cent, however, did not sound its bell to convene an assembly, concerned that it might precipitate disorders among the many curious people who had come out into the streets.[4] In the words of one Catalan nobleman, the arrests caused "the universal scandal of the people [*pueblo*], repeated complaints, public rumors, while the rabble [*la gente soez*] plotted in the squares."[5] Viceroy Santa Coloma warned that an anonymous song *(octavillas)* encouraged the general resentment against the arrest of the jurats, which had "stirred a great uneasiness" in the city. The king urged Santa Coloma to have the imprisoned diputat transferred to Perpinyà, but the viceroy could not do that without the city's assistance, and the Consell de Cent had refused to help.[6] Tamarit, Vergós, and Serra remained in Barcelona's royal prison.

During April and May 1640, the viceroy dispatched the Audiència's judges and other royal officers to towns and villages throughout northeastern Catalonia to enforce the billeting orders. Soon those efforts proved to be a disaster. Towns and villages complained that several royal judges and officials were extorting money.[7] But far more serious, clashes between the local population and royal troops resulted in extremely grave incidents. The one incident that produced the greatest outrage against the royal troops occurred on 27 April in the small community of Santa Coloma de Farners, just south of Girona. When news arrived at the village that one company would soon quarter there, the nervous inhabitants decided not to allow that to happen. The royal official responsible for carrying out the order turned out to be Joan Miquel Monrodón, the royal constable who had arrested the diputat in March. Upon his arrival at Santa Coloma de Farners, the village rose in opposition with cries of "Long live the land and death to the traitor who captured the noble diputat Tamarit!"[8] Monrodón and several of his men took cover in an inn, which was set on fire, killing everyone except one of Monrodón's servants. Within days, Philip IV tried

4. ACA CA llig. 286 no. 43: Santa Coloma to King, 19 March 1640, in *consulta*, 1 April 1640.

5. BC MS 500: Albert de Tormé i Liori, "Miscelláneos históricos, y políticos sobre la Guerra de Cataluña, desde el año 1639," fol. 6ov.

6. ACA CA llig. 286 no. 40: Santa Coloma to King, 15 March 1640, in *consulta*, 22 March 1640; no. 43: Santa Coloma to King, 19 March 1640, in *consulta* 1 April 1640; no. 41: Santa Coloma to King, 24 March 1640, in *consulta*, 1 April 1640.

7. ACA CA llig. 393: Felip Vinyes to King?, 7 July 1640.

8. BNM MS 897: Felip Vinyes, "Desengaños de los inquietos y amotinados de Cataluña en 1640–1641," fol. 203. The manuscript is incorrectly ascribed to José de Pellicer de Tovar.

to avoid further clashes by ordering the punishment of guilty soldiers and villagers, "but without starting a new war."[9] Yet that war had already begun.

News of the incident in Santa Coloma de Farners led to the formation of bands of between 800 and 4,000 armed men from the surrounding towns and villages, which began to attack the royal troops under the command of Leonardo Moles. On 3 May, as Moles's men fled from the rebels toward the coast, they burned the church of Riudarenes, where the villagers had placed their belongings for safekeeping. On 14 May, another company sacked and burned all but two of the houses in Santa Coloma de Farners as punishment for Monrodón's death. Those two attacks hardened the general indignation throughout Catalonia against the royal army. The bishop of Girona excommunicated the troops responsible for burning Ruidarenes's church. Rebels continued to chase and attack royal troops anywhere they were to be found.

The peasant revolt completely transformed the already tense atmosphere in Barcelona. Early on 21 May, 520 fleeing infantrymen and cavalry reached the city's port hoping to escape the rebels' wrath. As they tried to board galleys, the soldiers were shot at, and in the ensuing panic some men drowned as they jumped into the sea and left their horses behind.[10] There was great alarm in Barcelona that the presence of the soldiers might lead to trouble, and city officials made every attempt to prevent the troops from entering the city or anyone from the city from attacking the soldiers.

Around ten in the morning of 22 May, while authorities supervised the departure of soldiers who had taken refuge in the shipyard, a crowd of 1,000–2,000 peasants led by men carrying firearms arrived at Barcelona's Portal Nou and forced its way into the city. One witness affirmed that the crowd shouted "Long live the King, and death to traitors and bad government!" whereas a Genoese correspondent heard "Long live the Faith and the King, and death to bad government!"[11] The crowd then marched

9. Quoted in Elliott, *Revolt of the Catalans,* 423.

10. ACA CA llig. 285 no. 18: *consulta,* Consejo de Estado, 27 May 1640; AHCG Administració Municipal Correspondència amb Barcelona llig. 2 (1640–59): Ramon Xammar to Jurats of Girona, 23 May 1640. Captain Federico Spatafora claimed that first shots came from the city walls and then armed peasants attacked the soldiers; see BNM MS 1430: Federico Spatafora y Rufo, "Relación," fol. 19.

11. On the rioters' slogans, see AHCG Administració Municipal Correspondència amb Barcelona llig. 2 (1640–59): Ramon Xammar to Jurats of Girona, 23 May 1640; and AADD CP Espagne 21, fols. 16–17: Genoese report on events in Barcelona, 29 June 1640. The latter estimated the crowd at 1,600 peasants, although the number is unclear and it might be 2,600. Amazingly, Albert de Tormé i Liori, who was "two hundred paces" from the royal prison, claimed that the crowd of 1,000 moved silently; BC MS 500: "Misceláneos históricos," fol. 68. Dídac Montfar-Sorts later recalled only 600 rioters; AHCB MS B-153: "Catálogo [sic] o ceremonial dels Consellers de Barcelona y coses notables succeides en sos temps."

on to the royal jail and liberated all prisoners, including the diputat Tamarit and the two jurats Vergós and Serra, arrested for their opposition to the billeting and levy. The consellers, diputats, bishops of Barcelona and Vic, and a number of chaplains, accompanied by the city guard, eventually convinced the armed men to leave the city without further violence. In the end, only one guard was killed when he tried to stop the rioters.[12]

City, Catalan, and royal authorities gave different accounts of the protagonists in the riots and their motivations, intended in part to validate official responses and assign political responsibilities. The consellers, denying the involvement of anyone from the city, insisted that the rioters were exclusively the armed men *(somatens)* who had been attacking the royal troops responsible for the recent burning of churches. In their letter to the king describing the incidents, the consellers explained that a man carrying a cross with the crucified Christ led the demonstrators, who were crying "Long live the Holy Catholic Faith and the King of Spain!" and "Death to the heretics who burn churches!"[13] The consellers did not mention any calls for the death of "bad government." The diputats, who also insisted on the rioters' expressions of loyalty to the king and their faith, portrayed the armed crowds as respectful of city, Catalan, and religious authorities, and pointed out that the diputat Tamarit left prison only after learning that the viceroy had ordered his release. Afterward, the armed men escorted Tamarit to the cathedral to give thanks for his release, and then on to the palace of the Diputació, before the crowd left the city. The diputats estimated the crowd at three thousand and reported no deaths. Nor did they tell whether any other prisoners had been liberated from the royal prison.[14]

---

12. AHCG Administració Municipal Correspondència amb Barcelona llig. 2 (1640–59): Ramon Xammar to Jurats of Girona, 23 May 1640; BC MS 500: Tormé i Liori, "Miscelláneos históricos," fol. 68; Miquel Parets, *De los muchos sucesos dignos de memoria que han ocurrido en Barcelona y otros lugares de Cataluña*, in *MHE*, vols. 20–25 (Madrid, 1888–93), 20:157. On Parets's diary, see the English translation of his account of the 1651 plague in *A Journal of the Plague Year: The Diary of the Barcelona Tanner Miquel Parets, 1651*, trans. and ed. James S. Amelang (New York, 1991), and James S. Amelang, *The Flight of Icarus: Artisan Autobiography in Early Modern Europe* (Stanford, 1998).

13. *DACB*, 12:478–79.

14. *Dietaris de la Generalitat de Catalunya*, vol. 5 (1623–1644), ed. Josep Maria Sans i Travé (Barcelona, 1999), 1032–33. According to Parets, the rioters took hammers from workshops on Carrer de la Dagueria to break open the prison's doors, something neither city nor Catalan authorities mentioned; *De los muchos sucesos*, 20:157. According to a later chronicle, the leader of the rioters was Joan Carbonell, a peasant from the village of Sant Andreu, who was known as *el Negre* ("the black man"); Francesc Pasqual de Panno, *Motines de Cataluña*, ed. Isabel Juncosa and Jordi Vidal (Barcelona, 1993), 127.

In contrast, reports from persons with ties to the royal government put particular emphasis on the rioters' threats against royal authorities and on the support they enjoyed from the people of Barcelona. Viceroy Santa Coloma reported that early in the morning of 22 May leaflets were posted around the city stating that "since Monrodón had been done away with, the viceroy and all traitors should be done away with." He believed the crowd consisted of both "locals [*naturales*] and more than two thousand peasants," some of whom went to his residence crying "Death to the traitor!" and brought a barrel of gunpowder to blow up the palace. His brother Don Ramon, a canon, had the cathedral's doors closed when he heard that crowds gathered near the church of Sant Jaume wanted to sound the cathedral's bell and burn the viceroy's residence.[15] The attackers did not know that the viceroy had taken refuge in the shipyard and was ready to board a ship if necessary. Recalling the events months later, the Audiència judge Felip Vinyes, who was in Barcelona at the time, offered a rather different interpretation. On the eve of the riot, "rebels" from Barcelona allegedly went to the nearby village of Sant Andreu to ask the peasant rebels to enter Barcelona and liberate diputat Tamarit and the two jurats from prison.[16] When the peasants arrived at the city gates, the consellers did little to stop them, and people in the street gave them money and refreshments, urging them to free all prisoners and later taking part in a victory march to accompany diputat Tamarit to the Diputació's palace. In addition, it was people from Barcelona who urged rioters to burn the viceroy's palace, to attack the houses of the Audiència's judges, and to murder them.[17] Vinyes clearly blamed city and Catalan officials for the chaotic situation in Barcelona and refuted the consellers' claim that no one in the city had "said a word or taken action" in favor of the rebels.[18]

After 22 May, the mood in the city remained perceptibly tense as news of the revolt in the countryside continued to arrive and fears persisted about the presence of troops in Barcelona's port. On 3 June, a group of segadors (reapers) rioted inside the city after an unidentified student shouted the patriotic cry "Long live the land!" (*Visca la terra!*).[19] The following day Don Juan de Benavides, the royal army's inspector general, de-

---

15. ACA CA llig. 285 nos. 26 (Santa Coloma to King, 23 May 1640) and 18 (Council of State's *consulta*, 27 May 1640).

16. According to another Audiència judge, Ramon Rubí de Marimon, the diputats were the ones who asked the rebels to enter Barcelona to liberate Tamarit; see Elliott, *Revolt of the Catalans*, 429.

17. BNM MS 897: Vinyes, "Desengaños," fol. 204.

18. Consellers to King, 23 May 1640, in *DACB*, 12:479.

19. ACA CA llig. 393: Santa Coloma to Pedro de Villanueva, 3 June 1640.

scribed another serious incident at the port. A crowd that included sailors, women, and "people from the sea" (possibly fishers and port workers) from the Ribera neighborhood threatened the galleys under the command of the marquis of Villafranca as they tried to dock in the port. Benavides received warnings not to enter the city because there would be an "uproar" and he might be slaughtered. He heard cries of "Death to the Castilians!" and death threats against him.[20]

The incidents of 22 May seemed to confirm viceroy Santa Coloma's fear that the rebels pursuing the king's soldiers might try to slip inside Barcelona among the segadors arriving in the city for the spring harvest. He asked the Consell de Cent to prohibit their entry. Yet city authorities claimed that closing the gates would cause disorders and that it would prove difficult to control the large number of people.[21] Nevertheless, they canceled the annual procession for the feast of Corpus Christi on 7 June. Despite such precautions, the feast of Corpus Christi would be the bloodiest in Barcelona's history.

"Death to the Traitors!"

Around nine in the morning of 7 June 1640, five hundred segadors ran down Barcelona's Rambla crying, "Long live the Holy Mother Church!" "Long live the king!" "Death to the traitors!" and "Long live the land!"[22] They were protesting the stabbing of a segador not far from the viceroy's residence when a member of the company of velvet makers searched him for weapons. It was rumored that the man who killed the segador had been a servant of Miquel Joan Monrodón, the royal constable killed at Santa Coloma de Farners whose house was close to where the incidents were taking place.[23] The crowd ran to the Plaça (or *pla*) de Sant Francesc, across from the viceroy's residence near the port. As the segadors shouted their slogans, a shot was heard coming from the viceroy's palace, and another

20. ACA CA llig. 393: Juan de Benavides to Santa Coloma, 4 June 1640, and Santa Coloma to King, 6 June 1640.

21. AHCB CC II-149 (Delibs. 1639–40), fols. 188v–189r.

22. Federico Spatafora, who was not in Barcelona, said there were 100 peasants (*villanos*); BNM MS 1430: "Relación," fol. 24. For descriptions of the riots, see Antoni Rovira i Virgili, *El Corpus de Sang: Estudi històric* (Barcelona, 1932), and Elliott, *Revolt of the Catalans,* 446–51.

23. Felip Vinyes stated that the guard was a silk weaver; BNM MS 897: "Desengaños," fol. 205v. Another source says he was a ribbon maker (*passamaner*); APL Registre 855 Correspondència 1640–47: Domingo Calderó to Lleida's paers, 9 June 1640. According to Parets, the segador did not die; *De los muchos sucesos,* 20:162. Monrodon's house was on Carrer Ample near the Rambla.

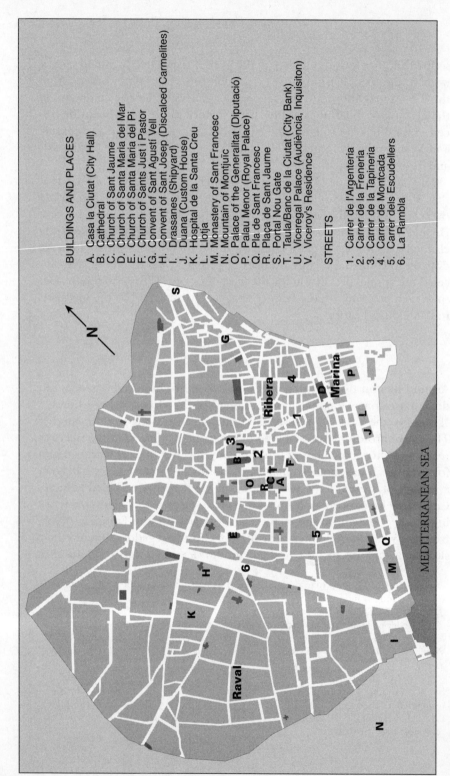

BUILDINGS AND PLACES

A. Casa la Ciutat (City Hall)
B. Cathedral
C. Church of Sant Jaume
D. Church of Santa Maria del Mar
E. Church of Santa Maria del Pi
F. Church of Sants Just i Pastor
G. Convent of Sant Agustí Vell
H. Convent of Sant Josep (Discalced Carmelites)
I. Drassanes (Shipyard)
J. Duana (Custom House)
K. Hospital de la Santa Creu
L. Llotja
M. Monastery of Sant Francesc
N. Mountain of Montjuïc
O. Palace of the Generalitat (Diputació)
P. Palau Menor (Royal Palace)
Q. Pla de Sant Francesc
R. Plaça de Sant Jaume
S. Portal Nou Gate
T. Taula/Banc de la Ciutat (City Bank)
U. Viceregal Palace (Audiència, Inquisiton)
V. Viceroy's Residence

STREETS

1. Carrer de l'Argenteria
2. Carrer de la Freneria
3. Carrer de la Tapineria
4. Carrer de Montcada
5. Carrer dels Escudellers
6. La Rambla

MAP 3. Barcelona

segador fell dead. The angry crowd then took wood from a nearby bakery and stacked it in front of the building to set it ablaze.[24] Minorite friars from the adjacent monastery of Sant Francesc prevented the fire by placing a crucifix on the wood pile and later by bringing out the consecrated host. Meanwhile, the consellers, diputats, and bishops of Barcelona, Urgell, and Vic helped to diffuse the riot. After city and Catalan authorities managed to make the rioters disperse to the Rambla, craft confraternity companies stood guard before the viceroy's palace.

Up the Rambla between 200 and 300 segadors assaulted the house of Audiència judge Gabriel Berart, who escaped to the nearby convent of Discalced Carmelites. Rioters ransacked the judge's house and burned all of his belongings, except religious paintings and images, in a big bonfire out in the street.[25] The extent of the destruction in Berart's home is striking. According to the judge's nephew, the rioters not only burned trial papers, books, furniture, and "sacks of silver and gold" but even destroyed the ceiling, all doors and windows, and cut down every tree in Berart's garden.[26] Other judges and royal officials suffered similar acts of violence.

Not far from judge Berart's house, rioters attacked the residence of another royal minister, Guerau de Guardiola. They sacked the house, destroyed all doors and windows, and burned everything they found inside in a bonfire in the street. Another crowd sacked a nearby warehouse, where the marquis of Villafranca, the commander of the royal galleys, kept his carriages, and brought everything they found to the bonfire in front of Berart's home. The clergy from the church of Santa Maria del Pi tried to stop the attack on Guardiola's house by displaying the consecrated host. But the crowd refused to stop, saying—according to the Barcelona master tanner Miquel Parets—that royal officials had "watched the Castilians burn churches and sacraments, [and] while they could have stopped it, they had done nothing; it was thus reasonable that they should pay for it."[27]

The consellers arrived at Guardiola's house and convinced the rioters to follow them outside the city. But as the crowd passed by the Portal de Sant Antoni, shots were fired at them near the marquis of Villafranca's residence. Villafranca's servants had feared that the crowd might attack the

24. Although several accounts claim that the shot came from the viceroy's palace, Parets did not think so; *De los muchos sucesos*, 20:163. See also Rovira i Virgili, *Corpus*, 37.

25. Parets, *De los muchos sucesos*, 20:164. For the number of rioters, see Bishop of Urgell to King, 7 June 1640, in Ferran de Sagarra, *Catalunya en 1640: Les lliçons de la història* (Barcelona [1930?]), 55.

26. ACA CA llig. 506: *memorial* by Gaspar Berart, 30 August 1640.

27. Parets, *De los muchos sucesos*, 20:165. Guardiola was the *mestre racional*, an officer involved with the administration of the royal patrimony in Catalonia.

house and opened fire to keep them away. The segadors reentered the city, assaulted the house, and set it ablaze; they then chased Villafranca's servants as they fled to nearby convents and killed five or seven of them in the Dominican Convent dels Angels. When the rioters entered the convent of the Discalced Carmelites, they found judge Berart and fatally stabbed him numerous times. He died later that evening.[28]

During the shoot-out between rioters and the marquis of Villafranca's servants, the third conseller, Josep Massana, apparently tripped and fell on the ground. Believing the conseller to be dead, someone cried: "Treason, our conseller has been killed!" Blaming Villafranca's servants, a crowd of three thousand formed by segadors and people from the city armed with firearms and sickles ran toward the drassanes, where the alleged assassins had supposedly fled in order to leave the city by sea.[29] When the rioters arrived at the shipyard, they set out to burn its gates. Other rioters assaulted an adjacent bastion, which a company of master stocking makers, booksellers, and glassmakers proved unable to defend. Once inside the bastion, one of the rioters threatened to shoot at Francesc Barra, a cooper and artillery officer, if he did not fire a cannon at a Genoese galley in the port. The shots missed the vessel, but it was forced to retreat. Barra later identified the man who threatened him as Josep Novis, a Barcelona barber-surgeon's assistant (*jove cirurgià*) and standard-bearer in one of the city's companies.[30]

Once the rioters had torn down the shipyard gates, they ran inside to capture the conseller's alleged murderers. Soldiers and nobles inside the shipyard fled to the rocky beach and ran in the direction of the mountain of Montjuïc. Among them, Don Ramon de Sagarriga survived by taking off his clothes and swimming away to a cave in Montjuïc, where he and others were later rescued.[31] Don Miquel de Salbà also ran along the beach while rioters shot at him. He was lucky that one "less cruel" rioter felt sorry for him and helped him escape by disguising him with different clothes.[32] But others failed to escape, among them the viceroy of Catalonia.

28. On the deaths at the Convent dels Angels, see letters to the king by the bishops of Barcelona and Urgell, in Sagarra, *Catalunya en 1640*, 54, 56; Parets, *De los muchos sucesos*, 20:166, 173–74. According to Berart's nephew, Gaspar Berart, his uncle received five harquebus shots; ACA CA llig. 224 no. 28: *memorial*, 10 October 1640.

29. Parets, *De los muchos sucesos*, 20:167–68; Rovira i Virgili, *Corpus*, 43–44.

30. Francesc Barra's deposition in *DACB*, 12:750–53.

31. In the middle of the night he managed to catch a boat that took him to a Genoese galley, where he accompanied Santa Coloma's son, Don Luis; ACA CA llig. 507: Sagarriga's *memorial*, n.d.

32. ACA CA llig. 506: Miquel de Salbà's *memorial*, Madrid, 30 August 1640. Salbà would become a key figure in the restoration of Spanish authority in Catalonia after 1652; see Pere Molas i Ribalta, *Catalunya i la Casa d'Àustria* (Barcelona, 1996), 133.

The viceroy's presence in the drassanes at the time of the attack was to some extent unexpected. After the riot that morning at his residence, Santa Coloma had gone to the shipyard escorted by the consellers, diputats, craft confraternity companies, and numerous nobles and dignitaries. Some of them urged the viceroy to board the Genoese galley in the port and sail away to safety. But uncertain about the best course of action, he made the fatal mistake of delaying his departure. When the galley had to retreat to avoid the cannon shots from the port, the viceroy lost his last chance to escape.

An obese Santa Coloma fled the shipyard and ran with great difficulty along the rocky shore, assisted by two servants. As they tried to evade the shots aimed at them, the viceroy and his servants took refuge behind a boulder. A third man accompanying the group, a Barcelona potter named Dalmau Prats, tried in vain to secure a boat in which to escape. But three or four of the rioters, among them a sailor *(mariner)* and other men from the city, finally caught up with the viceroy and found him lying on the sand, seemingly unconscious after he had fallen from the boulder; one of his servants was wounded in the arm, and the other feigned an injury.[33] At first, the rioters did not recognize the viceroy as they emptied his pockets and asked the servants to give them all of their money. As other rioters approached the scene, one of them, dressed like a segador, recognized one of the viceroy's servants. After the servant admitted that the man lying on his back was the viceroy, the segador offered them his protection. But when the sailor realized that the viceroy himself was there, he took his knife and stabbed him once in the belly. Another man, also dressed like a segador, began stabbing the viceroy repeatedly. "I swear," said the segador who had offered protection to Santa Coloma and his servants, "you've killed the viceroy, whom all of us had to defend!" He added that there was no use in continuing the stabbing, because the viceroy was clearly dead.[34] Leaving Santa Coloma's corpse on the beach, the rioters escorted the servants back to the city and left them at a barber-surgeon's home. "The traitor is already dead," announced the men who had witnessed Santa Coloma's death once

33. *DACB*, 12:740–42: testimony of Magí Steve (one of the servants accompanying Santa Coloma) in the investigation on Santa Coloma's assassination.

34. Magí Steve's testimony, in *DACB*, 12:742. According to the historian Rovira i Virgili (*Corpus*, 48), the men who first approached the viceroy were not segadors because they wore "Gascon capes," rather than "shepherd's capes" worn by most of the segadors. Santiago Domínguez de la Mora, another of Santa Coloma's servants at the scene of the murder, stated that many of the rioters were "segadors and Catalans *(gente de la tierra)*, as revealed by their clothing and looks"; he believed the first to stab the viceroy was "a native (*uno de la tierra*), . . . a beardless man, around twenty years old, dressed like a sailor"; transcribed in Sagarra, *Catalunya en 1640*, 65.

they reached the city.[35] The viceroy's corpse remained on the beach, along with those of several other men who perished that afternoon. Later that night, Santa Coloma's body was taken to the monastery of La Merced and buried there.

As the news of the viceroy's death spread, bands of armed rioters continued to roam the city. A crowd sacked the house of the Audiència judge Rafel Puig and burned his belongings. Regent Miquel Joan Magarola was more fortunate. According to him, that day there were three failed attempts to take his house, but the fact that it was located across from city hall and next to the city bank meant that there was a heavy presence of city guards in the area, which spared Magarola's home from the destruction suffered by the other judges.[36] Nevertheless, the master tanner Parets described the city as an apocalyptic vision: "While the events were taking place in the shipyard, the people and the segadors went about Barcelona with such fury, cries, and loud noises, that it seemed as though the world was coming to an end or as though the city had become the very stage of the Last Judgment."[37]

In the next three days, armed crowds carried out sporadic attacks on the homes of royal officers, unhindered by the impotent local authorities.[38] On Friday, 8 June, crowds of segadors and city people sacked the houses of Audiència judges Jaume Mir (where two thousand books were burned), Felip Vinyes, and Josep Massó, where the master tanner Parets believed locals openly pillaged the judge's belongings, so that "as much was stolen as was burned."[39] Also attacked was the home of former royal constable Miquel Joan Monrodón. Rioters also entered the Capuchin monastery of Santa Madrona at the foot of Montjuïc and killed a number of nobles who had taken refuge there after the assault on the shipyard the day before. On Saturday, rioters sacked and burned the contents of the house of yet another Audiència judge, Lluís Ramon. His brother-in-law lived across the street and went with some of his servants to stop the rioters, who proceeded to pillage and burn the brother-in-law's house too. On Sunday, crowds broke into the stables of two nobles and stole a large number of horses. But by then the violence had waned. The riots finally ended on Monday, 11 June, after city authorities announced that the conseller en cap needed volunteers to rescue the city of Girona. Many of the armed segadors joined the

---

35. *DACB*, 12:742.

36. ACA CA llig. 506: Miquel Joan Magarola's *memorial*, 1641; ACA CA llig. 286 no. 83: Felip Vinyes to Pedro de Villanueva, 11 June 1640.

37. Parets, *De los muchos sucesos*, 20:173.

38. On events during 8–11 June, see Parets, *De los muchos sucesos*, 20:174–82.

39. On the destruction of judge Mir's books, see ACA CA llig. 225: Mir's *memorial*, 22 August 1654; Parets, *De los muchos sucesos*, 20:182.

conseller and left the city. After four days of rioting, the final toll was about twenty dead and as many injured.[40]

The Identity of the Crowd

As in the riots of 22 May, we find different accounts of the identity of the rioters. Most witnesses described them vaguely as segadors (reapers) from outside the city and "people of the land," meaning people from Barcelona and other parts of Catalonia. Three eyewitnesses testified that on 7 June one segador from Vic called Josep Vicens (known as Vitxach), went around the streets of Barcelona claiming that he had killed the viceroy.[41] Shortly after the riots, judge Vinyes argued that among the segadors were rebel peasants from the northern Empordà region who had slipped inside the city pursuing the royal troops. One of their leaders was Sebastià Estraban (or Estralau). However, according to Vinyes the crowd in judge Berart's house consisted of segadors from the nearby Vallés region, where Berart had been ruthless in his efforts to levy soldiers. A leader from that group, Rafel Goday, headed a band of rebels from the nearby village of El Prat and organized the attacks on the houses of royal judges Puig, Mir, and Massó because they were trying a case against Goday. Vinyes is the source of these two leaders' names, which he left out of later accounts, where he reversed his earlier opinion and denied that any of the segadors were from the Empordà. He insisted instead that men pretending to be segadors were in fact people from Barcelona and armed rebels from the environs of the city who had arrived prior to 7 June and stayed with city residents.[42]

But the segadors did not necessarily have to come from far away. Not long after the 7–10 June riots, Jaume Duran, a wool clothier from Barcelona, testified that Joan Vert, a segador from El Prat, offered to sell him jewelry stolen from the dead viceroy Santa Coloma. The Barcelona wool clothier had been a segador, and he knew Vert because "together we

---

40. Rovira i Virgili, *Corpus,* 52.

41. The three witnesses were together; they were the carpenter Josep Font, the merchant (*negociator*) Melchior Perssians, and his wife Rafaela; *DACB,* 12:758–59.

42. ACA CA llig. 286 no. 83: Felip Vinyes to Pedro de Villanueva, 11 June 1640. For Vinyes's later account, see BNM MS 7595: "Desengaños a los pretextos y motivos que han tenido los inquietos y amotinados de la Ciudad de Barcelona y del Principado de Cataluña," fol. 17v. Parets stated that many of the segadors were from the Vallés, but did not mention Estraban; *De los muchos sucesos,* 20:164. On Estraban/Estralau and another galley slave called Estraheque, see Elliott, *Revolt of the Catalans,* 461. According to Francesc Pasqual de Panno, who did not witness the incidents and wrote later in the century, one of the leading rioters was the peasant from the nearby village of Sant Andreu—Joan Carbonell, known as "el Negre de Sant Andreu"; *Motines de Cataluña,* 137.

used to collect the harvest in the property that the *señor* regent Magarola has in El Prat."[43] This example is, no doubt, insufficient to prove or disprove the geographical origins of segadors who participated in the 7–10 June riots, but it underscores the arguments that ensued over the rebels' identity. Here, two segadors came, not from the areas ravaged by the royal army, but from Barcelona and the nearby village of El Prat. The one from Barcelona was an artisan—a wool clothier—who may have supplemented his income by working in the fields during the harvest season. Others in Barcelona could have also been segadors.

In the early sixteenth century, 6.7 percent of the city's households had trades in agriculture or husbandry; their proportion fell only to 6.1 percent in the early eighteenth century.[44] Barcelona had two old confraternities of master gardeners *(hortolans),* one of journeymen gardeners *(joves hortolans),* and one of master grain sifters *(garbelladors),* whose members were eligible for city offices.[45] Agustí Forés described the rioters who attacked his home in 1636 as "*segadores* or grain sifters [*garberos*]."[46] One eyewitness to the riots of June 1640 also used the terms segadors and "grain sifters" interchangeably.[47] We know virtually nothing about the composition and activities of any of these agricultural confraternities, although their members worked in the tracts of arable land within Barcelona's walls in the Raval neighborhood.

Identifying the people from Barcelona in the riot is just as difficult. One witness stated that a quarter of the population, all the dregs of the city, were

43. Duran's testimony, in *DACB*, 12:769. He resided in Barcelona's Raval neighborhood (*vico novo*), an area with plots of land dedicated to agriculture. Xavier Torres i Sans discusses the imprecision of the term *segador* in "Segadors i miquelets a la revolució catalana (1640–1659)," in *La revolució catalana de 1640*, 77–78; see also Eva Serra i Puig, "Segadors, revolta popular i revolució política," in *Revoltes populars contra el poder de l'estat* (Barcelona, 1992), 45–57.

44. James S. Amelang, *Honored Citizens of Barcelona: Patrician Culture and Class Relations, 1490–1714* (Princeton, 1986), 17, table I-1.

45. In 1498, there were two confraternities of gardeners, named after two of the city's gates: the *hortolans del Portal Nou* (also known as the *hortolans del Pi*), and the *hortolans de Sant Antoni;* Jaume Vicens i Vives, *Ferran II i la ciutat de Barcelona, 1479–1516,* 3 vols. (Barcelona, 1936–37), appendix, doc. no. 182; Margarida Tintó i Sala, *El gremis a la Barcelona medieval* (Barcelona, 1978), 55. Grain sifters became eligible for the office of fifth conseller in 1600; AHCB C VIII-12 (Llibres d'insaculacions): "Llibreta d'insaculacions" (1594–1657).

46. ACA CA llig. 236 no. 1: Forés to King, 14 June 1636.

47. APL Registre 855 Correspondència 1640–47: Domingo Calderó to Lleida's paers, 9 June 1640.

actively engaged in the disorders.[48] The master tanner Parets described the rioters as the worst characters from the city, "birds of prey" primarily interested in pillaging.[49] Other witnesses specifically described some of the rioters as people from the Ribera neighborhood.[50] Two artisans played a key role during the riots: the unidentified young sailor who stabbed the viceroy on the beach and Josep Novis, the barber-surgeon's assistant responsible for the cannon shots at the Genoese galley in the port. He was standard-bearer in the company of druggists and barber-surgeons, which had escorted viceroy Santa Coloma to safety only hours before Novis's actions ultimately prevented the viceroy from saving his life.[51] However, most master artisans in the city guard remained generally cooperative with city authorities in trying to restore order to the city. Authorities in Madrid acknowledged the need to distinguish between two kinds of people in Barcelona, the menestrals, "who are the more rational kind because they seek to carry on peacefully, which is not the case with the little people [*pueblo suelto*]."[52]

As in the 22 May riot, city and Catalan authorities preferred to call the rioters segadors without admitting the participation of anyone from the city, whereas royal officials insisted on the connivance and active participation of people from Barcelona.[53] Writing on 11 June, judge Vinyes insisted that the violence was not the work of segadors but of "rioters" *(amotinados)* who were "outsiders" *(forasteros)* acting "with the help of the people" of Barcelona: "The people were so insolent that they accompanied the outsiders and encouraged them by pointing out the houses of ministers; and many gave them [the rioters] money as a reward for their actions." According to Vinyes, the people of Barcelona purposely spread the rumor about the conseller's death "to finish off the viceroy." In addition, Barcelona's companies not only stayed away from the places where riots were taking place, but some of the guards "came over and helped steal the

48. Catalan rebel leader Felip Sorribes's statement, summarized in Elliott, *Revolt of the Catalans,* 449.

49. Parets, *De los muchos sucesos,* 20:175.

50. Eyewitness testimony by the Barcelona clothier (*abaixador* and *paraire*) Gaspar Ferriol, in *DACB,* 12:765. Barcelona's deacon (*degà*) Pau del Rosso also stated in his account of the 7 June events that "many people from la Ribera" joined the segadors in the rioting; transcribed in Eulogio Zudaire Huarte, *El Conde-Duque y Cataluña* (Barcelona, 1963), 464.

51. On the druggists and barber-surgeons' escort of Santa Coloma, see AHCB C III-5 (Política-Guerra, 1600–1641): "Motins o asonadas en la ciutat de Bar[celo]na: Motí succehit en lo dia de Corpus per los segadors" (Consellers' account of the 7 June riots for the investigation of Santa Coloma's assassination).

52. ACA CA llig. 287 no. 133: statement by Jerónimo de Villanueva in *consulta,* Junta de Estado y Ejecución, 18 June 1640.

53. *DACB,* 12:485 n. 3; *Dietaris de la Generalitat,* 5:1036–40.

clothes and goods taken from the houses of ministers." Likewise, Vinyes's fellow judge Ramon Rubí de Marimon accused the artisans in the guard of saying, "We won't fight our brothers," and refusing to stop the rioters.[54]

The identity of the rioters had great political implications for the debate over the motivations and political responsibilities for the events in Barcelona. City and Catalan authorities condemned the violence, but they insisted it was carried out by segadors from outside of Barcelona in reaction to the royal soldiers' attacks in the Catalan countryside. Terrible as the murders of viceroy Santa Coloma and judge Berart were, their deaths, along with the attacks on the houses of other royal ministers, appeared to underscore their political responsibility for allowing the royal troops into Catalonia in the first place. It made sense that the segadors cried "Long live the king and death to bad government!" because presumably they had suffered more directly from the abuses by royal soldiers and were therefore more angry at the government's failure to stop them and punish those responsible. In addition, Catalan villages and towns had suffered for years at the hands of Audiència judges who had ruthlessly levied soldiers and extorted contributions to the war under orders from Santa Coloma. As peasant rebels had done in the countryside, the segadors in Barcelona had merely acted in self-defense. This eventually became the official argument of the Consell de Cent, as expressed in *Proclamación Católica* (Catholic Proclamation), one of the key political texts of the 1640 revolt published in October of that year. Its author, the Augustinian priest Gaspar Sala, explained that the segadors' violence on 7 June resulted from the deaths early in the day of two of their men (the one allegedly killed by Monrodón's servant and the other shot during the protest at the viceroy's palace). Faced by such brutal attacks, "together with the memory of the insults and past oppression executed under the order and permission of the viceroy, it was no accident when they [the segadors] became angry."[55]

In the following weeks and months, critics of royal policies in Catalonia considered it essential to argue that the riots in Barcelona had been above all the work of peasants who had suffered atrocious abuses and for that rea-

---

54. ACA CA llig. 286 no. 83: Felip Vinyes to Pedro de Villanueva, 11 June 1640 (copy of ACA CA llig. 287 no. 131). For Rubí de Marimon's statement, see Elliott, *Revolt of the Catalans,* 450.

55. [Gaspar Sala Berart,] *Proclamación católica a la magestad piadosa de Felipe el Grande* (Barcelona, 1640), 69. For its author and date of publication, see AHCB CC II-149 (Delibs. 1639–40), fol. 337: 4 October 1640; and Gaspar Sala, *Secrets Públics, de Gaspar Sala, i altres textos,* ed. Eva Serra, vol. 2 of *Escrits polítics del segle XVII* (Vic, 1995).

son enjoyed legal and divine sanction. On the evening of 19 June, a stranger delivered a letter to the secretary of the Consell de Cent signed by a so-called Captain of the Christian Army. "The most uneducated and rural people," the letter read, "moved by the Holy Spirit (because God always communicates with the most humble) have formed a large army" that is capable of "formidable punishments." Declaring allegiance to the Catholic faith and the king, the Captain threatened the consellers with serious reprisals if they did not seek the punishment of royal troops and the removal of all those officials "moved by an evil spirit to violate the laws, privileges, constitutions, and liberties" of Catalonia.[56] Gaspar Sala later declared that the royal army's blasphemous acts and royal officials' negligence in stopping them had brought God's wrath upon them. According to Sala, the attack on royal officials had been in

> revenge for these intentional omissions, punishment in particular for the offenses to the Holy Sacrament. The Lord awaited his most solemn day of Corpus [Christi] to execute divine justice at the hands of some segadors . . . , who were invested with powers so great that three bishops, the diputats, and five consellers trying to find a solution with gentle means, and then with arms, found it impossible to stop their action.[57]

Not surprisingly, royal authorities argued that the rioters had merely used the royal troops' excesses as an excuse to kill and pillage. Since the city had not directly suffered any attacks by royal troops or billeted any troops, the self-defense motivations could not be true. Instead, those critics insisted that the real political motivations lay not with the rioters themselves but with the city and Catalan authorities, whose ultimate goal was to increase their own power by reducing the royal government's. The Consell de Cent and the Diputació had undermined royal authority—the argument went—by repeatedly defying the viceroy and ignoring royal orders under the pretext of defending the laws and privileges of the pàtria. Such disobedience

---

56. BC F. Bon. 6139: "Aquesta escriptura se dona a Jaume Agramunt Secretari de la Ciutat peraque se legis en Consell de Cent"; copy in BC MS 503, fols. 36–40; reprinted in *MHE*, 21:52–55. On the delivery of the letter, see AHCB CC VI-87 (LC 1640–41), fols. 10v–14v: Consellers to Pau Boquet, 31 July 1640. Regarding evil spirits during the 7 June attack on the marquis of Villafranca's house, rioters found a clock with a mechanical monkey that moved its hands and eyes. Calling it a "demon," they paraded it around the city as evidence of "its owner's spell" (*el encanto de su dueño*); see Duke of Cardona to King, 10 June 1640, in Sagarra, *Catalunya en 1640*, 57; Francisco de Melo, *Guerra de Cataluña*, ed. Joan Estruch Tobella (Barcelona, 1982), bk. 1, paragraph no. 100, p. 57.

57. *Proclamación católica*, 19–20 (erroneous foliation indicates 15–16), 66.

had presumably laid the ground for unruly people to unleash their extreme violence against royal officials. Writing less than a month after the June riots, judge Vinyes blamed the riots on the "doctrine" defended by the Diputació and the Consell de Cent that the royal tribunals could not be trusted anymore "because those judges always judge in favor of the king."[58]

However, these two radically opposed interpretations of popular violence shared one thing in common: if the riots had any political motivations, they lay not with the rioters but either with royal authorities or with city and Catalan officials. During the crucial months that followed, it would become evident that popular violence did have political motivations of its own that neither officials in Madrid nor those in Barcelona could control. Those motivations involved above all a visceral hatred of royal judges that contributed directly to the most important revolt against the Spanish monarchy during the seventeenth century.

The Rope Following the Lamb

After the riots of 7–10 June Catalonia remained on the brink of chaos.[59] Clashes continued between royal troops and locals in the Catalan countryside. Near Barcelona, there were sporadic attacks against royal officials, their relatives, and properties. But far more serious, the royal government was virtually paralyzed. The viceroy and judge Berart were dead, and other royal officials in Barcelona remained hidden wherever they could. Some took cover in churches and monasteries, such as the Dominican monastery of Santa Caterina, which gave refuge to the governor, Don Ramon de Calders.[60] Judge Rubí de Marimon recounted that he disguised himself as a monk, with his head and beard shaved, whereas judge Massó hid in a tomb in the monastery of Sant Francesc.[61] Judge Vinyes first hid in the Dominican monastery but eventually considered it safer to move to the palace of the Inquisition. From there he wrote to Madrid describing the difficult situation of his fellow magistrates in the Audiència: "We remain in hiding

---

58. ACA CA llig. 393: Vinyes to King?, 7 July 1640. Vinyes stated that the author of this doctrine was the renowned jurist Joan Pere Fontanella. On the latter's career and thought, see Joan Lluís Palos, *Els juristes i la defensa de les Constitucions: Joan Pere Fontanella (1575–1649)* (Vic, 1997).

59. On the events between late June 1640 and January 1641, see Elliott, *Revolt of the Catalans*, chap. 16; José Sanabre, *La acción de Francia en Cataluña en la pugna por la hegemonía de Europa, 1640–59* (Barcelona, 1956); Serra, "1640: Una revolució política"; Zudaire Huarte, *El Conde-Duque*, chaps. 13–16.

60. ACA CA llig. 289 no. 35: Calders's memorial, 11 June 1640.

61. For Rubí de Marimon's account, see Palos, *Els juristes*, 122.

in different places not knowing about the others," except for judge Carreras, who moved freely about the city, allegedly because of his ties to rioters.[62] At least thirteen of the surviving fifteen Audiència judges were hiding. The two surviving judges not hiding were Carreres and judge Rafel Joli, who was in Tortosa when violence broke out in Barcelona and stayed there; Gabriel Berart was dead.[63] With the Audiència of Barcelona unable to meet, the royal justice system in Catalonia practically ceased operations.

City, Catalan, and royal authorities in Barcelona and Madrid all agreed that the return of some semblance of order in the principality required the resumption of a judicial system, or in their words, "the restoration of justice." But they all had widely different ideas of how to accomplish that. On the one hand, the Consell de Cent and the Diputació insisted that the first step was the immediate removal of the royal troops from the principality and the appointment of judges who could command Catalans' respect. On the other hand, authorities in Madrid considered the presence of the troops indispensable in case of a French attack. Moreover, despite Catalan authorities' avowals of loyalty to the king and their condemnation of popular violence, the marquis of Castrofuerte argued at the Council of State that demands for the removal of royal troops from Catalonia resembled those that sparked the revolt in the Netherlands in 1566. Nearly a century before, rebels in the Netherlands "began like that, proposing the removal of foreign troops and then rising up."[64] And so, despite warnings that harsh measures might worsen the principality's situation, Madrid insisted on a speedy punishment of the viceroy's assassins as proof of the sincerity of Catalan authorities' intentions.

The disjunction between orders issued from Madrid and conditions in Barcelona had long shaped relations between the Spanish monarchy and Catalonia, but now the gulf between the two capitals seemed insurmountable. That gulf resulted in part from what the historian Geoffrey Parker has

62. ACA CA llig. 286 no. 83: Vinyes to Pedro de Villanueva, 11 June 1640. Carreras was supposedly a "relative" of Sebastian Estraban—whom Vinyes described as the chief of the Empordà's rebels during the 7 June riots—and a friend of Rafael Godoy, leader of the rebels from El Prat. For Vinyes's hiding place, see ACA CA llig. 289 no. 80: Vinyes's *memorial*, 11 August 1640.

63. ACA CA llig. 507: Joli to King, 9 August 1641. The judges hiding in Barcelona after 7 June 1640 were Ramon Rubí de Marimon, Lluís Ramon, Felip Vinyes, Jeroni Guerau, Onofre d'Argensola, Bernat Pons, Benet Anglasell, Jaume Mir, Francesc Corts, Josep Massó, Joan Baptista Gori, Rafel Puig, and Guillèm Meca. The Audiència's regent, Miquel Joan Magarola, was also in hiding.

64. ACA CA llig. 287 no. 133: Junta de Estado's *consulta*, 18 June 1640. For an overview of the opinions of royal ministers on the events in Barcelona, see Elliott, *Revolt of the Catalans*, 454–56.

termed "Public Enemy Number 1" in the Spanish monarchy, namely, the distance.[65] Compared with the colonies overseas, or even the Netherlands, Catalonia was relatively close to the heart of the empire. But in such a fluid situation the four to ten days that it could take for ministers in Madrid to receive and review correspondence from Barcelona might be too long. On 22 May 1640 viceroy Santa Coloma sent a letter to Madrid describing a spy's report about alleged plans by rebel peasants to capture him and other royal officials in order to extort a general pardon for the Catalan rebels in the countryside. The Council of Aragon discussed the matter on 8 June 1640, unaware that the viceroy had died the day before.[66] Madrid's insistence on the restoration of justice without removing any troops or royal judges evidenced its inability or unwillingness to grasp the precariousness of its officials in Catalonia, whose most pressing concern was to stay alive.

The hopeless task of restoring justice in Catalonia fell on the new viceroy, the duke of Cardona. From the start of his term, his chances of success appeared slim. The duke was seriously ill, and according to judge Rubí de Marimon, he had been bled forty-two times that year to relieve the pain from his gout. The governor, the treasurer, and six Audiència judges came out of their hideouts to witness his swearing-in ceremonies in Barcelona on 19 June. But if Cardona hoped the judges' presence might signal a return to normalcy, he soon realized that would not be the case. The next day he wrote to the king that the public appearance of royal officials and judges had generated "no small resentment" among the people of Barcelona, who according to another account denounced the judges as "traitors to the land."[67] Cardona could not guarantee the judges' safety and could offer only four ships to whisk off any judges wanting to flee the city. Apparently, the judges were too afraid to take up his offer. The viceroy pleaded with city and Catalan authorities to protect the judges, but they responded that this was simply impossible.[68] The Consell de Cent and the Diputació did agree to dispatch to Perpinyà the conseller en cap and the noble diputat Tamarit at the head of a sizable force of 1,200 to help the new viceroy stop the fighting between Catalans and royal soldiers.

---

65. Geoffrey Parker, *The Grand Strategy of Philip II* (New Haven, 1998), chap. 2.

66. ACA CA llig. 287 no. 40: *consulta,* 8 June 1640.

67. ACA CA llig. 287 no. 132: Cardona to King, 20 June 1640; AHCB MS B-148: Joan Francesc Ferrer, "Successos de Cathalunya en los anys de 1640 y 1641," fol. 258. Ferrer was a merchant elected fourth conseller in November 1640. On the viceroy's health and the number of judges at the swearing in ceremony, see Rubí de Marimon's quotation in Elliott, *Revolt of the Catalans,* 457.

68. *DACB,* 12:771, appendix 18; *Dietaris de la Generalitat,* 5:1049; on the four ships, see Cardona to King, Granollers, 23 June 1640, in *MHE,* 25:462.

Cardona's departure from Barcelona—against his doctors' recommendations—reflected the fact that it would be impossible to restore justice without first stopping the fighting between Catalans and royal soldiers. Rumors of troop movements fueled the fears of armed retaliation against Barcelona for Santa Coloma's death and left the city in a state of alarm. According to the master tanner Parets, it was said that on 17 August the king would launch a massive invasion of the principality. Allegedly, 20,000 soldiers and 4,000 cavalry, together with the 10,000 men already stationed in the Rosselló, would take Barcelona by October.[69] Writing from Barcelona, the ecclesiastic diputat Pau Claris stated that "the people here are very agitated because it is said that the soldiers in Catalonia, many others gathering in Aragon, and a large number of Englishmen arrived at La Coruña will invade Catalonia."[70] In early July, the Consell de Cent and the Diputació began military preparations against possible attacks and initiated secret negotiations with French authorities over their possible assistance.[71] Unable to restore justice or even reduce the clashes between Catalans and royal troops, Cardona died in Perpinyà on 22 July 1640.

In Barcelona, Cardona's successor as viceroy, the bishop of Barcelona, the Aragonese Don Garcí Gil Manrique, witnessed the city and the rest of the principality slip into lawlessness: the Audiència judges were hiding in fear; lower court judges could therefore do nothing; "the people [*el vulgo*] sees this, and evil ones feigning zeal for the public good do as they please."[72] Not a single Audiència judge attended the bishop's swearing-in ceremony on 3 August to avoid any disorders.[73]

The last hope of restoring justice vanished soon after. Between 12 and 19 June 1640, the only Audiència judge who dared to appear in public, Miquel Carreras, interrogated more than two dozen witnesses for an investigation of Santa Coloma's assassination.[74] Although the witnesses could not establish the precise identity of the assassins—this despite a reward of 4,000 lliures offered by the Consell de Cent—Carreras had enough evi-

69. Parets, *De los muchos sucesos*, 21:1–2.

70. Claris to Bernardí de Manlleu (Catalan ambassador in Madrid), 30 June 1640, quoted in Sanabre, *La acción de Francia*, 82.

71. On the start of negotiations with the French, see Sanabre, *La acción de Francia*, 93.

72. ACA CA llig. 233 no. 90: Bishop of Barcelona to King, 24 July 1640, in *consulta*, 2 August 1640.

73. *DACB*, 12:519; ACA CA llig. 288 no. 57: Bishop of Barcelona to King, 4 August 1640. A number of judges did meet after the ceremony at Carreras's home: Benet Anglasell, Bernart Pons, Onofre Argensola, and Francesc Corts.

74. Carreras's investigation was for the court of Barcelona's *veguer*, not the Audiència; see the transcription of the investigation's depositions in *DACB*, 12:737–71.

dence to prosecute someone indirectly involved in the viceroy's death. On 3 August, the day the bishop of Barcelona took his oath of office, the consellers ordered the arrest of the barber-surgeon Josep Novis. Several witnesses had identified him as the man who forced a city guard to fire a cannon at the Genoese galley attempting to rescue viceroy Santa Coloma not long before his assassination. News of Novis's arrest, however, caused great anger in the city, and a crowd outside the prison threatened to free the barber-surgeon by force. As a concession, the viceroy ordered the removal of chains put on Novis because his wife said he was very sick. But that did little to appease the crowds in the streets, and the Consell de Cent pleaded with the viceroy to liberate the barber-surgeon to avert a catastrophe. Even two Audiència judges recommended freeing Novis, because the angry crowds might slaughter all the royal judges. Finally, on 5 August the viceroy ordered Carreras to follow the Consell de Cent's wishes and let Novis out. On his way back from the prison, the judge said he feared for his life because of the "large numbers of people in the streets."[75]

But Carreras was not safe. The following day at eleven in the evening, seven men bearing firearms went to his home and asked him to surrender the documentation for Novis's case. Carreras insisted that he did not have it, while the second conseller, who was visiting the judge, tried to persuade the crowd to go away. The judge finally agreed to look for the papers in his bedchamber, and there he fled through a window to the street. Reviewing these and other events, the viceroy-bishop portrayed Barcelona as a city at the mercy of "the people" *(el vulgo),* which carried out

> atrocious crimes inside and outside the city, burning country homes, stealing, killing; and their evil intent reached the point of defrauding and extorting many individuals by sending messages demanding excessive sums with threats that, if they did not pay within a certain number of hours, they would be killed and burned.[76]

75. ACA CA llig. 233 no. 87: Dr. Rossell to Bishop of Barcelona, 5 August 1640; Bishop of Barcelona to King, 11–13 August 1640. The two judges consulted by the viceroy were Don Bernart Pons and Benet Anglasell; ACA CA llig. 288 no. 17: Bishop of Barcelona to Carreras, 23 August 1640 (copy). On the Consell de Cent's reward for the arrest of Santa Coloma's assassins, see *RB*, 2:334 (10 June 1640).

76. ACA CA llig. 233 no. 87: Bishop of Barcelona to King, 11–13 August 1640. The conseller was Antic Saleta i Morgades, an honored citizen related to Carreras's wife, who was ill at the time.

The release of the barber-surgeon and the continued reports of disorders in Barcelona and throughout Catalonia made ministers in Madrid conclude that there was now no chance of a peaceful restoration of justice in Catalonia. Evidently the viceroy could do nothing; and the consellers either did not have the means or did not have the intention to stop the lawlessness. The count-duke of Olivares convened Barcelona's emissary in Madrid, Pau Boquet, for a meeting in his chamber on 21 August at eight in the morning to accuse the consellers of preferring to avoid a scandal than to punish Novis. If there was no justice in the city, Olivares continued, it was because the consellers and the diputats had failed to defend it, when they should have given up their lives in its defense. Barcelona had allowed criminals to run loose, instead of taking actions so that "the rope would not follow the lamb."[77]

The next day the Council of Aragon discussed Novis's release and was appalled that the city did not dispatch the guard to defend the prison against any possible attacks. Thus, the ministers concluded, the consellers "cooperate in these actions, or at least their fear of the people is invincible." Consequently, the only remedy left was the recourse to force: "Five hundred musketeers in Barcelona would solve everything."[78] The royal government prepared an invasion of Catalonia that would start in November.

Catalan authorities refused to accept blame for the failure to restore order and faulted Madrid for the present situation. For more than two months they had pleaded with the king to remove the royal troops from Catalonia and to name new judges; until that happened, the popular violence would not stop. But perhaps the royal ministers in Madrid wanted the violence to continue as an excuse to use force. The consellers told the Catalan ambassador in Madrid that the repeated demands to carry out the impossible task of defending the royal judges seemed a trap: since it was not possible to do so, city authorities would be blamed if their efforts failed or if they responded that they could not defend the judges. In addition, the appointment of the bishop-viceroy only contributed to the paralysis of the Audiència because he lacked the papal dispensation to intervene in criminal matters.[79] The consellers and the Consell de Cent insisted that they had demonstrated their desire to restore order—even at the risk of their lives—by trying to stop the riots in the city since May, and more recently by seeking alternative legal venues to arrest the barber-surgeon. They had been forced to release the latter only to avert imminent catastrophe.[80]

77. Boquet's letter is transcribed in AHCB CC II-149 (Delibs. 1639–40), fol. 304.
78. ACA CA llig. 233 no. 81: *consulta*, 23 August 1640.
79. *DACB*, 12:527–28: Consellers to Bishop of Barcelona, 25 August 1640.
80. On the consellers' reasons for releasing Novis from prison, see AHCB CC VI-87 (LC, 1640–41), fol. 34: Consellers to Joan de Grau (Barcelona's agent in Madrid), 1 September

The royal government's claims that city and Catalan authorities may have welcomed the popular violence defied logic. They wanted to maintain order not only because they wished to demonstrate to the king their loyalty and respect for legality, but more importantly, because they feared the violence. Throughout Barcelona's history, street demonstrations and limited violence had occasionally bolstered the position of Catalonia's political elite vis-à-vis royal authorities. But that elite had never trusted popular politics beyond the confines of the city's institutions. Now as before, courting the people in the streets was to play with fire; and even if the violence against the "traitors to the land" targeted royal officials and judges, crowds could easily turn those accusations of treachery against city and Catalan authorities.

Hard-pressed between, on the one hand, royal demands for greater efforts to stop the lawlessness and, on the other, tremendous popular violence in the streets of Barcelona, Catalan authorities launched a political revolution that would bypass the paralysis in the principality's royal government in order to "restore justice." Yet that restoration now had a double meaning, referring both to the establishment of an independent judicial system and to the repression of violence.

The restored Catalan judicial system would be independent from royal authorities, based on Catalan laws and privileges, and answerable only to city and Catalan authorities. The consellers would hold unappealable criminal trials (*juí de prohoms*) to tackle the large backlog of criminal cases and expedite the punishment of delinquency.[81] This measure, however, did not fully make up for the absence of an appeals court. And so, between mid-September and early October, Catalan authorities set up an extraordinary court of six jurists presided over by one conseller, which acted as a new Audiència directly under Catalan authority.[82] Such actions, together with other profound changes in the fiscal and military organization of the principality, effectively marked the beginning of a political revolution that would ultimately lead to the break between Catalans and the Spanish monarchy. Referring to the consellers' efforts, the Council of Aragon asserted that "it was an even greater crime than the death of the count of

---

1640. The opinions expressed here sum up two letters by the consellers to the bishop of Barcelona dated 25 August and 18 September 1640 in *DACB*, 12:527–29, 536–39.

81. The *juí de prohoms* consisted of the consellers and twenty-four jurats, who went to the prison to judge criminal cases; AHCB CC II-149 (Delibs. 1639–40), fols. 290–95. Their decisions were unappealable, had to be immediately executed, and had a reputation for unusual harshness; Víctor Ferro, *El dret públic català: Les institucions a Catalunya fins al Decret de Nova Planta* (Vic, 1987), 175.

82. Serra, "1640: Una revolució política," 54–56.

Santa Coloma, since that was the killing of one minister . . . and this is to try to completely undo the name of the royal dignity and power."[83]

As for the repression of the violence, city and Catalan authorities tried to accomplish that by a dramatic display of force. Barcelona was divided into 10–15 districts, each patrolled by companies of 140 men. An armed force (*unió* or *germandat*) would try to prevent attacks inside the city and in the surrounding countryside and to prevent the repeated interception of mail by criminals. In addition, Catalan authorities ordered the construction of gallows at the Rambla, the Plaça del Rey, the shipyard, and other central locations "for the terror of criminals and the extirpation of delinquency."[84]

However, before Catalan authorities could implement this radical shift, they would have to contend with the political revolution launched in the spring from the streets of Barcelona, and which had thus far resulted in the death of the viceroy and judge Berart and the near paralysis of the royal government. It was also a revolution in the sense that it had transformed politics in the city. Unlike earlier street protests, the violence that had irrupted into the city in late May of 1640 had altered the traditional dynamics of Barcelona politics. It had become a seemingly implacable and uncontrollable force—like a monster, as will be seen later. Propelled by ideals of justice and the duty of rulers to govern well or suffer the revenge of the subjects, that revolution in the streets lacked a formal program. Yet its intent was clear enough: to rid Catalonia of bad government by eliminating the "evil ministers" who had betrayed the pàtria. Viceroy Santa Coloma and judge Berart were the first "evil ministers" killed in Barcelona, but several others remained hidden in the city.

By the end of the summer of 1640, the elimination of these so-called "traitors" had become all the more pressing because of the imminent royal invasion. Published pamphlets and leaflets, letters, and word of mouth brought alarming news of large numbers of royal troops lining up along the Catalan frontier. In addition, there remained the troops already inside of the principality, whose removal Barcelonese and Catalan authorities had failed to secure. It is therefore not surprising that despite their best efforts officials in Barcelona could do little to prevent the extraordinary tensions

83. ACA CA llig. 288: *consulta* 10 September 1640. The Council of Aragon rebuked the bishop of Barcelona for allowing the consellers to hold unappealable trials (*juí de prohoms*) when the law allowed this only during the viceroy's absence from Barcelona.

84. On the establishment of district patrols, see AHCB CC II-149 (Delibs. 1639–40), fols. 299–300 (25 August); on the *unió* (or *germandat*) and the gallows, see Basili de Rubí, *Les Corts Generals de Pau Claris* (Barcelona, 1976), 149–50 (21 September).

inside the city from erupting into violence aimed at punishing all traitors, but especially the Audiència judges in Barcelona.

On the evening of 15 September, a shooting took place at the Portal de Sant Antoni when guards tried to stop a carriage that had just left the city. A man came out of the carriage and shot one guard, and the other guards returned fire, seriously injuring the Audiència judge (and priest) Jeroni Guerau and killing his twenty-five-year-old son, Josep. Guerau, Josep, and another son seven years old were on their way to board a ship that would take them south to Tortosa, where Josep was a canon (and where the presence of royal troops may have offered them greater protection).[85] The injured judge Guerau took refuge in the gate until the consellers and diputats came the following day and took him to the nearby church of Sant Antoni. Then on the morning of 17 September, rioters broke into the church in search of the judge, who was allegedly heard to say that "if God gave him life, he would take revenge and hang many." The crowd found Guerau on a second floor and dragged him down the stairs to the street, where the attackers "gave him so many stabs that they disfigured him," saying all along, "Death to the traitors to God, the *pàtria,* and the king!" The judge lay dead on the street, with only his undershirt on.[86]

To critics of city and Catalan authorities, Guerau's brutal murder was proof that the principality had descended to mob rule. An anonymous pamphlet published on 26 September explained that "the rabble and the people [*el vulgo, y la plebe*] govern and rule, and the good ones and guardians of the common good are oppressed. Therefore, there is no justice, and all sorts of crimes go unpunished." No one obeyed the new viceroy, and all lived according to their vices and whims, "exceeding the Caribs," which is to say, worse than bloodthirsty savages. In short, Catalonia had become a "portrait of hell."[87] Without denying that justice had been "raped by ruinous and seditious people," Catalan authorities rejected any re-

---

85. AHCB MS B-148: Ferrer, "Successos de Cathalunya," fols. 259v–26or.

86. Rubí, *Corts Generals,* 135–36, 138–39. The reference to the "undershirt" (*camisa*) comes from Parets, who offers other details that underscore the extreme brutality of the violence much more than does the Diputació's diary, on which Rubí's text is based; Parets, *De los muchos sucesos,* 21:17–18n. According to Don Bartomeu Rodríguez, the priest who gave refuge to Guerau in his church, the rioters who entered into the church took advantage of the situation to steal; AHCB CC III-2 (Delibs. de Guerra 1640–41), fol. 130v.

87. BC F. Bon. 5246: *La estrecha amistad que professamos . . .* [1640], 2, 7. For the date of publication and the possible author, see Antoni Simon i Tarrés, *Els orígens ideològics de la Revolució Catalana de 1640* (Abadia de Montserrat, 1999), 233 n. 5.

sponsibility, insisting that those actions did not belong to the "community" as a whole but to "irrepressible individuals" *(particulars inquiets)*.[88]

In an attempt to repress the violence in the city and take the necessary measures to ward off imminent invasion by the king's army, Catalan authorities convened a joint meeting of the braços, known as the Junta de Braços, to open on 10 September in Barcelona. On that day, wrote the delegate from Cervera Rafel Moxò, the meeting took place in the morning because of the numerous crimes and shootings in the evenings. One month later, he saw more effective efforts to stamp out the violence. On 10 October, Moxò wrote, authorities "garroted one scoundrel from among the rioting thieves, who had stolen much silver . . . and kept him all day hanging in a cage. Today they have given lashes to another thief; and I'm told that each day we'll have new things on matters of justice. A great thing, because there was need for it." Three weeks later, on 27 October, he again reported to his superiors in Cervera the execution of another "rioter and thief," and added: "I write this as something new because you have seen how captive justice has been."[89]

In spite of such optimism, the violence continued and in fact reached its worst moment since the June riots. The detonator was the start of the royal army's invasion, which kept the city in a nearly permanent state of fear and turmoil. On 23 November, the marquis de los Vélez was sworn in as the new viceroy of Catalonia in the southern city of Tortosa, from where he launched the "conquest of Catalonia." As news of the advancing army reached Barcelona, serious disorders and rioting seemed to occur weekly. On 12 December, Montserrat Sanz, Vic's delegate to the Junta de Braços, wrote that news of one victory by the Spanish forces had made the people *(la plebe)* riot against the knights for not having gone to the front. Had it not been for the intervention of companies *(unió i germandat)* in Barcelona, there would have been "a second feast of Corpus," that is to say, another riot like that of 7 June.[90] Some of these incidents intended to force city and Catalan authorities to take swift action to stop the advance of the forces headed by los Vélez. Nevertheless, the invasion proceeded, taking the towns

88. BC F. Bon. 5241: *Justificacio en conciencia de aver pres lo Principat de Catalunya las armas* (Barcelona, 1640), 15. This pamphlet, written by a committee of theologians convened by the diputats, appeared on 22 October 1640; Rubí, *Corts generals*, 198.

89. AHCC Fons Municipal, Correspondència (1640–49): Rafel Moxò [or Rafael de Moixò] (*síndic* to Junta de Braços) to paers of Cervera, Barcelona, 10 and 27 October 1640. See also, AHCG Administració Municipal Correspondència amb Barcelona llig. 2 (1640–59): Antoni Martí and Rafel Vives (*síndics* to the Junta de Braços) to Jurats of Girona, 11 October 1640.

90. AMV Cartes a la Ciutat 13 (1636–40): Montserrat Sanz to Vic's Consellers, Barcelona, 12 December 1640.

along the route to Barcelona, the most important of which was the city of Tarragona on 24 December. The fall of Tarragona was a major military and symbolic loss. It was the seat of the primate of Catalonia and the second most important Catalan city after Barcelona. Still Catalan forces had failed to defend it, despite the presence of French troops for the first time since Catalan authorities signed a treaty making the principality a republic under the protection of King Louis XIII.[91] Within weeks, Spanish troops would reach Barcelona.

News of the surrender of Tarragona triggered three days of rioting in Barcelona—the worst since June.[92] On Christmas Eve, armed crowds searched for royal judges, who had allegedly betrayed secrets to the enemy forces. After failing to find any in the cathedral and the palace of the Inquisition, rioters located judge Josep Puig and stabbed him to death in the street. They also entered a house where the seventy-year-old Antoni Gori lay sick in bed and threw him out the window (perhaps after stabbing him) to die in the street. Judge Lluís Ramon tried to escape through the roof of his house, but rioters shot and killed him. In all three cases, rioters dragged the bodies of the dead judges around the streets of the city crying, "These are the traitors!" They then hung the disfigured corpses from the gallows at the Plaça del Rei recently built to end such violence and "to reaffirm justice."[93] There large crowds kept city authorities away from the corpses for two days, after which clergymen buried the dead judges. Riots also forced Catalan officials to free all of the prisoners from jail, where overnight someone hung a "For Rent" sign.[94]

As in earlier riots, accounts of the composition of the crowds and the ferocity of their actions varied. Crowds appear to have included refugees from the lands ravaged by war as well as city people, particularly from the Ribera; they were mostly men, but children may have dragged the corpses, and women took part as well. According to judge Rubí de Marimon, a woman bathed her hands in judge Gori's blood.[95] Judge Felip Vinyes—who had fled Barcelona back in August—explained that while his former col-

---

91. Sanabre, *La acción de Francia*, 116–17.

92. For a description of these events, see Rubí, *Corts Generals*, 291–95; AHCB MS B-148: Ferrer, "Successos de Cathalunya," fols. 266–67; Parets, *De los muchos sucesos*, 22:26–31; Luca Assarino, *Delle riuolutioni di Catalogna* (Bologna, 1645), 136–37.

93. Rubí, *Corts generals*, 292.

94. AHCB MS B-148: Ferrer, "Successos de Cathalunya," fol. 266v; Parets, *De los muchos sucesos*, 22:32–33.

95. For the participation of children (*minyons* or *muchachos*), see *DACB*, 12:580, and Parets, *De los muchos sucesos*, 22:27. On the woman's blood bath, see Rubí de Marimon's quotation in Palos, *Els juristes*, 134; and Assarino, *La rivolta*, 137.

leagues hung from the gallows, the crowds burned their beards, which were associated with judges and the legal profession.[96]

On Christmas Day, crowds of women and men looking for judge Rubí de Marimon attacked the palace of the duke of Cardona's widow, where he was hiding, but did not find him. The fourth conseller, Joan Francesc Ferrer, recounted that a number of "young women" *(unes donetes)* accused the conseller of housing traitors, but the presence of a company of soldiers spared his life and property.[97] Barcelonese and Catalan officials tried to pacify the city, while the consellers ordered two patrols of fifty men — accompanied by an executioner and a noose—to arrest and summarily execute any rioters, whose corpses would hang from a crane especially built for that purpose before city hall. The following night, two men were executed, among them a coachman in the Inquisition who had allegedly urged rioters to look for judges and soldiers hidden in the palace. Three more men were executed in the following days.[98] However, on 27 December, when one of the patrols went to the Ribera neighborhood, a riot broke out. According to the fourth conseller, "women came out and threw stones and other things from windows, and there were many gunshots." Rioters then killed the executioner and hung him with his own noose.[99]

Despite the draconian measures to stamp out the renewed violence, city and Catalan authorities espoused arguments that legitimized both rage against the royal judges and rebellion in the face of injustice. This was one of the central themes of a book that appeared in public only three days before the judges' murders. In *Noticia universal de Catalunya* (Universal News from Catalonia), Francesc Martí i Viladamor, one of the most influential writers of the revolt, argued that the rebellion was inevitable because every time Catalans sought justice "they always found the door of justice closed." Countering the claims that the violence against the royal judges had brought about the end of justice in the principality, Martí i Viladamor warned against equating justice with the royal judges. On the contrary, he

96. BNM MS 7595: Vinyes, "Desengaños," fol. 10r. In Francisco de Quevedo's *Sueños* (Dreams), written in 1612 although first published almost twenty years later, a hellish underworld teems with judges and lawyers, with extremely long beards; *Sueños y discursos,* ed. Felipe C. R. Maldonado (Madrid, 1972), 108–9.

97. Ferrer also stated that rioters cried out that "our father Adam died without a will, and that property ought to be common because no one should have more than others"; AHCB MS B-148: Ferrer, "Successos de Cathalunya," fol. 267v.

98. For the measures taken to punish rioters, see ACHB CC III-2 (Delibs. de Guerra, 1640–41), fols. 183–84; *DACB,* 12:580–82. For the coachman's execution, see Rubí, *Corts generals,* 301. For incidents after Christmas Day, see Sanabre, *La acción de Francia,* 124–25.

99. AHCB MS B-148: Ferrer, "Successos de Cathalunya," fol. 268r.

wrote, justice was in fact to force out of office judges who had failed to protect Catalans and their laws and privileges from abuse, and who in some cases had carried out abuses themselves. By such actions, the judges had effectively ceased to be ministers of justice and had "become private individuals without any authority."[100] At no point did Martí i Viladamor—or for that matter any Catalan writer or official—ever call for the murder of judges. However, he cited numerous legal and political authorities to demonstrate the legitimacy of popular violence:

> How can one call riots, sedition, and disorders the acts conducted under the authority of the law? And call "crimes" actions whose execution the law allows? The truth is that those who following the law seek the law's revenge are free from guilt, since that which is done under the authority of a just law is not a sin.[101]

It is impossible to establish a direct influence between such statements and the popular violence in Barcelona, but contemporaries certainly believed political texts and speeches could have widespread impact. For months, Catalan preachers and pamphlets had been launching verbal attacks against "evil ministers" and "bad judges" in response to equally harsh attacks on Catalans from royal officials. Both sides acknowledged the profound impact such statements could have, condemning the inflammatory language used, but often responding in kind.[102] Contemporary accounts describe the streets and squares of Barcelona as teeming with murmuring crowds *(corrillos)*, which perhaps discussed the constant flow of news and rumors in which it was not always easy to distinguish fact from exaggeration. One fact was indisputable, however: words could kill. Following the latest rioting, city authorities ordered that anyone who publicly accused someone else of treason would face harsh punishment, even execution.[103] But as Catalan authorities tried to clamp down on seditious language and

---

100. [Francesc Martí i Viladamor,] *Noticia universal de Cataluña* [Barcelona, 1640], 143, 165. For the author and the date of the publication, see Xavier Torres's edition of the text in *Escrits polítics del segle XVII,* vol. 1 (Vic, 1995), 10–12.

101. *Noticia universal,* 149–50.

102. On the role of preachers in the Catalan revolt, see Joaquim M. Puigvert i Solà, "Guerra i Contrareforma a la Catalunya rural del segle XVII," in *La revolució catalana de 1640,* ed. Eva Serra (Barcelona, 1991), 99–132. On the importance given by Philip IV and the count-duke of Olivares to countering the claims made in leaflets *(papeles)*, see ACA CA llig. 286: King's response to Junta de Ejecución's *consulta,* 17 July 1640; and Olivares's comments in ACA CA llig. 232 no. 50: copy Junta de Ejecución's consulta, 11 July 1640. For Catalans' own propaganda, see Simon i Tarrés, *Els orígens ideològics,* 204–19.

103. *DACB,* 12:580n.

actions, they continued to support the publication of pamphlets defending their own revolt against the Spanish monarchy.

Political texts such as those of Martí i Viladamor drew on notions of justice shared by Catalans and Spaniards of all social backgrounds and regions.[104] The people of Barcelona did not need to read jurists' books to know under which circumstances they felt entitled to punish bad judges. Therefore, political texts such as those of Martí i Viladamor and other writers can provide insights into deeper concerns that may have motivated the unusually ferocious attacks on royal judges. From the perspective of the artisans of Barcelona, the brutality and humiliation suffered by the Audiència judges between June and December 1640 seemed to respond to a double betrayal: they were traitors for allowing many abuses to go unpunished, as well as for betraying their "sacred duty" to dispense justice.[105] Yet if the judges were indeed guilty of the crimes they were accused of, they could expect severe punishments. According to one sixteenth-century Spanish jurist: "Judges shown to have been involved in vices and other evil acts, shall be stripped of their honor and the dignity of their office, placing them among the lowest and most infamous citizens, and shall suffer rigorous punishment."[106] Even more terrifying was the emblem in Juan de Horozco y Covarruvias's *Emblemas morales* (Moral Emblems), which went through several editions between 1589 and the early seventeenth century. His entry for "judges who are tyrants" displayed a gruesome illustration of a flayed judge, his disfigured corpse nailed to the bench (see Figure 6).[107]

This atmosphere of riots and constant rumors as the royal army approached Barcelona once more had a crucial impact on the relations between Catalonia and the Spanish monarchy. According to Bernard Du-Plessis Besançon, the chief French negotiator before Catalan authorities, the extraordinary violence in Barcelona meant "the impossibility of the plan to establish a political government in the shape of a republic, divided

---

104. For Barcelona artisans' notions of justice, see Chapter 6; for those of Catalan peasants, see Jordi Olivares i Periu, *Viles, pagesos i senyors a la Catalunya dels Àustria: Conflictivitat social i litigació a la Reial Audiència (1591–1662)* (Lleida, 2000). For popular notions of justice elsewhere in Spain, see Pedro L. Lorenzo Cadarso, *Los conflictos populares en Castilla (siglos XVI–XVII)* (Madrid, 1996); Ruth MacKay, *The Limits of Royal Authority: Resistance and Obedience in Seventeenth-Century Castile* (Cambridge, 1999); and Helen Nader, *Liberty in Absolutist Spain: The Habsburg Sale of Towns, 1516–1700* (Baltimore, 1990).

105. On the sacred nature of justice, see Chapter 6.

106. *Un práctico castellano del siglo XVI (Antonio de la Peña)*, ed. Manuel López-Rey y Arrojo (Madrid, 1935), 33.

107. Juan de Horozco y Covarruvias, *Emblemas morales* (Zaragoza, 1604), lib. 2, 45 (emblem 23).

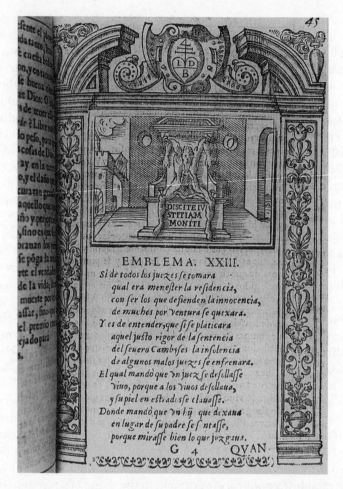

FIGURE 6 Gruesome punishment for evil judges. The text is an early modern retelling of Herodotus's story about the Persian king Cambyses, who ordered a judge to be flayed alive because by demanding payment for his decisions he had flayed the living. The judge's skin was then nailed to the bench as a warning to future judges. From Juan de Horozco y Covarruvias, *Emblemas morales* (Zaragoza, 1604), bk. 2, emblem 23. Courtesy of the Kenneth Spencer Research Library, University of Kansas.

between nobility and the multitude."[108] Under pressure from France, the annexation of Catalonia to the French monarchy became the only way to secure additional French support to forestall a disaster. On 23 January 1641 the Consell de Cent and the Junta de Braços approved the election of Louis XIII as count of Barcelona, making him Catalans' new king.

The election of Louis XIII coincided with the arrival of the troops commanded by the marquis de los Vélez, who reached the outskirts of Barcelona on 26 January 1641. That day, the invincible Spanish forces confronted a rebel army, formed mostly by the city's craft confraternity companies and the French troops, in Montjuïc, just south of the city walls. After an initial onslaught that seemed to favor the royal army, the rebel troops won a major victory, which sent los Vélez back to Tarragona. The victory at Montjuïc averted the fall of Barcelona and of the rebel government. The war, however, was not over. Hostilities between Catalans and Philip IV would continue until 1652, when Barcelona surrendered after a long siege and a devastating plague.[109] After twelve years of fighting, Catalans would resume their allegiance to the Spanish monarch.

By January 1641 one central aspect of the revolt in the streets of Barcelona had come to an end, namely, the persecution of royal judges. Five of them had been murdered, and most had escaped to Madrid or would do so within the next two years; only judge Carreras remained in Barcelona, now working for the Consell de Cent.[110] The riots declined significantly in number after the victory at Montjuïc, but did not end. Occasionally serious riots would once more threaten city and Catalan authorities, as well as the French.

In addition to the wider impact on the relations between Catalonia and the Spanish monarchy, another permanent remnant of the revolt in the streets of Barcelona was the restoration of the Sisé, the sixth conseller, on 30 November 1641 after a major riot in city hall. The additional conseller would restore artisans' political representation in the Consell de Cent to the level it had had before Ferdinand the Catholic's 1498 reforms. The Sisé guaranteed that the artistes and menestrals had their own conseller every year. This privilege had officially nothing to do with artisans' participation

---

108. AADD CP Espagne-Supplément, vol. 3, fol. 213.

109. See Parets, *Journal of the Plague Year.*

110. Dead judges: Berart, Guerau, Puig, Gori, Ramon, and Argensola (who died in hiding). Escaped: Joli (in Tortosa at the time of the 7 June 1640 riot), Vinyes (escaped in August 1640), Rubí de Marimon (escaped in January 1641), Mir (August 1641), Pons (1641), Corts (1642), Meca (1642), and Anglasell (1643). Judge Masso's fate is unknown; see Elliott, *Revolt of the Catalans,* 570–71, and Jordi Vidal Pla, *Guerra dels Segadors i crisi social: Els exilats filipistas (1640–1652)* (Barcelona, 1982), appendix 1.

in the street violence, but rather was a reward for their role in the election of Louis XIII and the war against the king of Spain. Yet after Barcelona returned to the Spanish monarchy Philip IV confirmed this privilege. Master artisans would have their two annual consellers until the abolition of the Consell de Cent in 1714.[111]

The Seven-Headed Monster

The events of 7–10 June 1640, given the name of Corpus de Sang, or "Corpus of Blood," in the nineteenth century, decisively pushed what had been a serious political crisis between Catalans and their king in the direction of an armed conflict.[112] Today, Catalans refer to the revolt and war between 1640 and 1652 as the "War of the Segadors." This epithet highlights the initiative of the Catalan peasants who first began the attacks against royal troops in the early spring of 1640. Likewise, the Catalan national anthem, "The Song of the Segadors," hails these valiant fighters who rose against Olivares's tyranny to free their land of its enemies "with a good sickle stroke!" As has been pointed out, however, the term "segador" not only is vague but also tends to obscure the participation of the inhabitants of the city of Barcelona, who, according to virtually all eyewitness accounts, had a prominent role during the Corpus of Blood. The peasant rebellion certainly ignited a conflict that would turn into a revolt and a war; but the tragic events of June 1640 in Barcelona catapulted that conflict into a major political crisis in the Spanish monarchy.

Seen within the larger context of popular politics in sixteenth- and seventeenth-century Barcelona, the Corpus of Blood follows a number of familiar patterns. First, it proved, once again, how violence in the streets of a territorial capital could transform tensions between "center and periphery" into a major crisis. As with the murder of the marquis of Almenara in Zaragoza in 1591, the murder of the viceroy in Barcelona in 1640 convinced the Spanish monarchy to use force to resolve what had otherwise been a serious but peaceful dispute. In 1588 and again in 1591–92, Barcelona managed to avoid the killing of royal officers, and this fact con-

111. Josep M. Torras i Ribé, *Els municipis catalans de l'Antic Règim, 1453–1808* (Barcelona, 1983), 73–75. On the support of artistes and menestrals in the Consell de Cent for the election of Louis XIII as count of Barcelona in December 1640, see BNP Français 705: "Estat de la Catalogne: Mémoire de Mr. l'Abbé de St. Cugat sur les affaires de la Principauté," fols. 71–73.

112. Rovira i Virgili, *Corpus,* 5.

tributed to sparing Catalonia an invasion by Spanish troops such as the one suffered by the kingdom of Aragon in 1591.

Second, the events of 1640 reflected the language, ideas, and actions characteristic of popular politics in the city. The violence toward Santa Coloma and the Audiència judges pointed to the deep resentment toward members of the royal justice system in Catalonia. The Corpus of Blood was the first occasion when Audiència judges were chosen as the target of attacks by crowds in Barcelona.. The extreme anger and humiliation vented on these men has long been seen as the result of the judges' harsh measures used to force Catalans to serve their king in the war against France from 1635 on. Given the importance to Barcelona's artisans of appealing to the Audiència, as well as the increasing difficulties of the tribunal from the 1620s on in meeting Catalans' demand for justice, the popular violence against royal judges was also revenge for the judges' failure to carry out their duties.

Moreover, according to supporters of the revolt, the viceroy and royal judges had demonstrated not only their inability to deliver justice but even more seriously their willingness to allow challenges to the laws and privileges of Catalonia and even to allow sacrilege against God. The writer Francesc Martí i Viladamor insisted that given all of those conditions, the "plebeians" *(la Plebe)* not only had legitimate reasons to resort to force but had an obligation to end so many abuses. Martí i Viladamor cited jurists, political writers, miracles, and supernatural events as evidence of the legal and divine sanction for the popular revolt against the failure of royal authorities to carry out their duties. For instance, in response to the abuses of royal troops, God afflicted Catalonia with a drought. "The revolts happened, the count [of Santa Coloma] died, and the judges fled, and then it rained."[113]

The accusations of treason leveled by rioters in Barcelona against viceroy Santa Coloma, the Audiència judges, and other royal officers recall the deeply ingrained commitment of the people of Barcelona to the defense of their city, their privileges, and their institutions. As on so many occasions between the 1580s and 1630s, the people of Barcelona had once more acted on their own to defend their city from its enemies, disregarding the calls of consellers and clergymen to return to order.

To those lay and religious authorities, the rioting was the antithesis of politics, the expected result of the participation of the people in politics. That "people," which the friar Bernardí de Manlleu, the Catalan ambassador in Madrid, described to the ecclesiastic diputat Pau Claris in 1639 as a

---

113. *Noticia universal,* 158–59.

FIGURE 7 Castile lifts the veil from Catalonia's eyes as she is about to fall down a precipice where the French lion awaits her. From a book by a Catalan exile and critic of the 1640 revolt, Alejandro de Ros, *Cataluña desengañada* (Naples, 1646). Courtesy of the Kenneth Spencer Research Library, University of Kansas.

"seven-headed monster composed of lies and calumnies and false ideas," had to be kept under tight control; otherwise, its natural passions would only bring about disaster.[114] By June 1640, the monster had become free from the bonds that kept society and the political order in place.

114. Manlleu to Claris, 27 August 1639, in *MHE*, 20:268 n. 1.

The image of the people as an unbound monster, however powerful and familiar to early modern societies, forces us to consider the place of violence in popular politics.[115] The behavior of crowds in 1640 constituted a radical departure from the more "normal" activities associated with popular politics. Riots in Barcelona, as elsewhere in early modern Europe, were not exceptional; yet it was far more common to find artisans participating in the meetings of the Consell de Cent and its committees, demanding justice from royal courts, even making written petitions to the king than raging against royal officials in the city's streets. Artisans were very active during the riots of June 1640; but there were also many other artisans serving in the city guard and in the Consell de Cent who tried to put an end to the disorders.

From another perspective, Barcelona's case raises a number of issues connected with identity and violence. On the one hand, Natalie Zemon Davis, E. P. Thompson, James Amelang, and others have shown how popular demonstrations and riots could reaffirm community identity by defending customs and values against attacks by "outsiders."[116] In other words, popular violence could represent a defensive expression of community identity. On the other hand, Suzanne Desan has warned that violence *within* the community might also lead to the opposite effect. Citing examples of religious violence during the French Wars of Religion and the French Revolution, Desan argues:

> Violence actually fundamentally transformed the urban community and entirely redefined it. Rather than asserting that existing perceptions of the body social defined violence, one could say that violence over religious beliefs destroyed the existing community and tore it apart in a bloody power struggle as each group fought to draw new communal boundaries. Violence forced urban dwellers to rethink traditional definitions of community.[117]

115. The discussion that follows derives in part from my "Violence and Identity in Sixteenth- and Seventeenth-Century Barcelona," *Mediterranean Studies* 7 (1998): 179–90.

116. Natalie Zemon Davis, "Rites of Violence," in *Society and Culture in Early Modern France* (Stanford, 1975), 152–87; E. P. Thompson, "The Moral Economy of the English Crowd in the Eighteenth Century" in *Customs in Common: Studies in Traditional Popular Culture* (New York, 1993), 185–258; James S. Amelang, "People of the Ribera: Popular Politics and Neighborhood Identity in Early Modern Barcelona," in *Culture and Identity in Early Modern Europe (1500–1800): Essays in Honor of Natalie Zemon Davis*, ed. Barbara Diefendorf and Carla Hesse (Ann Arbor, 1993), 119–37.

117. Suzanne Desan, "Crowds, Community, and Ritual in the Work of E. P. Thompson and Natalie Davis," in *The New Cultural History*, ed. Lynn Hunt (Berkeley, 1989), 65.

The examples of popular violence in Barcelona from the late 1500s to the 1640 revolt point to yet another possibility: a community as a whole might essentially agree with the identity defended by local authorities, but be divided over its meaning. To Barcelona's rulers, the city's political institutions and offices they dominated embodied the privileges and liberty of "the land"; to popular demonstrators those privileges stood for the protection and liberty of *all* city inhabitants as well as some measure of popular participation in its government. In addition, an "official" identity could be used as a standard to evaluate the work of rulers. Those who failed to conform to it might be labeled "traitors" and be treated as enemies of the community.

Conclusion

I began this book arguing that popular politics matters to the political history of early modern Europe in two areas: first, the relations between royal governments and the territorial elite in composite monarchies, and second, the everyday workings of government. On the first point, popular politics could have the greatest impact when violence pushed tensions between a monarchy and the territorial elite into major crises. This happened in the Netherlands in 1566, when Protestant crowds directed their "iconoclastic fury" against Catholic churches, precipitating the rift between the Spanish monarchy and the elite of the Netherlands known as the Dutch Revolt.[1] Likewise, riots in Zaragoza in 1591, in Barcelona in 1640, and in Palermo and Naples in 1647 and 1648 all produced major crises that culminated in revolts.[2] Historians have long recognized the significance of

1. Alistair Duke and D. H. A. Kolff, "The Time of Troubles in the County of Holland, 1566–67," in Alistair Duke, *Reformation and Revolt in the Low Countries* (London, 1990), chap. 6. See also Phyllis Mack Crew, *Calvinist Preaching and Iconoclasm in the Netherlands, 1544–1569* (Cambridge, 1978); Jonathan I. Israel, *The Dutch Republic: Its Rise, Greatness, and Fall, 1477–1806* (Oxford, 1995), 129–54.

2. For Zaragoza, see Jesús Gascón Pérez, "El 'vulgo ciego' en la rebelión aragonesa de 1591," *Revista de historia Jerónimo Zurita* 69/70 (1994): 89–113. For Palermo, see Luis A. Ribot, "Las revueltas sicilianas de 1647–1648," in *1640: La monarquía hispánica en crisis* (Barcelona, 1992), 183–99. For Naples and other revolts of the 1640s in the Spanish monarchy, see Rosario Villari, "Revoluciones periféricas y declive de la monarquía española," in *1640: La monarquía hispánica,* 169–82; and J. H. Elliott, "Revolts in the Spanish Monarchy," in *Preconditions of Revolution in Early Modern Europe,* ed. Robert Forster and Jack P. Greene (Baltimore, 1970), 109–30.

these incidents of popular violence but have generally treated them as spontaneous outbursts that affected, but were not directly involved in, the legal or political tensions between central and territorial authorities.

There was another way in which popular politics mattered to composite monarchies. Local authorities knew that maintaining popular support was essential to strengthening their position vis-à-vis the monarchy, the church, or the nobility. For this reason, rivals of those local authorities tried to undermine or coopt that support. In Barcelona the Consell de Cent lay claim to the loyalty of its subjects, which gave it considerable advantage over viceroys, the monarchy, and the Diputació. During the Fronde, the nobility of Languedoc, Provençal towns, and the Parlement of Paris also vied for popular support to confront what they decried as the French monarchy's excessive demands.[3] Securing such popular support, however, could not depend solely on easy promises during difficult times. Ties of allegiance depended on generations of patronage, familial connections, or long-standing associations, all of which had to be repeatedly reaffirmed to remain strong. Consequently, there were numerous opportunities for commoners, including artisans and peasants, to make demands and take part in the political affairs of their communities and states.

Regarding the everyday workings of government, popular politics could matter greatly if they resulted in the obstruction or nullification of orders, policies, or reforms. As has been pointed out, opposition to military service in Catalonia and Castile affected the Spanish monarchy's ability to maintain its preeminence in European politics. But throughout early modern Europe, overt and covert opposition to religious reform in Catholic and Protestant societies also resulted in serious challenges to rulers, whether to Lutheran princes or Catholic authorities in Germany and the Holy Roman Empire.[4] Likewise, high prices, the plague, or clashes among ethnic, religious, or professional groups affecting large numbers of people might require responses by officials in local, territorial, and central governments, which in turn might generate conflicts among those authorities. In France nobles sometimes supported their subjects' refusal to pay royal taxes because of dire economic conditions. Yet as seriously as authorities

3. Yves-Marie Bercé, *Histoire des Croquants: Étude des soulèvements populaires au XVIIe siècle dans le Sud-Ouest de la France*, 2 vols. (Geneva, 1974); Sharon Kettering, *Judicial Politics and Urban Revolt in Seventeenth-Century France: The Parlement of Aix, 1629–1659* (Princeton, 1978); René Pillorget, *Les mouvements insurrectionnels de Provence entre 1596 et 1715* (Paris, 1975); Orest Ranum, *The Fronde: A French Revolution, 1648–1652* (New York, 1993).

4. For Germany, see David Warren Sabean, *Power in the Blood: Popular Culture and Village Discourse in Early Modern Germany* (Cambridge, 1984); for the Holy Roman Empire, see R. Po-Chia Hsia, *Social Discipline in the Reformation: Central Europe, 1550–1750* (London, 1989).

saw any act of disobedience, not every single act of resistance signaled a failure of government. Terrible economic conditions that may have been expected to produce a crisis did not necessarily pose a threat to political or social order. But if resistance or problems persisted and worsened, then the political consequences could be extremely serious. Hardly any of the instances of popular resistance to military service in Catalonia and Castile in the 1630s and early 1640s produced crises on their own. However, the repetition of such actions, tied to other disputes among local and royal authorities, created a sense that the government of the Spanish monarchy was nearing a crisis, which in Catalonia contributed to the 1640 revolt. In contrast, the dismissal in 1643 of the count-duke of Olivares, the main architect of the war policies, may have helped to avoid a similar outcome. In evaluating the impact of popular politics on the workings of government, it is necessary to look for the broader implications of individual action as well as long-standing patterns behind particular moments of political tension or conflicts.

Although I have concentrated on the workings of composite monarchies and their government, these are not the only areas in which popular politics could provide new perspectives on the political history of early modern Europe. Popular politics may also help us better understand the nature of politics and political relations during this period. Two examples will help clarify my point: the nature of the relationship between rulers and subjects, and the notion of public opinion in early modern monarchies.

For decades, historians have studied the legal and constitutional bases of the relationship between rulers and subjects in early modern European monarchies. In this book, I have also found it necessary to discuss Barcelona artisans' relationship to their kings by examining their understanding of privilege and justice, as well as the legal strategies the artisans used to appeal to their monarchs and to royal judges. Yet popular politics also underscores another essential aspect of royal power that is more tenuous: the personal and affective ties between rulers and subjects. This aspect seems simple enough in relationships between monarchs and favorites, which contemporaries often described in the language of friendship and love.[5] Early modern rulers and writers also considered that love between a Christian ruler and his or her subjects was important to good government. But how could those affective and personal ties bind the

---

5. Antonio Feros, "Twin Souls: Monarchs and Favourites in Early Seventeenth-Century Spain," in *Spain, Europe, and the Atlantic World: Essays in Honour of John H. Elliott,* ed. Richard L. Kagan and Geoffrey Parker (Cambridge, 1995), 25–47.

monarch to ordinary subjects? Were those ties to be understood only metaphorically as expressions of ethical, rhetorical, or religious ideals?

From the perspective of popular politics, a monarch's ability to build personal and affective ties with all of his subjects was not only an ideal but of the greatest practical necessity. Political writers throughout Europe advised rulers that no government would last long if it relied exclusively on force. Even Machiavelli, who recommended that princes instill fear in their subjects, recognized that a ruler who was loved stood a far better chance of staying in power and increasing it.[6] During periods of great necessity, such as war or economic crisis, a monarch needed to instill feelings of loyalty and love in order to demand sacrifices from all subjects. Public ceremonies, the use of powerful symbols, and the performance of certain acts or gestures offered the possibility of inspiring such sentiments in the majority of the common men and women.

Affective and personal ties to their rulers were also beneficial to subjects. Peasants and women could not enjoy the same individual attention that monarchs gave to their counselors and aristocrats, but common men and women wanted their kings and queens to care about them and respond to their needs. Personal rule was not only an ideal notion; it was also a growing expectation of any good government. Such expectations had significant implications for early modern governments. In the Spanish monarchy, it translated into constant appeals to rulers that threatened to overwhelm them. Between 1583 and 1586, one thousand petitions passed Philip II's desk, and in 1587 the Venetian ambassador claimed that the king might have to sign as many as two thousand items in a single day.[7] It is significant that despite the impossibility of establishing such a personal relationship between ruler and all subjects, Philip II and his successors tried to keep that illusion alive, even at the cost of dramatically increasing royal bureaucracy and slowing down government.

Popular politics also offers a valuable perspective on the slippery concept of public opinion. The term has often proved difficult because it has not always been possible to determine with precision whose opinion this was and how it could function in an absolutist monarchy. Scholars of eighteenth-century France have devoted much attention to this issue, even arguing that

6. For example, "one of the best safeguards that a ruler has against plots is not being hated by the people" (book 19); and "the best fortress a ruler can have is not to be hated by the people" (book 20); *The Prince,* ed. Quentin Skinner and Russel Price (Cambridge, 1988), 64, 75.

7. Geoffrey Parker, *The Grand Strategy of Philip II* (New Haven, 1998), 28.

the rise of public opinion contributed significantly to the end of the ancien régime.[8] Historians of seventeenth-century Spain have also had to make use of the notion of public opinion to characterize the interaction between ruler and subjects described in numerous works of politics and expressed by the Habsburg monarchy.[9] In both cases, historians have taken public opinion to be that expressed by influential figures or publications, but not, as Lisa Graham has pointed out, popular opinion. It is true that vulgar opinion was repeatedly condemned by lay and religious authors alike as false and not worthy of the attention of rulers. However, experience seemed to argue that the opposite was true—that is to say, that rulers cared about the opinion of their subjects as a matter of expediency and necessity. Good government depended on their ability to compel their subjects to obey, and therefore no ruler could remain deaf to his or her subjects' strong opposition to certain ministers or policies. Riots, protests, rumors, placards, letters, and published pamphlets might all act as vehicles of such popular opinion, which could then reach local authorities and, through reports from royal officers, the monarch. It is not always possible to establish how that opinion shaped specific actions or decisions, but it is clear that rulers paid attention to it.

In short, an understanding of popular politics is essential to many areas of political history because it provides an important perspective from which to observe the past. Such a perspective will prove most profitable when following what the historian Giovanni Levi has described as the principal method of microhistory: "the reduction of the scale of observation, on a microscopic analysis and an intensive study of the documentary material."[10] For anyone studying the actions of so-called ordinary people, whose opinions were hardly ever written down in great detail (when recorded at all), it becomes almost essential to focus on events and issues that may appear at first incidental and thus insignificant. Yet it is their relative insignificance that is most helpful because it raises questions about what constituted politics and who were political actors in early modern Europe. An examination of popular politics tends to underscore the challenges involved in the practice of government, a subject of endless discussion among early modern political writers, but also the different meanings contemporary ideals—such as the common good, loyalty, obedience, and justice—had in differ-

8. For a discussion of this issue and additional references, see Lisa Jane Graham, "Crimes of Opinion: Policing the Public in Eighteenth-Century Paris," in *Visions and Revisions of Eighteenth-Century France*, ed. Christine Adams, Jack R. Censer, and Lisa Jane Graham (University Park, Penn., 1997), 79–103.

9. John H. Elliott, *Lengua e imperio en la España de Felipe IV* (Salamanca, 1994), 69.

10. Giovanni Levi, "On Microhistory," in *New Perspectives on Historical Writing*, ed. Peter Burke (University Park, Penn., 1992), 95.

ent contexts. To focus exclusively on the interpretation of major ideas and words by writers and political theorists would therefore ignore the subtleties and contradictions that were central to those societies. In addition, popular politics points to issues that might not appear at first to be political at all, but rather criminal or simply administrative. Only by broadening the definition of what was political in early modern Europe will we also be able to understand how common men and women could sometimes become political actors. Popular politics is essential to political history, and to ignore it is to miss the experience of most human beings in the past.

Trades and Crafts in Barcelona, 1450–1650

A. Craft Confraternities with Representation in the Consell de Cent
(capital letters indicate those that had had representatives since 1455)[1]

Artistes

1. *BARBERS-CIRURGIANS* (barbers-surgeons)
2. *CANDELERS DE CERA* (wax chandlers)
3. *ESPECIERS, ADROGUERS,* and *APOTECARIS* (apothecaries and druggists)
4. *NOTARIS,* including both *notaris reials* and *notaris de Barcelona* (notaries)

Menestrals

1. *ARGENTERS* (silversmiths)
2. *ASSAONADORS* (curriers)
3. *BALLESTERS* (crossbow makers)
4. *Barreters* and *capellers,* often called *sombrerers* (hatters)
5. *BEINERS* (scabbard makers)
6. *BLANQUERS* (tanners)
7. *BOTERS* (coopers)
8. *Calceters* (stocking makers)
9. *CANDELERS DE SEU* (tallow chandlers)
10. *Capsers* (box makers)
11. *Carnissers* (butchers)
12. *Cinters* (ribbon makers)
13. *CORREDORS DE COLL* (auctioneers)
14. *COTONERS* (cottoners)
15. *Escudellers* (crock pot makers)
16. *ESPARTERS* (esparto makers)
17. *ESPASSERS* (sword makers) joined by *viratoners* (arrow makers)

1. Jaume Vicens i Vives, *Ferran II i la ciutat de Barcelona: 1479–1516,* 3 vols. (Barcelona, 1936–37), Appendix, doc. nos. 4 (7 October 1455 privilege), 158, 182 (13 December 1498); AHCB C VIII-12 B (Llibreta de inseculacions, 1617?-1660): lists of candidates for municipal offices, 1504–1622 and 1617.

18. *FERRERS*   (blacksmiths)
19. *FLASSADERS*   (blanket makers)
20. *FRENERS*   (bridle makers)[2]
21. *FUSTANYERS*   (fustian makers)
22. *FUSTERS*   (carpenters)
23. *Garbelladors*   (sifters)
24. *GERRERS*   (jug or jar makers)
25. *HORTOLANS* del Portal Nou   (market gardeners of the Portal Nou)
26. *Llancers*   (spear makers)
27. *LLAURADORS*   (laborers)[3]
28. *Llibreters*   (booksellers)
29. *MARINERS*   (sailors)
30. *MATALASSERS*   (mattress makers)
31. *MERCERS,* also known as *botiguers de teles*   (mercers)[4]
32. *MESTRES DE CASES*   (masons)
33. *Molers*   (stonecutters and grindstone makers)
34. *Ollers*   (cooking pot makers)
35. *PARAIRES*   (wool clothiers)
36. *Passamaners*   (passementerie makers)[5]
37. *PELLERS,* or *peiers*   (old clothes dealers)
38. *PELLISSERS*   (furriers)
39. *RAJOLERS*   (tile makers)
40. *SABATERS*   (shoemakers)
41. *SASTRES*   (tailors)
42. *Tapiners*   (clog makers)
43. *TEIXIDORS DE LLANA*   (wool weavers)
44. *TEIXIDORS DE LLI*   (linen weavers)
45. *TINTORERS de drap de llana*   (wool dyers)
46. *Torners*   (turners)
47. *Velers*   (veil makers)
48. *Velluters*   (velvet makers)
49. *Vidriers*   (glassmakers)

B. Craft Confraternities in the City Guard but without Representation in the Consell de Cent[6]

50. *Taverners*   (tavern keepers)
51. *Hostalers*   (innkeepers)
52. *Hortolans de Sant Antoni*   (market gardeners of the Sant Antoni gate)
53. *Perxers*   (ribbon makers)
54. *Pescadors*   (fishers)

2. Belonged to the Confraternity of Sant Esteve (see below).
3. Did not exist as a confraternity by the late sixteenth century.
4. Belonged to the Confraternity of Sant Julià (see below).
5. Belonged to the Confraternity of Sant Julià.
6. BC F. Bon. 10848: *Orde militar dels puestos als quals las compañias y altras personas de la ciutat de Barcelona han de acudir en tems de guerra, ô rebatos* (Barcelona, 1623).

C. Large Confraternities Made Up of Several Crafts[7]

Estevens or members of the Confraternity of Sant Esteve (see *freners* above)

55. *Arnesers,* or *basters* (packsaddle makers)
56. *Batifullers* (metal beaters)
57. *Broquerers* (shield makers)
58. *Cervellerers* (helmet makers)
59. *Guadamassilers* (leather gilders)
60. *Oripellers* (brass workers)
61. *Pintors* (painters)
62. *Sellers* (saddle makers)

Julians or members of the Confraternity
of Sant Julià (see **mercers** and **passamaners** above)

63. *Corders* (string makers)
64. *Corretgers* (belt makers)
65. *Guanters* (glove makers)
66. *Naipers* (card makers)
67. *Pinters* (comb makers)
68. *Tireters* (makers of flaps for doublets)

D. Craft Confraternities Not in the Consell de Cent or in the Guard

69. *Ataconadors* (cobblers)
70. *Bastaixos* (longshoremen)
71. *Barquers* (boatmen)
72. *Calafats* or *mestres d'aixa* (shipwrights)
73. *Calderers* (cauldron makers)
74. *Corders de viola* (musical string makers)
75. *Corredors de besties* (cattle brokers)
76. *Daguers* (cutlers)
77. *Espardenyers* (sandal makers)
78. *Estampers* (printers)
79. *Giponers* (doublet makers)
80. *Moliners* (millers)
81. *Pastissers* (pastry cooks)
82. *Revenedors* (resellers)
83. *Retorsedors de seda* (silk twisters)

7. See Pierre Bonnassie, *La organización del trabajo en Barcelona a finales del siglo XV* (Barcelona, 1975), 201–2; Salvador Sanpere i Miquel, *Barcelona: Son passat, present i porvenir* (Barcelona, 1878); Abbott Payson Usher, *The Early History of Deposit Banking in Mediterranean Europe* (New York, 1943), vol. 1, pt. 2.

84. *Traginers de ribera* or *traginers de mar* (carriers of goods
    from the port to the city)
85. *Vanovers* (quilt makers)

E. Journeymen Craft Confraternities[8]

1. *Hortolans joves* (journeymen market gardeners)
2. *Joves mestres de cases i molers* (journeymen masons and stonecutters)
3. *Joves sabaters* (journeymen shoemakers)[9]
4. *Joves sastres* (journeymen tailors)
5. *Joves i fadrins fusters* (journeymen carpenters)
6. *Joves paraires* (journeymen wool clothiers)

8. Sources: AHCB Gremis 37-2: carpenters' confraternity council book, 25 April 1614;
Pere Joan Comes, *Libre de algvnes coses asanyalades, succehides en Barcelona y en altres parts*
(Barcelona, [1583] 1878), 635; BC MS 501: Berart-Congost, *Molt illustres, magnifichs, y savis
senyors* (Barcelona, 1623 [*sic* 1632?]); *RB*, 5:227.
   9. Formed a confraternity with the *ataconadors*.

Artisan Representation in Barcelona's Consell de Cent

The Consell de Cent had 64 artisan *jurats* equally divided between *artistes* and *menestrals*. Their election followed a complex process that had been established by a 1498 privilege and that underwent few changes in the next 200 years. The privilege assigned a fixed number of seats to specific professional colleges and craft confraternities.

A. *Artista jurats*[10]

notaris de Barcelona	10
notaris reials	4
especiers	10
candelers de cera	2
barbers-cirurgians	6
Total:	32

B. *Menestral jurats*

Group 1: *Jurats* elected every year

freners	2
sastres	2
paraires	2
sabaters	2
argenters	2
ferrers	2
fusters (caixers)	1
blanquers	1
assaonadors	1
Subtotal:	15

Group 2: *Jurats* elected in even years

fusters (bosquers)	1
calceters	1
boters	1
hortolans	1
mercers	1
mestres de cases and *molers*	1

Group 2: *Jurats* elected in even years
(*continued*)

teixidors de llana	1
teixidors de lli	1
candelers de sèu	1
fustanyers	1
ballesters and *viratoners*	1
pellers	1
cotoners	1
beiners	1
gerrers and *ollers*	1
rajolers	1
pellissers	1
Subtotal:	17

Group 3: *Jurats* elected in odd years

corredors de coll	1
mariners	1
matalassers	1
espassers and *llancers*	1
tintorers	1
esparters	1
flassaders	1
Subtotal:	7

The remaining 10 seats in odd years were distributed from among the jurats from Group 1 elected the year before.

10. See the *Privilegi de regiment d'insaculació*, 13 December 1498; reprinted in Vicens i Vives, *Ferran II*, Appendix, doc. no. 182, pp. 341–54.

The composition of the *menestrals'* estate was the following:

Even years:		Odd years:	
Group 1	15	Group 1	15
Groups 2 and 3	17	Group 3	7
		Returning *jurats* from Group 1	
Total:	32	elected the previous year	10
		Total:	32

C. *Artista* candidates for fifth conseller (based on 1498 privilege, alternating yearly between one *artista* and one *menestral* until 1641)[11]

notaris de Barcelona	18
notaris reials	4
apotecaris	14
candelers de cera	2
barbers-cirurgians	9
Total:	47

D. *Menestral* candidates for fifth conseller[12]

Group 1: Jurats elected every year

	Number of jurats	Number of candidates for jurat	Number of candidates for conseller
Estevens	2 (*freners*)	25 (*freners*)	2
sastres	2	24	3
paraires	2	32	12
sabaters	2	32	9 (2 of which were *tapiners*)
argenters	2	25	9
ferrers	2	40	8
fusters (*caixers*)	2	23	10 (for both *fusters caixers* and *bosquers*)
blanquers	1	17	6
pellissers	1	14	2

11. AHCB C VIII llig. B, no. 12: Llibreta de inseculats en las bossas de Consellers, 1617[?]–1660: list of candidates for 1617.
12. AHCB C VIII llig. C, no. 12: Llibre de insaculacions, 1590–94 [–1622].

Group 2: *Jurats* elected in even years

	Number of jurats	Number of candidates for jurat	Number of candidates for conseller
fusters bosquers	1	14	10 (for both *fusters caixers* and *bosquers*)
calceters	1	14/15?	1
boters	1	22	2
mercers	1	23	3 (2 of whom were *passamaners*)
mesters de cases and *molers*	1	30	2
teixidors de llana	1	36	1
teixidors de lli	1	12	2
candelers de sèu	1	18	1
fustanyers	1	7	2 (both of whom were *cordoners*)
ballesters and *viratoners*	1	10	0
pellers	1	14	4 (2 of whom were *barreters*)
cotoners	1	8	3
beiners	1	15	1
ollers	1		
rajolers	1	16	3 (1 of whom was an *escudeller*)
pellissers	1	14	3

Group 3: *Jurats* elected in odd years

	Number of jurats	Number of candidates for jurat	Number of candidates for conseller
corredors de coll	1	14	0
mariners	1	55	3
matalassers	1	19	2
espasers and *llancers*	1	12	0
tintorers	1	8	2
esparters and *vidriers*	1	23	3 (1 of whom was a *vidrier*)
flassaders	1	14	2/1?

Total number of menestral candidates for fifth conseller: 111

E. Other offices for which artisans were eligible[13]

Office	Number of officers	Number of candidates
Receptors and *pallolers* (tax collectors and administrators of the public granary)	varied	136 (merchants, *artistes,* and *menestrals*)
Credencers and *romaners* (bookkeeper-comptrollers and weighers)	varied	185 ''
Portalers, cauquilladors, and *pesadors de palla i lenya* (tax collectors and weighers of hay and firewood tax)	varied	285 ''
Subadministrator of markets and captain of the guard	1	63 (*menestrals* only)
Verguers and *correus* (standard-bearers and messenger)	2	85 ''
Porter del clavari (assistant to the city treasurer)	1	25 ''
Pessadors del Mostassaf (weighers)	4	36 ''

In addition there were a number of minor offices artisans could hold (e.g., the keeper of the city's clock, or *rellotger,* was a blacksmith).

13. AHCB C VIII llig. C, no. 12: Llibre de insaculacions, 1590–94 [–1622]; Vicens i Vives, *Ferran II,* 1:129–30, 139.

Officers in the Confraternity of Master Shoemakers

A. Confraternity administrators[14]

prohoms (chief officers)[15]	4
clavari (treasurer)[16]	1
credencers (bookkeepers)	2
receptor (dues collector)	2
oïdors (account auditors)	4
andadors (messengers)[17]	1
syndic	1
examiners	4 (in addition to the *prohoms*)

B. Company officers

standard-bearer	1
sergeant	1
cap de squadra (chief of squadron)	1
assistant to the sergeant	1
corporals	5

14. Source: AHCB Gremis 1-91 (Llibre de consells, 1578–82) and AHCB Gremis 1-92.

15. In July of 1578, the confraternity lifted a restriction that there could be only one *prohom* from each of the four city quarters.

16. The confraternity's council chose one *clavari* from four individuals nominated by the officers. A 1617 proposal to make the *clavari* an office for life failed.

17. The *andador* was in charge of maintaining the chapel and the confraternity house and announcing masses, burials, and council meetings. Candidates had to know how to read and write.

Glossary

Note: For many of the definitions below, I have especially relied on the glossary in J. H. Elliott's *The Revolt of the Catalans* and on Víctor Ferro's *El dret públic català*. For the names of Barcelona's trades, see Appendix 1.

Currencies

1 *ducat:* 30 *sous*
1 *lliura:* 20 *sous*
1 *ral:* 2 *sous*
1 *sou:* 12 *diners*

artista (pl. *artistes*): master artisan belonging to a one of a select group of "arts" organized into colleges: apothecaries and druggists, barber-surgeons, notaries (two groups), and wax chandlers. Artistes formed one of the two artisans' estates in the Consell de Cent.

Audiència: the royal court of appeals in Barcelona and Catalonia's supreme judicial body. Its official name was the Reial (royal) Audiència. After 1599, it consisted of three chambers with seventeen judges. The first chamber was presided over by a chancellor *(canceller)* and the second by a regent *(regent la cancelleria)*.

braç (pl. *braços*): one of the three orders of Catalan society: *braç eclesiàstic:* ecclesiastical estate; *braç militar:* noble estate; *braç reial:* representatives from towns and cities. The *braços* were represented in the Corts, where they deliberated separately. The ecclesiastical and the noble *braços* could also meet separately in Barcelona to discuss matters and advise the *diputats*. See also Junta de Braços.

cafís: measure used for dry goods (such as grains), equivalent approximately to 4 *quarteres,* approximately 280 liters.

carrer: street.

Committee of Twenty-Four on the Corts (*consell de vint-i-quatrena de Corts*): committee of the Consell de Cent charged with the authority to draft proposals for legislation and royal privileges and issue instructions to Barcelona's syndics to the Corts; it consisted of 24 jurats.

Consell de Cent: Council of the Hundred, Barcelona's governing body made up of 144 representatives or jurats elected annually. It was presided over by five consellers.

consellers: Barcelona's five (six from 1641 on) counselors or executive officers who presided over the Consell de Cent; the first conseller was known as conseller *en cap* (chief counselor).

consulta: a document drawn up by royal ministers, offering advice to the king.

Corts: the principality's parliamentary assembly formed by representatives from the three *braços.* Its official name was the Cort General.

Council of Aragon (Catalan: Consell d'Aragó; Spanish: Consejo de Aragón): the royal council (usually in Madrid) that reviewed royal policy for Catalonia and the other territories of the Crown of Aragon. Its chief ministers were five regents, at least one of whom was Catalan.

Council of State (Spanish: Consejo de Estado): royal council (usually in Madrid), primarily, although not exclusively, concerned with external affairs.

Crown of Aragon: the eastern territories of the Spanish monarchy that included the kingdom of Aragon, the kingdom of Valencia, and the principality of Catalonia (see Map 1).

Diputació: the permanent committee of the Corts located in Barcelona, charged with the collection of taxes voted at the Corts and with the defense of Catalan laws and privileges; its official name was the Diputació del General, but it was also called the Generalitat.

diputats: the three deputies (one from each of the *braços*) who presided over the Diputació; they were elected every three years.

dissentiment: a formal protest before the Corts that effectively paralyzed all parliamentary proceedings until it was resolved.

drassanes: the shipyard located in Barcelona's port.

Junta de Braços: extraordinary joint meeting of the *braços* convened by the *diputats* and *oïdors* in Barcelona for consultation on urgent matters.

Junta de Ejecución: a small junta consisting of the count-duke of Olivares and other principal ministers, set up to avoid the delays and cumbersome process of government through the Consejo de Estado; the most powerful administrative organ at Madrid in the later years of Olivares's government.

jurats: the 144 councilmen of the Consell de Cent, divided into four estates *(estaments):* first estate (honored citizens, knights, and doctors of law and medicine); second estate: merchants; third estate: artistes; and fourth estate: menestrals. In a number of other Catalan cities and towns (such as Girona), the jurats were the town counselors, akin to Barcelona's con-sellers.

memorial: memorandum.

menestral (pl. *menestrals*): a master artisan belonging to Barcelona's "mechanical arts" organized into about 70 craft confraternities, such as shoemakers, tanners, carpenters, resellers, etc.; menestrals formed one of the two artisans' estates in the Consell de Cent.

mercès: favors (such as royal privileges and other honors) granted in recognition of "services" performed (such as military or civil service).

motu proprio: a papal declaration addressing a particular issue (such as the con-demnation of hoarding).

oficials: a somewhat vague term referring specifically to journeymen, but also more generally to "men of the trades."

oïdors: the three keepers of accounts (representing each of the *braços*) in the Diputació. They were second in importance only to the *diputats*. They were elected every three years.

paers: counselors in a number of Catalan towns and cities (such as Cervera and Lleida), akin to Barcelona's consellers.

pàtria: fatherland, country.

plaça: public square.

poble menut: the "little people" (akin to the French *menu peuple*), that is to say, ordinary men and women.

prohoms (or *promens*): equivalent to the notion of "elders" (as in a community). In a number of Barcelona's craft confraternities, this was the term used for their chief officers.

quartera: measure used for dry goods (such as grains) equivalent approximately to 70 liters.

regent: see Audiència and Council of Aragon.

remences: Catalan serfs who won their freedom from serfdom in 1486.

segador: reaper.

serveis: services (such as military or civil service).

síndics: Syndics, delegates, or agents (from cities, craft confraternities, etc.); the *síndics de Corts* were delegates to the Corts.

Syndicate of the Three Estates and the People (*Sindicat dels Tres Estaments i del Poble*): a special delegation formed primarily by merchants and master artisans from Barcelona's colleges and craft confraternities in the mid-fifteenth century to appeal to the king for political reforms in the city's government.

Taula de Canvi: Barcelona's deposit bank, replaced in 1609 by the Bank of Barcelona.

Trentenari: committee of the Consell de Cent charged with the examination of ordinances, particularly those affecting Barcelona's colleges and craft confraternities. It consisted of 36 jurats who rotated every three months.

unió (pl. *unions*):   special force composed of armed men from cities and towns temporarily convened to combat criminals and bandits and to restore order; also called *germandat.*

veguer: in Barcelona, the royal officer charged with judicial and policing duties.

viceroy (Catalan: *virrei;* Spanish: *virrey*):   the king's alter ego in the territories of the Spanish monarchy charged with administrative, judicial, and military duties; in Catalonia, the viceroy resided in Barcelona.

vitualles: a term roughly equivalent in English to "victuals" or "goods."

Bibliography

Published Primary Sources

Ágreda, María de Jesús de. *Cartas de la Venerable Madre Sor María de Ágreda y del Señor Rey Felipe IV.* Ed. Francisco Silvela. 2 vols. Madrid, 1885–86.

——. *Cartas de Sor María de Jesús de Ágreda y de Felipe IV.* Ed. Carlos Seco Serrano. Vols. 108–9 of *Biblioteca de Autores Españoles.* Madrid, 1958.

Assarino, Luca. *Delle riuolutioni di Catalogna.* Bologna, 1645.

Blecua, José Manuel, ed. *Pliegos Poéticos del s. XVI de la Biblioteca de Cataluña.* Madrid, 1976.

Bosc, Andreu. *Sumari index o epítome dels admirables y nobilíssimis títols de honor de Cathalunya, Rosselló, i Cerdanya.* Perpinyà, 1628. Fascimile edition, Barcelona-Sueca, 1974.

Bruniquer, Esteve Gilabert. *Relació sumaria de la antiga fundació y cristianisme de la Ciutat de Barcelona.* Barcelona, 1885.

——. *Rúbriques de Bruniquer. Ceremonial dels Magnífichs Consellers y Regiment de la Ciutat de Barcelona.* Ed. Francesch Carreras y Candi and Bartomeu Gunyalons y Bou. 5 vols. Barcelona, 1912–16.

Cavallers i ciutadans a la Catalunya del cinc-cents. Ed. Antoni Simon i Tarrés. Barcelona, 1991.

Caverel, Philippe de. *Ambassade en Espagne et en Portugal, en 1582.* Arras, 1860.

Cock, Henrique. *Relación del viaje hecho por Felipe II en 1585, á Zaragoza, Barcelona y Valencia.* Ed. Alfredo Morel-Fatio and Antonio Rodríguez Villa. Madrid, 1876.

Comes, Pere Joan. *Libre de algvnes coses asanyalades, succehides en Barcelona y en altres parts.* Barcelona, [1583] 1878.

Constitutions y altres drets de Catalunya. 3 vols. Barcelona, 1704.

Coras, Jean de. *Discours des parties et office d'un bon et entier iuge.* Lyon, 1605.

Despalau, Frederic. *Diari.* In *Cavallers i ciutadans a la Catalunya del cinc-cents.*

Dietaris de la Generalitat de Catalunya. Vols. 3–5. Ed. Josep Maria Sans i Travé. Barcelona, 1996–99.

Gremios y cofradías de la antigua Corona de Aragón. Ed. Francisco de Bofarull y Sans. Vol. 41 of *Colección de documentos inéditos del Archivo de la Corona de Aragón.* Barcelona, 1910.

Guicciardini, Francesco. *Viaje a España.* Trans. José María Alonso Gamo. Valencia, 1952.

Horozco y Covarruvias, Juan de. *Emblemas morales.* Zaragoza, 1604.

Iorba, Dionysio Hieronymo de [Dionís Jeroni Jorba]. *Descripción de las excellencias de la muy insigne ciudad de Barcelona.* 2d ed. Barcelona, 1589.

Llibre de les solemnitats de Barcelona. Ed. Agustí Duran i Sanpere and Josep Sanabre. Vol. 2. Barcelona, 1947.

Machiavelli, Niccolo. *The Prince.* Ed. Quentin Skinner and Russel Price. Cambridge, 1988.

Manual de novells ardits vulgarment apel.lat Dietari del Antich Consell Barceloní. Ed. Frederich Schwartz y Luna and Francesch Carreras y Candi. Vols. 5–13. Barcelona, 1892–1911.

A manuell, or a justice of peace his vade-mecum. Cambridge, 1641.

[Martí i Viladamor, Francesc]. *Noticia universal de Cataluña.* Barcelona, 1640.

——. *Noticia universal de Cataluña.* Ed. Xavier Torres. Vol. 1 of *Escrits polítics del segle XVII.* Vic, 1995.

Melo, Francisco de. *Guerra de Cataluña.* Ed. Joan Estruch Tobella. Barcelona, 1982.

Memorial Histórico Español. Vols. 20–25. Madrid, 1888–93.

Navagero, Andrea. *Il viaggio fatto in Spagna et in Francia.* Venice, 1563.

Panno, Francesc Pasqual de. *Motines de Cataluña.* Ed. Isabel Juncosa and Jordi Vidal. Barcelona, 1993.

Parets, Miquel. *De los muchos sucesos dignos de memoria que han ocurrido en Barcelona y otros lugares de Cataluña.* In *MHE,* vols. 20–25.

——. *A Journal of the Plague Year: The Diary of the Barcelona Tanner Miquel Parets, 1651.* Trans. and ed. James S. Amelang. New York, 1991.

Peña, Antonio de la. *Un práctico castellano del siglo XVI (Antonio de la Peña).* Ed. Manuel López-Rey y Arrojo. Madrid, 1935.

Pere Gil, S.I. (1551–1622) i la seva Geografia de Catalunya. Ed. Josep Iglésies. Barcelona, 1949.

Pérez, Antonio [Baltasar Alamos de Barrientos]. *Aforismos sacados de la historia de Publio Cornelio Tácito.* Ed. Modesto Santos. Barcelona, 1991.

Pérez de Herrera, Cristóbal. *Amparo de Pobres.* Ed. Michel Cavillac. Madrid, 1975.

Platter, Thomas. *Journal of a Younger Brother: The Life of Thomas Platter as a Medical Student in Montpellier at the Close of the Sixteenth Century.* Trans. Seán Jennett. London, 1963.

Pujades, Jeroni. *Dietari de Jeroni Pujades.* Ed. Josep Maria Casas Homs. 4 vols. Barcelona, 1975–76.

Quevedo, Francisco de. *Sueños y discursos.* Ed. Felipe C. R. Maldonado. Madrid, 1972.

Ros, Alejandro. *Catalvña desengañada.* Naples, 1645.

Rozmital, Leo of. *The Travels of Leo of Rozmital.* Trans. Malcolm Letts. Cambridge, 1957.

Rubí, Basili de. *Les Corts Generals de Pau Claris.* Barcelona, 1976.

Saavedra Fajardo, Diego de. *Empresas políticas.* Ed. Francisco Javier Díez de Revenga. Barcelona, 1988.

——. *Idea de un principe politico christiano representada en cien empresas.* Munich, 1640.

Saconomina, Jeroni. *Memòries.* In *Cavallers i ciutadans a la Catalunya del cinc-cents.*

[Sala Berart, Gaspar.] *Proclamación católica a la magestad piadosa de Felipe El Grande.* Barcelona, 1640.

——. *Secrets Públics, de Gaspar Sala, i altres textos.* Ed. Eva Serra. Vol. 2 of *Escrits polítics del segle XVII.* Vic, 1995.

Salazar, Juan. *Siguese un caso notable, y verdadero de cono* [sic] *los dsablos* [sic] *se han llevado a un mercader agavellador de trigo, porque no se quiso confesar.* Barcelona, 1603.

Viatge a l'infern d'en Pere Porter. Ed. Josep Maria Pons i Guri. Barcelona, 1999.

Secondary Sources

1640: La monarquía hispánica en crisis. Barcelona, 1992.

Amelang, James S. "Barristers and Judges in Early Modern Barcelona: The Rise of a Legal Elite." *American Historical Review* 89 (December 1984): 1264–84.

——. "El Carrer de Montcada: Canvi social i cultura popular a la Barcelona moderna." *L'Avenç* 18 (1979): 56–60.

——. *The Flight of Icarus: Artisan Autobiography in Early Modern Europe.* Stanford, 1998.

——. *Honored Citizens of Barcelona: Patrician Culture and Class Relations, 1490–1714.* Princeton, 1986.

——. "People of the Ribera: Popular Politics and Neighborhood Identity in Early Modern Barcelona." In *Culture and Identity in Early Modern Europe (1500–1800): Essays in Honor of Natalie Zemon Davis,* ed. Barbara Diefendorf and Carla Hesse. Ann Arbor, 1993. 119–37.

Anderson, M. S. *War and Society in Europe of the Old Regime, 1618–1789.* New York, 1988.

Arrieta Alberdi, Jon. *El Consejo Supremo de la Corona de Aragón (1494–1704).* Zaragoza, 1994.

Bada, Joan. *Situació religiosa de Barcelona en el s. XVI.* Barcelona, 1970.

Baker, Keith Michael, ed. *The Political Culture of the Old Regime.* Vol. 1 of *The French Revolution and the Creation of Modern Political Culture.* Oxford, 1987.

Banks, Philip. "The Origins of the 'Gremi de Sabaters' of Barcelona." *Quaderns d'arqueologia e història de la ciutat* 18 (1980): 109–18.

Batlle Gallart, Carmen. "La 'busca.' Aspecto de la reforma municipal de Barcelona." In *Homenaje a Jaime Vicens Vives.* 2 vols. Barcelona, 1965–67. 1:337–50.

——. *La crisis social y económica de Barcelona a mediados del siglo XV.* 2 vols. Barcelona, 1973.

——. *L'expansió baixmedieval (segles XIII–XV).* Vol. 3 of *Història de Catalunya.* Ed. Pierre Vilar. Barcelona, 1988.

——. "La ideología de la 'Busca.' La crisis municipal de Barcelona del siglo XV." *Estudios de Historia Moderna* 6 (1955): 165–95.

——. "La proyectada reforma del gobierno municipal de Barcelona (año 1386)." In *VII Congreso de Historia de la Corona de Aragón.* 3 vols. Barcelona, 1962. 3:143–52.

Batlle, Mar. *Patriotisme i modernitat a La fi del Comte d'Urgell.* Barcelona, 1999.

Beik, William. *Absolutism and Society in Seventeenth-Century France.* Cambridge, 1985.

Belenguer i Cebrià, Ernest. "Un balance de las relaciones entre la corte y el país: los *greuges* de 1599 en Cataluña." *Estudis* 13 (1987): 99–130.

——. "La legislació político-judicial de les Corts de 1599 a Catalunya." *Pedralbes* 7 (1987): 9–28

Bensch, Stephen P. *Barcelona and Its Rulers, 1096–1291.* Cambridge, 1994.

Bercé, Yves-Marie. *Histoire des Croquants: Étude des soulèvements populaires au XVIIe siècle dans le Sud-Ouest de la France.* 2 vols. Geneva, 1974.

——. *History of Peasant Revolts: The Social Origins of Rebellion in Early Modern France.* Trans. Amanda Whitmore. Ithaca, 1990.

Betrán, José Luis. *La peste en la Barcelona de los Austrias.* Lleida, 1996.

Bisson, T. N. *The Medieval Crown of Aragon: A Short History.* Oxford, 1986.

Black, Antony. *Guilds and Civil Society in European Political Thought from the Twelfth Century to the Present.* Ithaca, 1984.

Blickle, Peter. *The Revolution of 1525: The German Peasants' War from a New Perspective.* Trans. Thomas A. Brady Jr. and H. C. Erik Midelfort. Baltimore, 1985.

Bofarull y Brocá, Antonio de. *Historia crítica (civil y eclesiástica) de Cataluña.* 9 vols. Barcelona, 1876–78.

Bonnassie, Pierre. *La organización del trabajo en Barcelona a fines del siglo XV.* Barcelona, 1975.

Bossenga, Gail. *The Politics of Privilege: Old Regime and Revolution in Lille.* Cambridge, 1991.

Braudel, Fernand. *The Mediterranean and the Mediterranean World in the Age of Philip II.* Trans. Siân Reynolds. 2 vols. New York, 1972.

Bromley, J. S. "Outlaws at Sea, 1660–1720: Liberty, Equality, and Fraternity among the Caribbean Freebooters." In *History from Below: Studies in Popular Protest and Popular Ideology,* ed. Frederick Krantz. Oxford, 1988. 293–318.

Brown, Jonathan, and J. H. Elliott. *A Palace for a King: The Buen Retiro and the Court of Philip IV.* New Haven, 1980.

Burke, Peter. *Popular Culture in Early Modern Europe.* London, 1978.

Burns, J. H., with Mark Goldie, ed. *Cambridge History of Political Thought 1450–1700.* Cambridge, 1991.

Cabestany i Fort, Joan-F. "Els mestres sabaters i la Confraria de Sant Marc (segle XIV)." In *Homenaje a Jaime Vicens Vives.* 2 vols. Barcelona, 1965–67. 2:75–84.

Calbet i Camarasa, Josep M. and Jacint Corbella i Corbella. *Diccionari Biogràfic de Metges Catalans.* 2 vols. Barcelona, 1982–83.

Capmany, Aurelio, and Agustín Duran y Sanpere. *El gremio de los maestros zapateros.* Barcelona, 1944.

Capmany y de Montpalau, Antonio de. *Memorias históricas sobre la marina, comercio y artes de la antigua ciudad de Barcelona.* Ed. E. Giralt and C. Batlle. 3 vols. Barcelona, 1961–63.

Carrera Pujal, Jaime. *Aspectos de la vida gremial barcelonesa en los siglos XVIII y XIX.* Madrid, 1949.

——. *Historia política y económica de Cataluña: Siglos XVI al XVIII.* 3 vols. Barcelona, 1946–47.

Català i Roca, Pere. *El virrei comte de Santa Coloma.* Barcelona, 1988.

Chartier, Roger. *The Cultural Origins of the French Revolution*. Trans. Lydia G. Cochrane. Durham, N.C., 1991.

Colas Latorre, Gregorio, and José Antonio Salas Ausens. *Aragón en el siglo XVI: Alteraciones sociales y conflictos políticos*. Zaragoza, 1982.

Coroleu é Inglada, José, and José Pella y Forgas. *Las Cortes Catalanas*. Barcelona, 1876.

Corteguera, Luis R. "Barcelona en 1591: Historia de una revuelta evitada." *Cuadernos de ALDEEU* 9 (November 1993): 267–77.

——. "El motín: ¿Una institución de la política popular en la Barcelona del XVI–XVII?" In *Tercer Congrés d'Història Moderna de Catalunya: Actes*. 2:235–41.

——. "The Painter Who Lost His Hat: Artisans and Justice in Early Modern Barcelona." *Sixteenth Century Journal* 29 (1998): 1021–40.

——. "Violence and Identity in Sixteenth- and Seventeenth-Century Barcelona." *Mediterranean Studies* 7 (1998): 179–90.

Crew, Phyllis Mack. *Calvinist Preaching and Iconoclasm in the Netherlands, 1544–1569*. Cambridge, 1978.

Davis, Natalie Zemon. "Rites of Violence." In *Society and Culture in Early Modern France*. Stanford, 1975. 152–87.

Desan, Suzanne. "Crowds, Community, and Ritual in the Work of E. P. Thompson and Natalie Davis." In *The New Cultural History*, ed. Lynn Hunt. Berkeley, 1989. 47–71.

Diefendorf, Barbara B. *Beneath the Cross: Catholics and Huguenots in Sixteenth-Century Paris*. Oxford, 1991.

Duke, Alistair and D. H. A. Kolff. "The Time of Troubles in the County of Holland, 1566–67." In *Reformation and Revolt in the Low Countries*, by Alistair Duke. London, 1990.

Duran i Sanpere, Agustí. *Barcelona i la seva història*. 3 vols. Barcelona, 1972–75.

Elliott, John H. *The Count-Duke of Olivares: The Statesman in an Age of Decline*. New Haven, 1986.

——. "A Europe of Composite Monarchies." *Past and Present* 137 (November 1992): 48–71.

——. *Lengua e imperio en la España de Felipe IV*. Salamanca, 1994.

——. *The Revolt of the Catalans: A Study in the Decline of Spain, 1598–1640*. Cambridge, 1963.

——. "Revolts in the Spanish Monarchy." In *Preconditions of Revolution in Early Modern Europe*, ed. Robert Forster and Jack Greene. Baltimore, 1970. 109–30.

——. *Richelieu and Olivares*. Cambridge, 1984.

——. *Spain and Its World, 1500–1700: Selected Essays*. New Haven, 1989.

Estèbe, Janine. *Tocsin pour un massacre: La saison des Saint-Barthélemy*. Paris, 1968.

Farr, James. *Hands of Honor: Artisans and Their World in Dijon, 1550–1650*. Ithaca, 1988.

Feliu Montfort, Gaspar. *Precios y salarios en la Cataluña moderna*. 2 vols. [Madrid], 1991.

Fernández-Santamaría, José Antonio. *Reason of State and Statecraft in Spanish Political Thought, 1595–1640*. Lanham, Md., 1983.

——. *The State, War, and Peace: Spanish Political Thought in the Renaissance, 1516–1559*. Cambridge, 1977.

Feros, Antonio. "Twin Souls: Monarchs and Favourites in Early Seventeenth-Century Spain." In Kagan and Parker, *Spain, Europe, and the Atlantic World.* 25–47.

——. " 'Vicedioses, pero humanos': El drama del rey." *Cuadernos de Historia Moderna* 14 (1993): 103–31.

Ferro, Víctor. *El dret públic català: Les institucions a Catalunya fins al Decret de Nova Planta.* Vic, 1987.

Flynn, Maureen. "Mimesis of the Last Judgment: The Spanish *Auto de fe.*" *Sixteenth Century Journal* 22 (1991): 281–88.

Foucault, Michel. "On Popular Justice: A Discussion with Maoists." In *Power / Knowledge: Selected Interviews and Other Writings.* Ed. Colin Gordon. New York, 1980. 1–36.

Freedman, Paul. "The German and Catalan Peasant Revolts." *American Historical Review* 98 (February 1993): 39–54.

García Espuche, Albert. *Un siglo decisivo: Barcelona y Cataluña, 1550–1640.* Madrid, 1998.

García i Espuche, Albert, and Manuel Guàrdia i Bassols. *Espai i societat a la Barcelona pre-industrial.* Barcelona, 1986.

Gascón Pérez, Jesús. "Defensa de los fueros y fidelidad a la Monarquía en la rebelión aragonesa de 1591." In *Monarquía, imperio y pueblos en la España moderna,* ed. Pablo Fernández Albaladejo. Alicante, 1997. 459–75.

——. "El 'vulgo ciego' en la rebelión aragonesa de 1591." *Revista de historia Jerónimo Zurita* 69 / 70 (1994): 89–113.

Geertz, Clifford. *Negara: The Theatre State in Nineteenth-Century Bali.* Princeton, 1980.

Gil Pujol, Xavier. "Aragonese Constitutionalism and Habsburg Rule: The Varying Meanings of Liberty." In Kagan and Parker, *Spain, Europe, and the Atlantic World.* 160–87.

——. "Catalunya i Aragó, 1591–1592: Una solidaritat i dos destins." In *Primer Congrés d'Història Moderna de Catalunya: Actes.* 2 vols. Barcelona, 1984, 2:125–31.

——. "Noves visions sobre velles realitats de les relacions entre la capital i els territoris a les monarquies europees dels segles XVI i XVII." In *El Barroc Català: Actes de les jornades celebrades a Girona, desembre 1987.* Barcelona, 1989. 23–45.

——. "Olivares y Aragón," In *La España del Conde Duque de Olivares,* ed. John Elliott and Angel García Sanz. Valladolid, 1990. 575–602.

——. "Visió europea de la monarquia espanyola com a monarquia composta, segles XVI i XVII." *Recerques: Història, Economia, Cultura* 32 (1995): 19–43.

Giralt Raventós, Emilio. "La colonia mercantil francesa de Barcelona a mediados del s. XVII." *Estudios de Historia Moderna* 6 (1956): 215–78.

González Fernández, Mònica. "Barcelona i la vint-i-quatrena de Corts a les Corts de Montsó de 1585." In *Tercer Congrés d'Història de Catalunya: Actes.* 1:299–307.

Gordon, Daniel. *Citizens without Sovereignty: Equality and Sociability in French Thought, 1670–1789.* Princeton, 1994.

Graham, Lisa Jane. "Crimes of Opinion: Policing the Public in Eighteenth-Century Paris." In *Visions and Revisions of Eighteenth-Century France,* ed. Christine Adams, Jack R. Censer, and Lisa Jane Graham. University Park, Penn., 1997. 79–103.

Gramsci Antonio. *Selections from the Prison Notebooks of Antonio Gramsci.* Ed. and trans. Quentin Hoare and Geoffrey Nowell Smith. New York, 1971.

Haliczer, Stephen. *The Comuneros of Castile: The Forging of a Revolution, 1475–1521.* Madison, Wis., 1981.

Hamilton, Earl J. *American Treasure and the Price Revolution in Spain, 1501–1560.* Cambridge, Mass., 1934.

Hernández, Bernat. "Un assaig de reforma del sistema fisco-financer de la monarquia a Catalunya: L'impost del quint sobre les imposicions locals, 1580–1640." *Manuscrits* 14 (1996): 297–319.

Hill, Christopher. "The Many-Headed Monster in Late Tudor and Early Stuart Political Thinking." In *From the Renaissance to the Counter-Reformation: Essays in Honour of Garrett Mattingly,* ed. Charles Howard Carter. London, 1966.

Hobsbawm, E. J. *Primitive Rebels: Studies in Archaic Forms of Social Movement in the Nineteenth and Twentieth Centuries.* 1959; reprint, New York, 1965.

Israel, Jonathan I. *The Dutch Republic: Its Rise, Greatness, and Fall, 1477–1806.* Oxford, 1995.

Kagan, Richard L. *Lawsuits and Litigants in Castile, 1500–1700.* Chapel Hill, 1981.

———. *Lucrecia's Dreams: Politics and Prophecy in Sixteenth-Century Spain.* Berkeley, 1990.

Kagan, Richard L., and Geoffrey Parker, eds. *Spain, Europe, and the Atlantic World: Essays in Honour of John H. Elliott.* Cambridge, 1995.

Kamen, Henry. *Philip of Spain.* New Haven, 1997.

———. *The Phoenix and the Flame: Catalonia and the Counter Reformation.* New Haven, 1993.

———. *The Spanish Inquisition: A Historical Revision.* New Haven, 1997.

Kantorowicz, Ernst H. *The King's Two Bodies: A Study in Mediaeval Political Theology.* Princeton, 1957.

Kettering, Sharon. *Judicial Politics and Urban Revolt in Seventeenth-Century France: The Parlement of Aix, 1629–1659.* Princeton, 1978.

———. *Patrons, Brokers, and Clients in Seventeenth-Century France.* Cambridge, 1986.

Koenigsberger, H. G. "The Crisis of the Seventeenth Century: a Farewell?" In *Politicians and Virtuosi: Essays in Early Modern History.* London, 1986.

Lalinde Abadía, Jesús. *La institución virreinal en Cataluña (1471–1716).* Barcelona, 1964.

Le Roy Ladurie, Emmanuel. *The Beggar and the Professor: A Sixteenth-Century Family Saga.* Trans. Arthur Goldhammer. Chicago, 1997.

Levi, Giovanni. "On Microhistory." In *New Perspectives on Historical Writing,* ed. Peter Burke. University Park, Penn., 1992.

Lisón Tolosana, Carmelo. *La imagen del rey (monarquía, realeza y poder ritual en la Casa de los Austrias).* Madrid, 1991.

Lloyd, Howell A. "Constitutionalism." In Burns, *Cambridge History of Political Thought.* 254–97.

Lorenzo Cadarso, Pedro L. *Los conflictos populares en Castilla (siglos XVI–XVII).* Madrid, 1996.

Lovett, A. W. *Philip II and Mateo Vázquez de Leca: The Government of Spain (1572–1592).* Geneva, 1977.

Luebke, David Martin. *His Majesty's Rebels: Communities, Factions, and Rural Revolt in the Black Forest, 1725–1745.* Ithaca, 1997.

———. "Of Emperors and the Queen of Heaven: The Seditious Uses of 'Naive Monarchism' and Marian Veneration in Early Modern Germany." *Past and Present* 154 (February 1997): 71–106.

Lynch, John. *The Hispanic World in Crisis and Change: 1598–1700.* 2d ed. Oxford, 1992.

———. *Spain 1516–1598: From Nation State to World Empire.* 2d ed. rev. Oxford, 1991.

MacKay, Ruth. *The Limits of Royal Authority: Resistance and Obedience in Seventeenth-Century Castile.* Cambridge, 1999.

Maravall, José Antonio. *Teoría del estado en España en el siglo XVII.* 2d ed. Madrid, 1997.

Marcos Martín, Alberto. *España en los siglos XVI, XVII y XVIII.* Barcelona, 2000.

Martz, Linda. *Poverty and Welfare in Habsburg Spain.* Cambridge, 1983.

Molas Ribalta, P. *Catalunya i la Casa d'Àustria.* Barcelona, 1996.

———. *Los gremios barceloneses del siglo XVIII.* Madrid, 1970.

Monter, William. *Frontiers of Heresy: The Spanish Inquisition from the Basque Lands to Sicily.* Cambridge, 1990.

Moore, Barrington, Jr. *Injustice: The Social Bases of Obedience and Revolt.* White Plains, N.Y., 1978.

———. *Social Origins of Dictatorship and Democracy.* Boston, 1966.

Moreu-Rey, Enric. *Els immigrants francesos a Barcelona (segles XVI al XVII).* Barcelona, 1959.

Nadal, Jorge, and Emilio Giralt. "Barcelona en 1717–18: Un modelo de sociedad pre- industrial." In *Homenaje a Don Ramón Carande.* 2 vols. Madrid, 1963. 2:277–305.

———. *La population catalane de 1553 à 1717: L'immigration française et les autres facteurs de son développement.* [Paris], 1960.

Nader, Helen. *Liberty in Absolutist Spain: The Habsburg Sale of Towns, 1516–1700.* Baltimore, 1990.

Olivares i Periu, Jordi. *Viles, pagesos i senyors a la Catalunya dels Àustria: Conflictivitat social i litigació a la Reial Audiència (1591–1662).* Lleida, 2000.

Palos, Joan Lluís. *Catalunya a l'imperi dels Àustria: La pràctica de govern (segles XVI i XVII).* Lleida, 1994.

———. *Els juristes i la defensa de les Constitucions: Joan Pere Fontanella (1575–1649).* Vic, 1997.

Parker, Geoffrey. *The Army of Flanders and the Spanish Road, 1567–1659: The Logistics of Spanish Victory and Defeat in the Low Countries' War.* Cambridge, 1972.

———. *The Grand Strategy of Philip II.* New Haven, 1998.

———. *Philip II,* 3d ed. Chicago, 1995.

———. *The Thirty Years' War.* Ed. Geoffrey Parker. London, 1997.

Peck, Linda Levy. *Court Patronage and Corruption in Early Stuart England.* London, 1993.

Pérez Bustamante, Ciriaco. "La España de Felipe III: La política interior y los problemas internacionales." In vol. 24 of *Historia de España,* ed. Ramón Menéndez Pidal and José María Jover Zamora. 2d ed. Madrid, 1983.

Pérez García, José Manuel. "Economía y sociedad." Chap. 4 of *La crisis del siglo XVII,* vol. 6 of *Historia de España,* ed. Antonio Domínguez Ortiz. Barcelona, 1998.

Pérez Latre, Miquel. "'Llevar la corona del cap a sa Magestat': Juntes de Braços i Divuitenes a la Diputació del General de Catalunya (1587–1593)." Licenciate thesis, Universitat de Barcelona, 1994.

——. "Les torbacions de Catalunya (1585–1593): De les Corts a la suspensió del nou redreç de la Diputació del General." *Afers* 23–24 (1996): 59–98.

Pillorget, René. *Les mouvements insurrectionnels de Provence entre 1596 et 1715.* Paris, 1975.

Po-Chia Hsia, R. *Social Discipline in the Reformation: Central Europe, 1550–1750.* London, 1989.

Poni, Carlo. "Norms and Disputes: The Shoemakers' Guild in Eighteenth-Century Bologna." *Past and Present* 123 (May 1989): 80–108.

Post, Gaines. *Studies in Medieval Legal Thought: Public Law and the State, 1100–1322.* Princeton, 1964.

Puigvert i Solà, Joaquim M. "Guerra i Contrarreforma a la Catalunya rural del segle XVII." In *La revolució catalana de 1640.* Barcelona, 1991. 99–132.

Ranum, Orest. *The Fronde: A French Revolution 1648–1652.* New York, 1993.

Riba, Carlos. *El Consejo Supremo de Aragón en el reinado de Felipe II.* Valencia, 1914.

Ribot, Luis A. "Las revueltas sicilianas de 1647–1648." In *1640: La monarquía hispánica en crisis.* 183–99.

Riera i Melis, Antoni, and Gaspar Feliu i Monfort. "Activitats econòmiques." In Sobrequés i Callicó, *Història de Barcelona.* 3:137–272.

Roca, Josep Maria. *Discursos llegits en la Real Academia de Buenas Letras de Barcelona en la solemne recepció pública de Joseph Ma. Roca el dia 20 de maig de 1918: En Jaume Ramon Vila heraldista catalá de començaments del segle XVIIé.* Barcelona, 1918.

Roper, Lyndal. " 'The Common Man,' 'the Common Good,' 'Common Women': Gender and Language in the German Reformation Commune." *Social History* 12 (1987): 1–22.

Rovira i Virgili, Antoni. *El Corpus de Sang: Estudi històric.* Barcelona, 1932.

Rudé, George. *The Crowd in History: A Study of Popular Disturbances in France and England, 1730–1848.* New York, 1964.

——. *Ideology and Popular Protest.* Reprint, with a foreword by Harvey J. Kaye. Chapel Hill, 1995.

Sabean, David Warren. *Power in the Blood: Popular Culture and Village Discourse in Early Modern Germany.* Cambridge, 1984.

Sagarra, Ferran de. *Catalunya en 1640: Les lliçons de la història.* Barcelona, n.d. [1930?].

Sales, Núria. *Els segles de la decadència (segles XVI–XVIII).* Vol. 4 of *Història de Catalunya,* ed. Pierre Vilar. Barcelona, 1989.

Sanabre, José. *La acción de Francia en Cataluña en la pugna por la hegemonía de Europa, 1640–59.* Barcelona, 1956.

Sanpere i Miquel, Salvador. *Barcelona: Son passat, present y porvenir.* Barcelona, 1878.

Scott, James C. *Weapons of the Weak: Everyday Forms of Peasant Resistance.* New Haven, 1985.

Serra, Eva. "1640: Una revolució política: La implicació de les institucions." In *La revolució catalana de 1640.* Barcelona, 1991.

——. "Notes sobre l'esforç català a la campanya de Salses: Juliol 1639, gener 1640." In *Homenatge al Doctor Sebastià García Martínez.* 3 vols. Valencia, 1988. 2:7–28.

——. *Pagesos i senyors a la Catalunya del segle XVII: Baronia de Sentmenat, 1590–1729.* Barcelona, 1988.

——. "Segadors, revolta popular i revolució política." In *Revoltes populars contra el poder de l'estat.* Barcelona, 1992. 45–57.

Serra i Puig, Eva, and Xavier Torres i Sans, eds. *Crisi institucional i canvi social: segles XVI i XVII.* Vol. 4 of *Història, política, societat i cultura dels Països Catalans.* Barcelona, 1997.

Simon, Antoni, and Jordi Andreu. "Evolució demogràfica (segles XVI i XVII)." In Sobrequés y Callicó, *Història de Barcelona.* 4:103–63.

Simon i Tarrés, Antoni. *Els orígens ideològics de la Revolució Catalana de 1640.* Abadia de Montserrat, 1999.

Smith, Robert S. "Barcelona 'Bills of Mortality' and Population, 1457–1590." *Journal of Political Economy* 44 (1936): 84–93.

——. *The Spanish Guild Merchant: A History of the Consulado 1250–1700.* Durham, N.C., 1940.

Sobrequés i Callicó, Jaume, ed. *Història de Barcelona.* 8 vols. Barcelona, 1991–97.

Sonenscher, Michael. "Journeymen, the Courts, and the French Trades, 1781–91." *Past and Present* 114 (February 1987): 77–109.

Stradling, R. A. *Philip IV and the Government of Spain, 1621–1665.* Cambridge, 1988.

Strong, Roy. *Art and Power: Renaissance Festivals, 1450–1650.* Berkeley, 1984.

Te Brake, Wayne. *Shaping History: Ordinary People in European Politics, 1500–1700.* Berkeley, 1998.

Tercer Congrés d'Història de Catalunya: Actes. Special issue of *Pedralbes* 13 (1993). 2 vols. Barcelona, 1993.

Thompson, E. P. *Customs in Common: Studies in Traditional Popular Culture.* New York, 1993.

Thompson, I. A. A. "Castile, Spain and the Monarchy: The Political Community from *Patria Natural* to *Patria Nacional.*" In Kagan and Parker, *Spain, Europe and the Atlantic World.* 125–59.

——. "Patronato real e integración política en las ciudades castellanas bajo los Austrias." In *Imágenes de la diversidad: El mundo urbano en la Corona de Castilla (s. XVI–XVIII),* ed. José Ignacio Fortea Pérez. [Santander], 1997. 475–96.

——. *War and Government in Habsburg Spain, 1560–1620.* London, 1976.

Tintó i Sala, Margarida. *El gremis a la Barcelona medieval.* Barcelona, 1978.

Torras i Ribé, Josep M. *Els municipis catalans de l'Antic Règim, 1453–1808.* Barcelona, 1983.

Torres i Sans, Xavier. *Els bandolers (s. XVI–XVII).* Vic, 1991.

——. *Nyerros i cadells: Bàndols i bandolerisme a la Catalunya moderna (1590–1640).* Barcelona, 1993.

——. "Segadors i miquelets a la revolució catalana (1640–1659)." In *La revolució catalana de 1640.* Barcelona, 1991. 66–96.

Usher, Abbott Payson. *The Early History of Deposit Banking in Mediterranean Europe.* Vol. 1, pt. 2. New York, 1943.

Vázquez de Prada, Valentín, and Pere Molas. "La indústria llanera a Barcelona. Segles XVI–XVII." In *Economia i societat al segle XVIII,* by Pere Molas. Barcelona, 1975. 143–59.

Ventalló Vintró, José. *Historia de la industria lanera catalana.* Tarrasa, 1904.

Vicens i Vives, Jaume. *Ferran II i la ciutat de Barcelona, 1479–1516.* 3 vols. Barcelona, 1936–37.

Vicente, Marta. "Images and Realities of Work: Women and Guilds in Early Modern Barcelona." In *Spanish Women in the Golden Age,* ed. Magdalena S. Sánchez and Alain Saint-Saëns. Westport, Conn., 1996. 127–39.

Vidal Pla, Jordi. "Les formes tradicionals de l'organització armada a la Catalunya dels s. XVI i XVII: Suggerències per a una investigació." *Manuscrits* 3 (1986): 105–16.

———. *Guerra dels Segadors i crisi social: Els exilats filipistes (1640–1652).* Barcelona, 1982.

Vilar, Pierre. "The Age of Don Quixote." Trans. Richard Morris. In *Essays in European Economic History,* ed. Peter Earle. Oxford, 1974. 100–113.

———. *La Catalogne dans l'Espagne Moderne.* 3 vols. Paris, 1962.

Vilar Berrogain, Jean. *Literatura y economía: La figura satírica del arbitrista en el Siglo de Oro.* Madrid, 1973.

Villanueva López, Jesús. "Los orígenes carolingios de Cataluña en la historiografía y el pensamiento político del siglo XVII." Licentiate thesis, Universitat Autónoma de Barcelona, 1994.

Villari, Rosario. *Elogio della dissimulazione: La lotta politica nel Seicento.* Rome, 1987.

———. *The Revolt of Naples.* Trans. James Newell with John A. Marino. Cambridge, 1993.

———. "Revoluciones periféricas y declive de la monarquía española." In *1640: La monarquía hispánica en crisis.* 169–82.

Zudaire Huarte, Eulogio. *El Conde-Duque y Cataluña.* Barcelona, 1963.

Index